Publications of the

MINNESOTA HISTORICAL SOCIETY

RUSSELL W. FRIDLEY
Editor and Director

JUNE DRENNING HOLMQUIST
Associate Editor

Newspapers on the Minnesota Frontier 1849-1860

By George S. Hage

MINNESOTA HISTORICAL SOCIETY • 1967

For Anne

Foreword

THE TEACHING of journalistic writing, in which I have been engaged since 1946, is a vocation committed to the contemporary. So complete is this commitment that it is possible to spend most of one's waking hours on the University of Minnesota campus in a building named for William J. Murphy without knowing much more about the man than the fact that he published the *Minneapolis Tribune* late in the nineteenth century. There comes a time when that is not enough. Bulldozers threaten the ageless oak outside the window, but one does not want to move on without having known how one got here.

I began research in the history of Minnesota's newspapers while on a sabbatical year in 1962, naïve in the hope of spanning a century before the year's leave should run out. Many a researcher digs purposefully into old newspaper files but finds himself unable to resist the irrelevant. I dug, fearing that everything might be relevant. And the mine of the Minnesota Historical Society's newspaper collection is seemingly without limit. At the end of my leave, the first tenth of my project mocked me from note cards and a rough draft of several interminable chapters. And there it lay until 1966 when June Drenning Holmquist, the Minnesota Historical Society's associate editor, prodded me to complete a study dealing with the period from 1849, when Minnesota's first paper made its appearance, to 1860, when the telegraph reached the newly established state. For that prod — and so much more — I am deeply grateful. The society's McKnight Foundation grant for 1966 enabled me to complete the writing.

One of the first things one learns about the Minnesota fathers is that *they* knew how they got where they were, and they wanted the events recorded. Rising before the pioneer lawmakers in the fall of 1849 to deliver his first message to the territorial legislature, Governor Alexander Ramsey urged them to provide for the preservation of every newspaper published in the territory — the "day-books of history" he called them. The lawmakers responded by chartering the Minnesota Historical Society and making it a repository for all the newspapers issued in the area. Six months earlier the first issue of the *Minnesota Pioneer* had appeared on the streets of St. Paul. Thus the beginning date for my study was set.

The terminal date of 1860 is not so capricious as it might appear, for on August 29, 1860, St. Paul was linked to the rest of the nation by telegraph, ending an era of frontier isolation which had been only partially relieved by the state's admission to the Union two years earlier. The degree of that isolation is difficult for us to comprehend in this era of Telstar.

One approaches research in a specialized segment of regional history hoping it is justified as a part of the whole. For the nation, the 1850s were assertive years, years of common-man equality and human perfectability, westward expansion and the ever-mounting tension between North and South. Years articulated poetically by Walt Whitman's *Leaves of Grass* and journalistically by Horace Greeley's *New York Tribune*. I found Minnesota's first newspapers not only part of the whole, but forming the cement by which the new annex adhered to the old structure. Two kinds of material made up most of their earliest content: reminders of what life had been back in Ohio and Pennsylvania and New York, clipped from Eastern newspapers weeks after their publication; and glowing descriptions of what life was like in Minnesota, written in the hope of being clipped in turn by Eastern newspapers to attract settlers to the new country. The tone was assertive and expansive. And even such parts of the whole as were missing — most notably, early acknowledgment of the slavery crisis — were missing because the first editors reasoned that the bond between nation and territory would be stronger if divisive influences were ignored.

It is good to find out where we have been, especially in an anniversary year. The past should be known in order to be celebrated. It is fitting that this book should appear in 1967, a year gala with anniversaries. One hundred years have elapsed since the Minnesota Newspaper Association and the *Minneapolis Tribune* were founded, and 1967 is also the fiftieth anniversary of the beginning of journalism education at the University of Minnesota.

A surprising number of former students turned up to make this enterprise enjoyable. Alan Ominsky, an imaginative onetime *Gopher* yearbook editor, could not have foreseen that he would one day design a book on frontier journalism; Dorothy Drescher Perry and Marjorie Kreidberg ferreted out mislaid facts and checked them with better grace than ever I checked their student news stories and editorials.

Other members of the Minnesota Historical Society's staff also deserve my sincere thanks. Mrs. Holmquist, an English major who first won my respect with a magazine article on the Republican national convention in Minneapolis in 1892, and now a seasoned editor whose patience was not belied by her muttering one day: "I hope that I shall never see/another newspaper family tree;" Eugene D. Becker, picture curator, his assistant Dorothy Gimmestad, and Sue E. Holbert, editorial assistant, who worked on the picture section of this book; Mrs. Phyllis Sandstrom, who typed the manuscript; and Luther Thompson of the newspaper staff who tirelessly searched for the missing bits and pieces of information which added so much to the book's appendix.

My wife, Anne Hage, provided sound criticism and the encouragement that kept me at the task. To all I am grateful. The mistakes, I should note, are all teacher's.

GEORGE S. HAGE

March 20, 1967

Contents

Newspapers
on the
Minnesota Frontier
1849–1860

Auferat hunc librum nullus
hinc omne per ævum cum
Antinoo partem quisquis habere
cupit.

CHAPTER 1

Pioneers and Promoters

HORACE GREELEY'S *New York Tribune* of April 28, 1849, fretted about the unpreparedness of gold seekers setting out for California. James Gordon Bennett's *New York Herald* commented on the revolutionary turmoil in Europe. William Cullen Bryant's *New York Evening Post* deplored the slave market in the nation's capital. And in the nation's capital Joseph Gales' and William W. Seaton's *National Intelligencer* noted the receipt of "the first number of the first newspaper" published in the new territory of Minnesota on April 27 and quoted from "its seductive account of the charms of this youngest daughter of the Union." The publisher of this new newspaper, called the *Minnesota Register,* the *Intelligencer* said, was A. Randall and Company of St. Paul.

But out in St. Paul in newly created Minnesota Territory, an impetuous newcomer named James Madison Goodhue would have fumed had he read the *Intelligencer* item. For on that same day — April 28, 1849 — he had run off the first number of the *Minnesota Pioneer,* whose claim to precedence he was not going to have slighted as long as he could hire a printer to set a stick of type. As he later asserted whenever the question arose, Randall's first issue, dated St. Paul, April 27, 1849, was published in Cincinnati, Ohio, for distribution in Minnesota Territory; his press didn't get to St. Paul until May, and Randall himself never did make it.[1] Goodhue's *Pioneer* was the first newspaper published in Minnesota Territory.

Goodhue had reason to be jealous of his claim to priority. Seven other weeklies were to appear — some of them only briefly—in the territory within the next four years, and the contest for official printing contracts with the territorial government was to be bitter. In these fights Goodhue's aggressive claim to precedence may have swung some votes. Without the territorial printing, it is doubtful that the *Pioneer* could have survived its early years on the frontier to become the longest-lived newspaper in the state.[2]

Goodhue had gone to Minnesota determined to publish the first newspaper and to exploit the advantage. For this thirty-eight-year-old native of New Hampshire, the new territory was to be the end of a personal westward movement that was strikingly representative of the restless, optimistic progress of many a frontiersman. After graduation from Amherst, he had tried schoolteaching in Elmira, New York, then practicing law, supplemented by farming, first in Plainfield, Illinois, then in Platteville and Lancaster, Wisconsin. A growing enthusiasm for writing led him gradually to abandon the law for newspaper work. But in Lancaster, as editor of a paper awkwardly named the *Wisconsin Herald and Grant County Advertiser,* he had learned how insubstantial was the living to be made from a weekly paper dependent upon advertising, circulation, and job printing in a frontier community. In the promise of territorial status for Minnesota in 1849, Goodhue saw another opportunity to improve his situation. The move to Minnesota, like all the others, cast him in the role of the final frontier type: the professional man following the trail forged by the explorer, the hunter, and the land-breaking settler.[3]

Goodhue must have hoped that his vision had not betrayed him as he stood on the deck of the steamboat "Senator" while it sidled into the lower landing at St. Paul. The day was a raw and cloudy April 18, 1849, and the first boat of the season had arrived nine days earlier with the news that Congress had created Minnesota Territory. Had some other ambitious editor preceded him? He scanned the faces of the curious villagers lining the shore.

They, in turn, sizing up Goodhue along with the other passengers, saw a man of medium height, solidly built, and probably wearing a frock coat. The black choker cravat topping the expanse of white shirt front emphasized the roundness of a face framed by dark hair worn long enough to almost hide the ears. The eyes were pensive. Only the set of the chin and the down-turned corners of the wide mouth suggested the strength of will that the territory was soon to recognize as a dominant character-istic of James M. Goodhue.

He needed a resolute will. After supervising the unloading of his heavy Washington hand press and cases of type, he had to leave them at the only warehouse on the landing until he could find a building to house them. It was even difficult for the editor to find a place to sleep — J. W. Bass's St. Paul House at Third and Jackson streets, the only public house in the village, being "crowded full, from cellar to garret." Of the thirty-odd log and frame shanties that lined the dirt trails of the infant city, only one afforded a vacant room that could be used as a print shop. It was, Goodhue said later, "open as a corn-rick," and hogs, root-ing under its board floor, threatened the equilibrium of a printer standing at a type case. "We print and issue this number of the Pioneer, in a building through which out-of-doors is visible by more than five hundred apertures," the editor confided in his first issue, "and as for our type, it is not safe from being *pied* on the galleys by the wind." [4]

But better the wind than the hot breath of competition which might blow in on the next steamboat. Goodhue simmered in frustration at one inescapable delay in producing his paper. On unpacking his equipment, he discovered that a news chase, the heavy iron frame which locked a page of type for printing, had been left behind, and he had to wait several days for blacksmith and wagonmaker William H. Nobles to make a new one. Even so the Pioneer reached the streets a full month before its first competition appeared in the form of the Minnesota Chronicle on May 31. When the second issue of the Register was published in St. Paul on July 14, Minnesota Territory had three news-papers — all of them published in its capital city. [5]

The frontier press in Minnesota was to fulfill two primary functions, both promotional. The first was to attract settlers to the territory, the second, to advance the cause of a political party. Other functions — informing the community about itself and the outside world, mounting watch on government, advertising goods and services, instructing and entertaining readers — got less attention from editors in the early years. For Goodhue, promoting the territory came first. "There is nothing more certain than that the interests of Minnesota require an able and efficient press, to represent abroad our wants and to set forth our situation, our resources and our advantages," he wrote in the leading editorial of his initial issue on April 28. And while Goodhue far surpassed his competitors in this effort, he was not alone in the emphasis.

The *Register* had two objectives, Andrew Randall said in his salutatory on April 27: to promote settlement of the territory and to establish a good constitution for statehood. The first issue of the first paper to be published in what is now Minneapolis — the *St. Anthony Express* of May 31, 1851 — told its patrons that "the primary, leading object of the *Express* will be to advocate the interests of the Territory in general, and especially those of the village of St. Anthony." Even the *North-Western Democrat,* which made its appearance at St. Anthony on July 13, 1853, declared in its first issue that "we *must* blow our own trumpet if we would have our Territory *and our village,* known and the country about us settled," before noting as its second objective that "the Democrats of St. Anthony have long felt the need of an organ to represent them and their principles." Two more weeklies which began publication in St. Paul in the early years of the territory were primarily interested in partisan politics. They were the *Minnesota Democrat,* first issued on December 10, 1850, which was, as its name implies, devoted to the interests of the Democratic party, and the *Minnesotian,* introduced on September 17, 1851, which supported the Whigs.[6]

Goodhue, at the outset, hoped to avoid the partisan function. Taking his cue from Henry Hastings Sibley, the territory's first delegate to Congress, he maintained that political partisanship was a luxury that could not be afforded in a territory inevitably dependent upon the good will of Congress and the national administration. "Our political relations to the Union as a Territory not only exempt us from the necessity, but preclude us from the propriety of enlisting in the great warfare of national politics," he proclaimed in the *Pioneer* of April 28, 1849. It was a comfortable theory, but living up to it was to prove impossible for the hotheaded editor.

Goodhue never had reason to withdraw, however, from the role he saw as primary. On April 17, 1851, the eve of the *Pioneer's* third year of publication, he amplified his viewpoint in a leading editorial headed "The Uses of the Press." "The most important purpose of the newspaper press, especially on the frontier, is to mirror back to the world, the events, the peculiarities and the whole features of the new world by which it is surrounded. . . . The frontier press, is more influential indirectly than directly: by being copied and multiplied in the enormous city papers, which penetrate every corner of the world. . . . We would rather, now, present a daguerreotype of Saint Paul, sitting now in our office, as we see it springing up fresh and vigorous, like the skeleton of a great city, where but yesterday stood a forest, filled with wild Indians — we would rather represent to the world abroad, the sounds of the hammer and the saw and the axe, which greet our ears now from every quarter of the town, or paint the shining river that flows under the bluff, one hundred feet below Bench street, from which a stone may be thrown into it, or describe the tumultuous joy with which the multitudes of our people, old and young, flocked down to the levee, to greet the landing on Friday week, of the first boat of the season, the Nominee, than to write a political homily as long as the Mississippi river, and twice as turbid."

In the picture of the new world mirrored back to the old by the *Pioneer,* the peculiarities inevitably eclipsed the "whole features." It was a world whose new inhabitants exulted in vast prairies and forests and in the clear-running rivers that gave access to them. But even as the settlers thrilled at the new land, they found in it features that reminded them of more familiar landscapes in Vermont or Pennsylvania or Ohio. The steamboat "Anthony Wayne" was acclaimed in the summer of 1850 for an exploratory excursion up the St. Peter's (now the Minnesota) River because "she afforded hundreds of our citizens and many strangers actual, visual proof, that through the very heart of Minnesota, east and west, extends a country, not surpassed in fertility by the lands of the Wabash valley — well wooded, beautiful as Paradise to the eye, the fairest, loveliest land, by the united testimony of all, that ever the light of the sun shone upon."[7]

Yet how isolated was Paradise, especially for five months of the year, and how resentful its residents when the interval between mails from Galena, Illinois, down the river stretched from one week to two or three. "Ice-olated as we are, with a mail only semi-occasionally — hibernating we may say, the press must subsist through the month of March, without the aliment of news," wrote Goodhue in the *Pioneer* of March 27, 1850. "In vain is our vision strained down the river, looking for the mail train to turn the bend. . . . Here sits Saint Paul, impatient as a young widow waiting for her nuptials, for the hour that shall unite her again with the world — looking down into the ice-covered channel of the long, long river . . . sighing as she turns to the South and fancies that even now the impatient steamboats may be knocking at the frozen gate of Lake Pepin. These facts remind us, of course they do, that we need and *must have* here, the telegraphic wires from the south; and that we must also have, at no distant day, a railroad to Dubuque."

It was a world in which the fur trade that had drawn the first white inhabitants was already declining, but one in which editor Goodhue still found it necessary to defend the American Fur Company from the charge of all-powerful monopoly. It was a world of millions of acres of unsettled potential farmland to which barrels of pork and flour were brought up the river from Dubuque and Galena and even St. Louis. This world was new, but it was already challenged by reforms: early temperance adherents even sought to change the name of the Rum River.[8]

St. Paul, the capital of Minnesota Territory, was no less remarkable for its seeming inconsistencies. Each steamboat from below carried new arrivals who eyed covetously the rich lands of the Sioux west of the Mississippi. The town's most familiar Indian figure, however, was no regal chieftain, but rather a squaw known as Old Bets who roamed St. Paul's streets appealing for handouts.[9] Since no "cases of importance" were heard in the district courts in 1849, the first session of the territorial supreme court had no cases on its docket, but any issue of the

Pioneer, the later *Chronicle and Register, Minnesota Democrat,* or *Express* carried business cards of more than a dozen lawyers. The first session of the legislature in 1849 chartered the Minnesota Historical Society, and the second the University of Minnesota. Within a year after the achievement of territorial status in 1849, the capital boasted a bookstore. Yet as late as July 29, 1852, Goodhue complained that despite the two schools in St. Paul, it was "swarming with children, little untaught brats, swarming about the streets and along the levee in utter idleness, like wharf rats." He lectured parents for permitting them to run wild on the levee — "a free school" from which they would soon get "a diploma from the Devil."

If indeed the "peculiarities" tended to obscure the "whole features" in the *Pioneer's* picture of the territory, it was not through any lack of devotion or energy on the part of the editor. Goodhue was indefatigable as traveler and reporter. Week after week during his first summer in the territory, he set out from St. Paul on horseback, by steamboat, or by canoe to explore for a day or two some new corner of the surrounding area. And week after week Goodhue's leading article in the *Pioneer* would run through two, three, or four columns of solid type describing for eastern eyes what he had observed. Stillwater and the St. Croix River, the settlements of St. Anthony, Mendota, Red Rock, and Cottage Grove, the lakes of White Bear and Bald Eagle, Fort Snelling and the military reserve — all these and more he surveyed with imagination and a sharp eye for detail, returning to the little print shop on Third Street to write in an angular scrawl glowing accounts of what he had seen. The territory had no better salesman.

The pioneer editor even beat the drums for St. Anthony — at least until that village set out to challenge St. Paul's claim to the headwaters of navigation on the Mississippi.[10] "The importance of the subject, and our want of full and definite information about it, is the only reason we have not yet attempted to describe the Falls [of St. Anthony] and to set forth the unrivalled advantages of that locality for business," he wrote in the *Pioneer* of August 9, 1849. "Here it is, that after a progress of four hundred miles from above, through a channel in which no obstructions occur to steamboat navigation worth mentioning, that the whole volume of the Mississippi pours down in a precipitous sheet from a bench of limestone rock, to the depth of eighteen or twenty feet. Of the sublimity of the Falls we will not now speak; although in this respect the cataract of St. Anthony is but little less wonderful than that of Niagara. The roar of this immense volume of falling water is often distinctly audible at St. Paul, a distance of eight miles, and probably at a much greater distance."

Goodhue's own voice was sustained through two columns of description and praise for the water power of the falls, the extent of the pine forests beyond, navigation on the Mississippi above the falls, and business interests at St. Anthony. In true booster spirit, he concluded with this description of the country: "A finer agricultural region than that which surrounds St. Anthony, cannot be found. On the east side of the river, down to the junction of the St. Croix and the Mississippi, is a wide expanse of prairie and oak openings, diversified with lakes and patches of natural mowing. On the west side, the eye extends over a vast expanse of fertile table lands of surpassing beauty, extending to the St. Peters river on the south, and as far west in the wide range of the buffalo as you may choose to go. In fact, whichever way you may travel from the Falls, you will pass over a region of country designed by nature for the most profitable employment of Agriculture. Farmers must and will turn their attention this way. There is certainly no spot in our country where farming is likely to be so well rewarded as here. To say nothing of the payment of Indian annuities and the demand for produce for the lumber trade, it is plain that extensive mills and manufactories must soon be built at St. Anthony, which will employ multitudes of hands in the manufacture of all articles of heavy transportation, and build up that most valuable of all trade, the trade of exchanges between the town and the country. Considering the bracing climate of this region as well as the prolific soil, it is very doubtful whether as many bushels can be produced per annum by the labor of one man in any other part of our continent. All crops do well. Corn is a sure and an abundant crop. If we were to specify the crop that is most excellent and abundant, however, it would be the potato crop. Farmers, especially of New England,

if they could but once see our lands, would never think of settling on the bilious bottoms and the enervating prairies south of
us. What is fertility, what is wealth, without vigorous health and
activity of body and of mind? These are considerations that will
weigh more in future with the immigrants, than they hitherto
have: a clear, bracing air, an invigorating winter to give elasticity
to the system — and water as pure and soft as the dews of heaven,
gushing from hill and valley.

"When we consider how soon the upper Mississippi will be
placed in direct communication with the Atlantic by railroad
extending east from Galena and by steamboat through the Wisconsin and Fox rivers and the Lakes — a work already well in
progress — is it too much to predict for this young Territory and
for the manufacturing interest of St. Anthony, a rapidity of
growth unparalleled even in the annals of Western progress?"

Such promotional pieces sometimes served for more than one
issue of the paper. Settlers, obligated to write to family and
friends back east about their new surroundings, found Goodhue
fulfilling the task more glowingly than they could. But extra
copies of an issue for such correspondents were not always available, and so the obliging editor would occasionally republish
an article in a subsequent issue and run off additional copies to
meet the demand.[11]

Nor was Goodhue the only writer thus engaged in recording
impressions of the new land for eastern readers of the *Pioneer*.
The paper frequently carried long letters from missionaries,
Indian agents, and other observers who found an outlet for their
literary urge by writing to the editor. Sometimes these correspondents covered ground already explored by Goodhue, but the
editor was not at all proprietary in this respect. He welcomed to
his columns all who would help spread the gospel of immigration to Minnesota.

Other early territorial weeklies also ran articles extolling the
virtues of countryside and village, but they were neither so frequent nor so detailed as Goodhue's. And none of them conveyed
his enthusiasm. The paper that came closest was the *St. Anthony
Express*. Its second issue touted the advantages of the Mississippi
above St. Anthony. Its fourth proclaimed: "We want FARM-

ERS . . . Mechanics . . . Lawyers . . . ministers . . . Physicians . . .
Last, though not least, *young ladies* are wanted." The writer left
no doubt that the young ladies should be prepared to do a day's
work; fashion's darlings were not welcome. But a few issues later
his paper was ready to let down the barricade: "We venture to
predict, that in less than twenty years, St. Anthony Falls will be
the most noted fashionable resort in the United States." The
reasons advanced for this optimism were the healthfulness of the
climate and the beauty of the Mississippi all the way from Galena
to St. Anthony.[12]

Less than a year later the *Express* revised its estimate of at least
that portion of the route known as St. Paul. On April 30, 1852,
the *Express* noted that anyone so unwise as to disembark at St.
Paul's lower landing and struggle up the bluff would get a view
less than enchanting: "Before you an amphitheatre of barren
hills, enclosing a greater number of bogs, morasses, ditches, and
impassable ledges of rock than you have ever before seen in so
narrow a compass." The view at the register of deeds office was
no better. "Examining the records of that establishment, you
find churches, hotels, manufacturing establishments, buildings
both public and private, buried under monstrous piles of mort-
gages, judgments, liens, and various other encumbrances, to
relieve from which, and derive a profit, would require an advance of at least a thousand per cent on cost."

Naturally the new arrival should take the next stage for St.
Anthony — the land of promise. "In the centre of this unrivalled
panorama, two miles distant, though seeming at your very feet,
extending along the bank of the river on as beautiful a site as
you ever beheld, lies the town of St. Anthony, its white houses
gleaming in the sunlight, the mighty Father of waters, rushing,
roaring, foaming, leaping at its feet, tearing out its 40,000 feet
of lumber daily (with the new saws,) and eager to propel an infi-
nite amount of machinery, as soon as supplied by the hand of
enterprise and industry."

The Father of Waters was seen in a different light by the writer
of a boostering bit published in various papers, including the
Register of July 21, 1849. It was a poem written by that widely
admired, genteel lady scribbler, Mrs. L. H. Sigourney, without

benefit, apparently, of a visit to the territory. Its first four lines ran:

> We've a child out at nurse, where the waters run clear,
> And the Falls of St. Anthony ring on the ear, —
> And there, where the breezes are bracing and free,
> She's as healthful and happy as baby can be[13]

Poems and articles were not the only evidence of infatuation with the territory welcomed by early editors. Like his later Minnesota counterparts, Goodhue also welcomed the farmer who brought to his office the returns from a particularly bountiful harvest. Such indications of the region's fertility were always reported in the columns of the *Pioneer,* sometimes with a note of asperity for eastern editors. "For producing wheat, oats and potatoes," Goodhue wrote on September 11, 1851, "Minnesota may safely challenge the world. Every word of this is true; but not a newspaper in all New England or New York will copy it, for fear of turning the attention of people there to the free, fertile, healthful Northwest."

Goodhue was particularly aware of the eastern reader looking over his shoulder when it was necessary to report or comment on some unfavorable aspect of life in the territory — especially the weather. Did the thermometer occasionally register twenty below zero in St. Paul? Said Goodhue in the *Pioneer* of December 19, 1849, "In fact, we have no wind; so that we actually suffer less in the coldest weather, than they do in the cutting winds of Illinois, at a much milder temperature. . . . Where there is no wind, the body soon generates and carries along with it, a warm atmosphere. Our cold weather is dry, bracing, exhilarating — gives us an appetite and makes us fat." Visitors inclined to be caustic about Minnesota winters in their correspondence to eastern papers he dismissed contemptuously as "eastern exquisites." And when he felt obliged to call attention to the community's need for a cemetery, he took pains to put that need in a reassuring context. "Healthful as it is here, beyond parallel on the face of the globe, free from every symptom of bilious diseases, to the very margin of our lakes and rivers, without a solitary disease that may be considered in any way peculiarly incidental to our region, we shall nevertheless, in the course of nature, have to bury friends, and in our appointed time shall ourselves die and be buried." Goodhue thought a tract of, say, forty acres "a convenient distance from town" would be ample.[14]

The similarity of the frontier editor to the modern chamber of commerce did not stop with initiating good news of his area or minimizing the bad. Prospective immigrants wanted answers to specific questions about the territory, and what better source to query than the newspaper editor? When these inquiries first turned up in his mail pouch, Goodhue answered them individually, either in the columns of the *Pioneer* or by personal letters. But in the *Pioneer* of August 16, 1849, he commented that "they flock in so fast that we now adopt the expedient of caging what we have on hand together, and sending the answers back in one covey."

Typical of the queries was that of a man from Crawford County, Pennsylvania, who wanted to know if the Odd Fellows had any lodges in the territory. A writer in Calhoun County, Michigan, asked: Is your land susceptible of growing wheat generally? Can fruit be raised? Are your winters long and severe? Are there many settlements in the country around St. Paul? Are building materials to be got nearby? Are the people of St. Paul mostly from the East? Have you a full supply of mechanics and tradesmen? How many stores, hotels, tinshops, and groceries? Is there a regular line of steamboats daily up the Mississippi? Could a stock of ready-made clothing be sold this fall? If not, what commodity can be disposed of readily? What is the price of board per week? Would the climate be congenial to bilious and rather delicate constitutions?

"We will proceed," Goodhue told his readers on August 16, 1849, "to answer these several interrogatories, by way of a general statement respecting Minnesota and her prospects, without going far into detail.

"First, Minnesota is large enough for every body. All her lands east of the Mississippi, except the comparatively small number of sections already entered, are in market. Probably, in the course of a year or two our enviable domain will include the lands now occupied by the Sioux Indians. When the Indian title is extinguished, all that tract of country included within the northern line of the State of Iowa, and the Mississippi and Missouri rivers, extending as far west as Nebraska, will be open to settlers, like other parts of Minnesota. . . .

"St. Paul, which is the principal commercial town on the Mississippi, is situated upon a bluff some seventy-five or a hundred feet above the river on its outward sweep, commanding a view of the stream for a distance of some two miles. The face of the country in the rear, that is, north of the town, is quite uneven; and is made up of oak-openings, mirrored by numerous little ponds.

"St. Paul has about eight hundred inhabitants, most of whom have sprouted up within the last few months. We have already most of the material comforts of life; we are usually visited by four steamboats a week, and Galena, Dubuque and St. Louis, though the latter town is some eight hundred miles south of us, seem like neighbors. Their citizens frequently 'drop up' to make us a call. The mechanic arts in St. Paul are in many of the departments abundantly represented. We have no immediate want of ordinary carpenters nor blacksmiths, though their journey work obtains from $1.50 to $2 per day. . . .

"We need no more merchants. There is already too great a supply of all sorts of merchandise adapted to this market. If any merchant is so set upon trying this market as not to take our word for it, let him come and see.

"We want farmers. We are almost ready to offer a bounty on farmers. And we recommend to them to come — come as soon as they can. Corn and oats have retailed here during most of the present season at 50 and 75 cents. Potatoes at 75 and $1. A ready market will be found for agricultural produce during the whole time the Territory is being settled, and probably long afterwards, for the supply of the lumber trade. Three nations of Indians, too, are supplied with provisions yearly, by the U. S. Government which now brings their supplies from below.

"The Territory is settling very fast with immigrants from the eastern and middle States. We should probably have had a fuller flood of immigration had it not been for the cholera in the towns along the way. Young men can do well to work for wages almost anywhere in the Territory, and in the pine region they can get from $15 to $26 per month.

"Whether winter wheat is a sure crop, we can find but one citizen who has resided here long enough to inform us. He has a small extent of ground sowed with winter wheat which bids as fair as can be desired. Apples can be raised here unquestionably in great perfection. We doubt whether peaches would survive the winters. The winters are long and cold, but the temperature is so equable, that they are said to be agreeable. . . . The climate is almost precisely like that of New England. Bilious diseases are rare, and agues have no home here. Our country is proverbially healthy.

"Town and suburb lots are for sale . . . Lands in the suburbs of St. Paul are worth from ten to one hundred dollars per acre.

"As to the order of Odd Fellows, we have not heard of any, but there are a great many smart bachelors, who will have to continue odd if their other halves do not come along with you immigrants.[15]

"We have hotels enough and a good tin shop. Board at the hotels is about one dollar a day, and from two and a half to five dollars per week. Washing is from seventy-five cents to one dollar and a half per dozen. We have some eighteen stores and twenty-five groceries of the first water; we have several excellent ministers and one good school."

As letters of inquiry continued to pour in, Goodhue occasionally indulged in lusty humor. On June 10, 1852, he told a correspondent that the trip to Minnesota would cost him eight dollars by railroad and stage from Chicago to Galena and five dollars more by steamboat from Galena to St. Paul. And he added: "You would save the fare of a woman, by marrying one here. We have many fine white girls, and some mixed, to any shade required; and a plenty of olive, copper and red — real native bloomers, built all the way from the ground up — valued at from a pair of three point blankets, to a pony and a pound of powder, with red leggins, coal black hair and eyes, warranted to kindle at the touch of the first spark." To the question "Is your country increasing fast in population?" he replied succinctly, "It is. The means are faithfully used, at any rate, in Saint Paul."[16]

So much for the *Pioneer's* reflection of the territorial world. What of the mirror itself?

The *Pioneer* was a better paper than its contemporaries, but it was not different from them. In appearance, content, news, and business policies and practices, the early papers of Minnesota Territory were markedly similar.[17] And, like Goodhue, their editors and publishers, almost without exception, were trained in newspaper or law offices or printing shops back east.

The men who guided the *Register* and the *Chronicle* — papers that became the *Pioneer's* first competitors — are a case in point. Andrew Randall, the *Register's* restless founder, and Nathaniel McLean and John P. Owens, who bought him out, all had newspaper experience in Ohio. Also from Ohio was James Hughes, a lawyer who edited the *Chronicle* briefly before it merged with the *Register* in August, 1849. Lorenzo A. Babcock, a native of Vermont who for a few months succeeded Owens as publisher of the *Chronicle and Register,* and William G. Le Duc, another Ohioan who replaced McLean as editor of the combined *Chronicle and Register* in September, 1850, were both lawyers. Charles J. Henniss, who succeeded them in November, 1850, was also a lawyer who had been junior editor of the *Philadelphia North American and United States Gazette.*[18]

"Colonel" Daniel A. Robertson, who founded the *Minnesota Democrat* in 1850, was a native of Nova Scotia. He had been admitted to the New York bar in 1839 but deserted law for journalism. Before going to Minnesota in 1850, he owned and edited the *Mount Vernon* (Ohio) *Democrat,* and then became editor of the *Cincinnati Enquirer.* John C. Terry and George W. Moore, successive publishers of the *Minnesotian* in 1851 and 1852, were printers from Ohio and Pennsylvania, respectively. The backgrounds of the team of Prescott and Jones, who founded the *North-Western Democrat* in 1853, are obscure. Prescott may have been George W. Prescott, a Maine lawyer who moved to Minnesota in 1850. He practiced law in St. Paul and St. Anthony, taught school for some years in St. Anthony, and became territorial superintendent of public instruction. Not even so tentative a guess can be made about Jones.[19]

An exception to the lawyer-editor-printer pattern was Elmer

Tyler, a tailor who believed that St. Anthony needed "an organ" and set about to give it the *Express*. In 1851 he persuaded lawyer Isaac Atwater to edit the paper and then went to Chicago where he hired the Woodbury brothers, H. and J. P., printers, to run the shop. Within three months part ownership of the *Express* passed from Tyler to the Woodburys, next to Atwater, and then in May, 1852, to George D. Bowman, who had edited the first paper published in Schuylkill County, Pennsylvania, before coming to Minnesota.[20]

The involvement of most of these men in newspaper work was episodic. Goodhue, in one sense the most stable of the group, died in August, 1852, after only three years of editing the *Pioneer*. The longest editorial career — 1849 to 1857 — was that of John P. Owens, and it was divided among the *Register*, the *Chronicle and Register*, and the *Minnesotian*. His endurance was perhaps remarkable, for he was an intensely partisan editor, first as a Whig and then as a Republican, and his gift for invective provoked physical assault on at least one occasion.[21]

All the territorial newspapers were much the same in physical appearance. They were published on good rag paper and consistently contained four pages of six or seven columns each. Headlines, if any, were set in minute type and were never more than a single column wide. Illustrations — a rarity at first — appeared infrequently as line drawings in advertisements.[22] The only individuality lay in the paper's choice of type for the logo: the *North-Western Democrat* achieved distinction with a lacy Old English, the *Minnesotian* with a startlingly modern type face that would not look out of place in today's *McCall's*.

The first pages of the initial editions of these early weeklies invariably had the over-all gray look of type set solid, and they usually offered foreign news, a short story, or articles clipped from *Putnam's Monthly Magazine, Godey's Lady's Book,* or *Harper's New Monthly Magazine*. If the paper survived, the scissored material on page one gradually gave way to the business cards of lawyers, doctors, and real estate dealers. Page two was the editor's. Rarely did advertisements invade it, and articles written by the editor were usually published under a single-column masthead with leads between the lines to provide white space. Page three featured items clipped from the *National Intelligencer,* the *New York Tribune,* the *Galena Advertiser,* or other papers with which the editor exchanged subscriptions. If his paper was prospering, such items shared page three with advertisements. Page four was usually solid with business cards and advertisements of merchants at Galena, Dubuque, and sometimes St. Louis, as well as at St. Paul, Stillwater, and St. Anthony.

The advertisements were restrained in appearance, set in small type and only a single column wide. They were also modest in language. "Genteel Vests, and well-fitting pants, have much to do with the success of mankind." "WILLIAM TAYLOR, BARBER AND HAIR-DRESSER, Has built and fitted up a SHAVING SALOON, on Third street, next door west of the new Post Office in Saint Paul, up to the increasing luxury, style and elegance, of the growing metropolis of Minnesota." "TO THE LADIES OF ST. PAUL. Deeply sensible of past favors, I again invite your attention to my MILLINERY ESTABLISHMENT, confidently assured that I can show you a variety of materials and trimmings that will repay inspection. . . . M. A. Marvin."[23]

Many of these advertisements were unchanged week after week, month after month, to take advantage of annual rates. Consequently, when the month-old *Minnesotian* came out on October 29, 1851, with an advertisement that ran two columns wide and proclaimed "STOVES" in thirty-point type, the effect was like a cherry bomb in a funeral chapel. If the reader recovered from the shock of that flamboyant display and turned to the back page, he discovered a second two-column advertisement in even larger type, running a half-page deep. In addition to two pictures of stoves ("Irving's Air Tight" and "Queen of the Prairies"), the ad was surmounted by a drawing of an eagle spread against a star-spangled sky. But did the other papers and their advertisers follow the leader and break out the big type? They did not. Instead, as the *Minnesotian* became better established and its advertising columns more widely patronized, the two-column ads disappeared, and stoves became as chaste as undergarments. Big, splashy ads were all very well when space was not at a premium.

Advertising rates did not vary among the papers. A year's contract for weekly insertions ranged from five dollars for a business card of not over six lines to fifty dollars a column. For a single insertion, the rate was one dollar a square (twelve lines or less) and fifty cents for each additional insertion. Advertisers were expected to bring their copy to the shop.[24]

The advertiser who arrived at the shop, copy in hand or head, was likely to find the editor bent over a slant-topped desk, writing in longhand the editorial or article for page two or the short local item picked up on his forays around town or countryside. Beyond him one or more printers stood at chest-high type cases, setting by hand the type for ads or straight matter. At the back of the room stood the Washington hand press, that small marvel of unautomated efficiency which produced at best about 250 impressions an hour. When printers had set all the type for pages one and four — usually Monday afternoon for a paper published Wednesday or Thursday — one of them would lock the type into an iron form on the bed of the press, roll ink onto the type, and then lay a sheet of paper over the form. By turning a hand crank, he could roll the bed along a track to a point half an inch below the platen. A pull on a lever would lower the platen to enforce the inked impression. The bed was then returned along the track, the sheet of newsprint removed, and the printer repeated the process.[25]

The equipment seems primitive judged by today's standards, but it was the best then available. Press, type, paper, and ink were produced by plants hundreds of miles from St. Paul, miles which could be traversed only during the summer season when rivers and lakes were open; the costs of overland transportation in winter would have been prohibitive. The Mississippi River was the trade artery that carried not only many editors but also the supplies they needed to Minnesota. Funneling into it from the east was the Ohio River as well as the important Erie Canal route through the Great Lakes. Such supplies as paper could be obtained at St. Louis and shipped northward by steamboat. The newsprint for Goodhue's *Pioneer*, for example, was purchased in St. Louis in 1849. Goodhue's first press was made in Cincinnati, his second in Boston, where he also obtained type.[26]

The frontier printer had to be resourceful. If he ran out of ink, he concocted some to his own recipe. He also made the rollers needed to spread ink over the form from a combination of heavy glue, sugar or molasses, and glycerine. When an angry subscriber once sought to stop the publication of the *Freeborn County Standard* (Albert Lea) by removing the lever from the press, the editor "merely substituted a fence rail for the missing lever and got out his paper." If the frontier printer misjudged his paper needs or if a supplier failed to fill his order, he was forced to publish in alternate weeks or to reduce the size of his paper. Not until 1859, after Minnesota had become a state, was newsprint manufactured locally by a paper mill on Hennepin Island at the Falls of St. Anthony.[27]

The subscription price of the *Pioneer* did not increase in the five years from 1849 to 1854 — two dollars a year paid in advance. Both Goodhue and the *Minnesotian* tried a rate of three dollars if not paid in advance and concluded that the plan did not work. "Crediting out newspapers over the whole extent of our land of magnificent distances, is a ruinous business to the publisher," Goodhue wrote in the *Pioneer* of April 10, 1850, to explain why he had discontinued the three-dollar rate.

Newspaper publishing in Minnesota Territory was unlikely to make a man rich, Owens of the *Minnesotian* intimated to his readers on April 2, 1853, but he added that the "people of Minnesota are remarkable for the liberality with which they support their local newspapers. The three establishments of St. Paul all appear to be doing a prosperous business. The aggregate investment in printing offices in this place we presume amounts to $12,000."[28]

Certainly not the least prosperous of the three offices was the *Pioneer's*. Goodhue had brought two printers with him from Wisconsin, and on September 6, 1849, he advertised for a printer "to work by the piece." Two years later, when the legislature was in session, his shop employed ten men. He paid them nine to ten dollars a week.[29]

He might well have given them a bonus, for one of the *Pioneer's* claims to excellence was its printing and composition. Column after column, page after page, issue after issue was innocent of a dropped line, a wrong font, or a transposed letter.

The *Minnesota Democrat,* the *Minnesotian,* and the *Express* may have had more white space and a somewhat less gray appearance than the *Pioneer* (the *Minnesotian* actually began publication using some two-line headlines in fourteen-point type), but they were all more vulnerable to mechanical error.

The *Pioneer* under Goodhue had other virtues as well. The legislature's award of official printing made it a newspaper of record, but the essential serious-mindedness and ability of its editor largely determined its other strengths: a selection of exchanges that fairly consistently favored the significant over the sensational, a responsible advertising policy, and vigorous, often colorful writing.

As official printer, Goodhue published in the *Pioneer* the proceedings of both houses of the legislature and the texts of the laws it passed. These consumed more than half of the paper's four pages during and immediately following a session. The proceedings were usually dull reading, but the record was there. In addition, the *Pioneer* and its contemporaries published the texts of important territorial and federal documents, such as presidential messages to Congress, the territory's Organic Act, Governor Alexander Ramsey's proclamation of the organization of territorial government, and his report as superintendent of Indian affairs.

Contributing further to the serious tone of the *Pioneer* was the material Goodhue selected to republish from papers with which he exchanged subscriptions. A description of a storm on Vesuvius, an incident from the Mexican War, a speech by Senator Thomas H. Benton on railroads, a summary of a new postal law, an article about the Mormon migration, the new wealth of California, "Americans in Brazil," "Americans in Japan," railroad progress, steam and water power, "Pressure of the Ocean," the economic situation in the East, "The Night Attack on Fort Erie," "A Sunday on the Dead Sea," American credit and European finance, John C. Frémont's reports on "The Great Basin"— these are typical of the longer articles clipped by Goodhue from eastern newspapers and magazines. This is not to say that the "melancholy-accident" item, or the short piece of sentimental fiction that abounded in the press of the period — on the frontier and elsewhere — was entirely missing from the *Pioneer*. A steamboat explosion was always good for several paragraphs no matter where it occurred, and a column-long article on a serious subject was occasionally spiced by a paragraph with a leadin such as "More Blood — Man Killed Last Night." Indeed, on June 20, 1850, Goodhue's scissors went berserk, and *Pioneer* readers were fairly bathed in the gore of "Horrible Murder and Suicide," "Body Found," "A Wild Girl in Connecticut," "Deliberate Suicide," "Seduction and Adultery," "Severe Fight and Death at Macon, Miss.," "Arrest of a Murderer," "U. S. Troops Murdered by the Comanche Indians," "A Fearful Leap" — all on the front page of one issue. But by September 19 the flow was stanched, and the *Pioneer* returned to serious fare by devoting almost its entire front page to "Reminiscences of Congress."

A similar sense of responsibility — with similar deviations therefrom — governed the advertising policy of the *Pioneer*. The paper's advertising columns were relatively free of extravagant claims for quack remedies, and its news columns contained few puffs for advertisers. "The press is abominably prostituted to the use and profit of quack medicine venders," Goodhue editorialized on July 25, 1850, doubtless with one eye on the competition. "Publishers ought to refuse to advertise many of the infernal nostrums that are extensively advertised, whatever price may be offered, and whatever array of certificates may be appended. It is our own determination to advertise no remedy which we would ourselves refrain from taking; for although a journal is a sort of common carrier — and advertising omnibus — into which almost any thing is entitled to go for pay, the publisher cannot be required to make his journal unclean as well as common, by admitting anything, however vile or pernicious."

One of the few patent medicines regularly advertised in the *Pioneer* was Ayer's Cherry Pectoral, and its claims were fairly restrained. As for editorial puffings of advertisers, so common in some newspapers of the period, "It is not our practice to notice those who advertise with us, editorially," Goodhue wrote on May 31, 1849, in apology for a rare exception to his rule. On one of the few occasions when he did give editorial space to an advertiser, it was derogatory. Accompanying a notice for "A New Volume of the American Phrenological Journal" by Fowler and Wells in the *Pioneer* of September 4, 1851, was the bristling comment: "We publish to-day the advertisement of Fowler & Wells, because it is sent to us to publish. But we assure our readers, that in our opinion, a more arrant humbug was never hatched than this same Phrenology. It has neither fact nor philosophy to sustain it — nothing but the prurient vanity of mankind. We never saw yet a disciple of Fowler, who was not an empty, conceited fool."

This denunciation suggests another of the *Pioneer's* virtues — vigorous, colorful language. Goodhue was sometimes overly exuberant in the length of his sentences and always in his use of commas, but he had a nice flair for apt figures of speech. In one vivid image, he could convey the desolation of the entire community at the departure of the season's last steamboat: "Finally she went off, with a tear in her eye, and disappeared around the bend, Mr. [Edward D.] Neill's church steeple standing on tiptoe to catch the last glimpse of her."[30] His humor, too, was sharpened by compression, as when he reported the feat of one Sergeant Findley of the United States Dragoons at Fort Snelling. "Our readers know of those successive flights of wooden stairs, leading down from the end of Bench street, by Mr. Randall's store, to the Lower Steamboat Landing," he wrote in the *Pioneer* of November 28, 1850. "Sergeant Findley, who was down from the fort, rode his horse, pell mell down all those flights of stairs, to Mr. Randall's store door, and then took the horse back up the stairs, by the same way he came down, without injury to horse or rider. The horse must have been perfectly sober."

Such editorial comment was not limited to "brighteners" in either the *Pioneer* or its contemporaries. The journalistic conventions of the time encouraged a practice that the modern reader would declare a serious fault. Today's reader, accustomed to the strict divorce of news from comment in his newspaper, might take offense at the unvarying interposition of the personality and opinions of the editor. The frontier reader, raised on Greeley and Bennett, expected it. If a band of Sioux ambushed and scalped a small company of Chippewa, these editors both reported and deplored the event in the same stickful of type.

After a ball at the Central House, Goodhue noted on January 23, 1850, the number of couples and in the same paragraph lectured the dancers. ("Dancing, properly conducted, with chaste, correct music, has a tendency, not only to improve the manners, but to elevate, to etherialize the mind.")

The practice had its charms, especially in the hands of an editor who could juxtapose two accidents in this manner: "On Sunday last, the Rev. Mr. Neill and lady of St. Paul, were overturned in a buggy, in driving down the hill from this side to the ferry at Fort Snelling; but were providentially only slightly injured. The same day, a soldier from the fort, named Robert Downing, was going down the same hill with a cask of whiskey on his shoulder, fell down, and the cask falling upon him, broke three of his ribs, his thigh and his spine; so that he soon died — an awful commentary upon the text, that 'The way of the transgressor is hard.'" [31]

Yet some twentieth-century sensation-mongers of the press might emulate Goodhue's restraint, if not his syntax, in reporting a local crime. "Last Friday, Feb. 22d, Alexander McLeod, a well known voyageur, living near St. Paul, beat a man to death with his fist, who was driving oxen and whose name was Gordon. We forbear any comments, as the matter will come before a judicial tribunal." Even telegraphic dispatches, lifted from other papers, did not escape the editor's personal touch. "We are constrained, reluctantly forced to believe, that Gen. Taylor, President of the United States, died on the evening of the 9th of July, by a sudden attack of chronic diarrhea, which he contracted in the Mexican campaign," wrote Goodhue. "The sad news reached us last Monday, by the steamboat Yankee; which bro't from the Galena Advertiser, the following telegraphic dispatches." [32]

Equally strange to the modern reader is the tendency of these papers to bury the news, to report it inadequately, or to ignore it completely. The *Minnesota Democrat* of April 13 and the *Pioneer* of April 14, 1853, after a column of material of marginal interest, got around to reporting that the passengers of the "West Newton" — the first boat up the Mississippi that season — had heard via the telegraph just before leaving Galena that Willis A. Gorman of Indiana had been appointed the second governor of Minnesota Territory. One wonders, too, about the local reader's reaction to this brief item, quoted in its entirety from the *Pioneer* of November 11, 1852. "Henry M. Rice. It is with deepest regret that we announce the probable demise of this gentleman in the course of a few hours." Murder? Or perhaps the reader had seen the *Democrat* of the preceding day: "Henry M. Rice is supposed to be dying, which spreads a gloom over this community. May God, in His mercy, cast aside the bitter cup, and rescue his family, friends, and Minnesota from this threatened calamity." (Mr. Rice was a Democrat.) If the reader depended on the *Pioneer* for his news, he had to wait until the following week to learn that it was illness not murder that had threatened Mr. Rice. "H. M. Rice. It is with the greatest satisfaction, that we are enabled to announce in this number, the recovery of this gentleman from his recent attack of disease, and that he is now in a fair way to soon be in the enjoyment of his usual health."

None of the St. Paul papers, and only the *Express* in St. Anthony, made a pretense of covering local government. The "Town of St. Paul" was incorporated by the territorial legislature in November, 1849, and its government entrusted to a president and board of trustees.[33] But aside from an occasional demand that these officials do something about the streets, the St. Paul papers tended to ignore their existence. Ramsey County's board of commissioners and the sessions of the district courts also received little attention.[34] For example, although there had been forty-six cases on the docket of the first district court at Stillwater, Judge Aaron Goodrich presiding, the *Chronicle and Register* of August 25, 1849, reported that the grand jury returned ten bills of indictment: "one for assault and battery, . . . one for perjury, four for selling liquor to Indians, and four for keeping gaming houses." The paper noted that only the assault case was tried, the others being laid over to the next term. The *Chronicle and Register* did not report the outcome of the assault case, the name of the defendant, or the names of any of the persons charged in the other nine cases. Instead, the paper admired the "vigilance and firmness" of prosecuting attorney Morton S. Wilkinson in dispatching his business and remarked on the hospitality of the citizens of Stillwater during the six-day court term.[35]

Such omissions were doubtless the result of oversight. But policy determined a more significant omission from the columns of the *Pioneer* during its first year. What one misses most in its pages is any sense of involvement in the great conflict that was building up in the nation in the 1850s. In Washington the House of Representatives, meeting in December, 1849, was so split by factions that it needed sixty-three ballots to elect a speaker. The Senate heard the impassioned oratory of Henry Clay, John C. Calhoun, and Daniel Webster in debate on the Compromise of 1850. In September Congress passed the essential bills embodying that compromise — the admission of California, the fugitive slave law, the organization of New Mexico and Utah territories, and the abolition of the slave trade in the District of Columbia. Only faint echoes of these stirring events carried to Minnesota via the *Pioneer,* and its editor offered no comment. His policy was consistent but parochial; ever conscious of eastern readers, the territory's prime booster did not want to risk offending either northern or southern lawmakers who would pass on territorial appropriations.

CHAPTER 2

Pioneers and Partisans

THE POLITICAL SITUATION during the first five years of the territory was as fluid as its rivers and considerably less clear. The contest for political control of the future state was fought only secondarily between Democrats and the less numerous Whigs. The basic struggle during this period was between the territory's two most powerful businessmen — Henry Hastings Sibley and Henry Mower Rice — both of whom were Democrats. The prize was the post of territorial delegate to Congress. As the sole official representative of Minnesota in Washington, the delegate could be expected to exercise great influence in awarding patronage. Underlying the Sibley-Rice political enmity was their rivalry in the diminishing fur trade, a rivalry that had grown out of an American Fur Company partnership dissolved in rancor in 1849. The private correspondence of the period bristled with charges of personal disloyalty and political betrayal. Sibley had the advantage of longer residence in the area (he had been a fur trader at Mendota since 1834) and the friendship of the territory's first governor, Alexander Ramsey, a Whig appointee of the national administration. He also had the support of Goodhue's *Pioneer*.[1]

Whether conducted by Democrats or Whigs, the earliest papers in the territory — the *Pioneer*, the *Register*, the *Chronicle*, and the combined *Chronicle and Register* — initially took a nonpartisan stance cued by Sibley, and then abandoned it. Later territorial papers — the *Minnesota Democrat*, the *St. Anthony Express*, the *Minnesotian*, and the *North-Western Democrat* —

were partisan in varying degrees of intensity from their first issues.

In Wisconsin, Goodhue had published a Whig paper and he had been active in Whig politics. His friends expected his new Minnesota paper to be Whig in its persuasion. When Goodhue arrived in St. Paul, however, he found that the political tone had been set by Sibley in the preceding fall of 1848 when he defeated Rice in the first contest for territorial delegate.[2] That tone was spirited but nonpartisan. Accordingly the first issue of the *Pioneer* carried the editor's declaration of neutrality along with the noncommittal legend, "Sound Principles, Safe Men and Moderate Measures." Similarly the first issue of the *Register* on April 27, 1849, had declared itself opposed to "party faction," and McLean and Owens — though Whigs — did not change that position when they took over from Randall. The *Chronicle* at the start of its two-month career on May 31, 1849, declared itself to be mildly Whiggish in its intention to give "cordial support of the principles of the administration of General [Zachary] Taylor." In the union of these two, *Register* neutrality won out over *Chronicle* cordiality. "We as citizens and as whigs, are willing to leave it for the future to determine which of these parties are to sway the destinies of our Territory," announced the *Chronicle and Register* on August 25, 1849.

Members of the first territorial legislature were elected in August, 1849, on a nonpartisan basis, but when they assembled in St. Paul on September 3, the signs of Whig organization began to be apparent. Territorial Secretary Charles K. Smith, who like Ramsey was a Whig appointee, had charge of disbursing the $13,700 appropriated by Congress to defray the expenses of the legislature, and he wanted at least part of the printing to go to the *Chronicle and Register*. Goodhue, in the meantime, had borrowed money from Sibley to purchase the new press he needed to support his bid for the official printing. He continued to affirm his neutrality in a leading article announcing that bid in the *Pioneer* of August 30, 1849. His brother Isaac N. Goodhue, who was temporarily associated with him in publishing the *Pioneer*, asked Sibley to use his influence with the legislators on behalf of the *Pioneer*. "We feel that you are the man to save us," Isaac wrote Sibley. After protracted maneuvering, the 1849 legislature split the printing between the *Pioneer* and the *Chronicle and Register*.[3]

In October, 1849, Rice supporters held a convention to attempt the organization of the Democratic party in the territory — a move designed by Rice in part to embarrass Sibley but defended by Goodhue in the *Pioneer* of October 18 as necessitated by the partisan operations of the Whigs. Sibley, invited to attend, discreetly regretted that business kept him at Mendota. He had been re-elected on August 1, 1849, to a second term as territorial delegate by an undivided vote of the people, he wrote, so he could not depart from neutrality. As a private citizen, however, he declared himself to be a "Democrat of the Jeffersonian school." The *Pioneer*, in reporting the convention and Sibley's stand, recorded on October 25 that it had been named the organ of the party in the territory, and in that issue the legend "Sound Principles, Safe Men and Moderate Measures" gave way to a trinity exclusively Democratic. In November, after Sibley had gone to Washington to attend the opening of Congress, Goodhue wrote to him: "The Whigs here are more bitter against you than against any one else, not excepting myself — alleging that you made my politics — which is rather too true for a pleasant joke." He may have been defending himself not merely against Whig denunciations but also against charges by Sibley's friends that he had sold out to Rice.[4]

If Delegate Sibley made Goodhue's politics Democratic, Secretary Smith confirmed them in anti-Whiggery. Smith's interference in the award of the official printing had incensed Goodhue, and worse was to come. McLean and Owens of the *Chronicle and Register* presented bills of $742 for part of their share of the printing, and Smith apparently paid them promptly. When the legislature adjourned late in October, Goodhue's larger bill had been only partially paid, and Smith indicated that he would have to wait a long time for the balance.[5] Smith probably did not suspect that the innocent round face of the editor masked poisonous fangs. In a *Pioneer* editorial on November 8, 1849, entitled "Licensed Thieving," the fangs were bared. "When, long after his official duties required him to be here, Secretary [of the

Interior Thomas] Ewing's Secretary of the Territory of Minnesota stole into Saint Paul, last summer, we supposed, not
only from the influences which secured his appointment, but also
from the hang-dog looks of the fellow, that he would steal *in*
Saint Paul. That he was snappish, unmannerly and mean, as
unfit to occupy a public post as a soreheaded dog is to occupy a
parlor, he has daily demonstrated since his arrival. The record
of his meanness, in all private transactions, would fill a volume;
and can be substantiated by all who have dealt with him."

Goodhue proceeded to fill part of a column with an alleged
record of Smith's public transactions, citing excessive expenditures for stationery and firewood as well as refusals to pay for
honest services. "For the incidental printing as well as for a large
amount of advertising done for the Executive Department before
the Secretary had yet arrived in Minnesota — printing done at
an enormous expense and amounting to more than $2,700, we
have received only six hundred dollars — an amount insufficient
to cover our bills now due in Saint Louis, for stationery. As it
does not appear, by all we can ascertain, that the Secretary has
paid out more than five or six thousand dollars, and he does not
condescend to explain what he has done with the rest of the
$13,500 [*sic*], nor deny that he has received it, we feel constrained
to believe that he intends to make a *clean grab* of all that re-
mains, or else that he has invested the money in some *private
speculation*. We are ready to bet that he will prove a defaulter;
and that he has given mere straw security in his bond; and that
this poor pettifogger, who was raked out of the kennel in Ohio
by Secretary Ewing, on purpose to plunder the Treasury, and
with the absolute certainty that he could touch nothing valuable
that would not stick to his fingers, after stealing into the Territory and stealing *in* the Territory, will steal *out* of it with all he
can plunder and with the united execration of all honest men."

Goodhue was tenacious. For the next several months, hardly
an issue of the *Pioneer* did not direct at least one shaft at the
secretary. But after castigating the national administration for
imposing Smith upon the territory, Goodhue had a second
thought. "We certainly do not believe in the total depravity of
the Whigs at Washington," he added on November 15, 1849.

"Smith was appointed without being known. It is rash to conclude that the Senate would ever have confirmed his nomination, if he had shown his face in Washington, looking, as it does, like a caricature of the eighth commandment violated." A week later on November 22, noting that in the temporary absence of Ramsey, Secretary Smith was serving as acting governor, Goodhue howled: "God of Heaven! to what lower depths of degradation can a young territory be thrust? Steeped in the foul pool of political corruption — with such whiggery as this surrounding you like an element — spreading out every way, every where, in, upon, above, beneath, around everything, like the lice of Egypt, can democrats be bamboozled any longer with this stuff about neutralism?" On December 5 even the weather report carried the attack: "The snow which fell the other day, has melted and mixed with the surface of the earth, producing mud as tenacious as — the fingers of the Secretary."

In his issue of December 12, Goodhue became more specific in his charges against Smith. After quoting from the United States statutes on embezzlement, Goodhue asserted that a number of legislators, whom he named, had been paid per diem allowances and mileage by the secretary in foreign coins of less value than the amounts due them. For this "embezzlement," he called on Washington to remove Smith.

Nor was he content to limit his campaign against the secretary to the pages of his newspaper. To Sibley in Washington, he wrote: "If it is a possible thing to get Secretary Smith removed, I hope it will be done. He pays me nothing — and if this continues much longer, I am ruined. Six hundred dollars is all he has paid me — which is not as much money as the *paper* cost, bought by me since August." And less than a month later: "$200 more, is all I have yet recd. from the Secretary. He *must* be removed and *shall* be. In my paper of this week you will see what charges are preferred against him. . . . By the next mail, I shall forward to you, fuller and more specific charges — sworn to, in due form; which I wish you to lay before the Secretary of Treasury."[6]

The charges were forwarded, but Goodhue waited in vain for action. Smith, he reported to Sibley, was getting his vouchers

"patched up." Another correspondent explained to the delegate
that Smith had paid the balances due the legislators and got new
certificates of receipt. "These certificates without any date the
Secretary may attempt to use to invalidate the charge and place
the Editor of the Pioneer in a false light. Of course the facts are
too well known here for him to attempt it, but where all the
facts are not known it might produce an impression."[7]

It is obvious that Goodhue's animus toward Smith was personal and grew out of his pecuniary interest. A number of Sibley's correspondents commented on Goodhue's drive for the
dollar, and some of them intimated that the delegate should
restrain his journalistic ally. At least one of them — Joseph R.
Brown — minimized the vendetta between the secretary and the
editor, assuring Sibley that "as both are wrong, and considered
to be more particularly in their sphere when dealing in Billings-
gate, but little attention is paid to the feud." In any case, Goodhue's efforts did not immediately result in Smith's removal, and
he seethed privately for a year.[8]

The town may have grown inured to Goodhue's campaign
against Smith, but the editor's attack on another Whig official
aroused such heat that he was set upon physically and the affair
boiled to a climax in a pair of citizens' indignation meetings.
Today's newspaper reader marvels that the courts of the period
were not clogged with suits for libel. Territorial statutes said
little about it, merely describing the forms of the complaint and
the indictment and establishing truth "with good motives and
justifiable ends" as an adequate defense in a prosecution for
criminal libel. No libel cases reached the territorial supreme
court; indeed the first such suit was not heard by the state's
highest court until 1864. One suspects that such suits were scarce,
in fact, because the injured parties found their remedies in
direct action rather than in recourse to law. A solid punch to
the jaw may have given greater satisfaction to the aggrieved. As
we shall see, Goodhue was to experience even more severe physical punishment.[9]

The incident grew out of a confused election in September,
1850, in which the territory was to choose its third delegate to
Congress. Rumors abounded: Rice would oppose Sibley; Sibley

would not be a candidate to succeed himself; Sibley would run as the Democratic nominee; Rice would back Colonel Alexander M. Mitchell, Whig appointee to the post of territorial marshal, as the Whig candidate. Again Sibley's friends privately voiced their suspicions of Goodhue's loyalty. "I have every reason to believe he is leagued in with the Rice faction," Dr. Thomas R. Potts, close family friend and physician, wrote Sibley in January. On February 4 Joseph R. Brown, a Sibley trusty, advised the dele-, gate conspiratorially, "you would do well not to confide too far, even in the Pioneers of the country. This I repeat and doubt not you will understand my meaning. . . . There are still men who will sell themselves and all they possess *for a price*, but if subsequently a higher price can be obtained, they are ever ready to betray their master 'with a kiss.'" Franklin Steele, Sibley's brother-in-law and another power in the frontier area, wrote the following month: "I am sorry that you should have written for its [the *Pioneer's*] colums [*sic*] for I believe it to be subservient to Rice and his faction." Interspersed with these allegations, letters from Goodhue complained to Sibley of his financial plight and suggested that the breach with the Rice faction could be healed. The implication seemed plain. But by June Rice was openly promoting the candidacy of Mitchell, and Goodhue had disowned him. "Rice is virtually read out of the party and cannot annoy us much more," he wrote Sibley with typical optimism. ". . . Although I have thought it good policy not to make any attack upon Rice, in print, I have spared no pains to have his treachery to the party properly understood by all democrats."[10]

On July 31, 1850, a group of Rice Democrats and unorganized Whigs, calling themselves a "Territorial Convention," nominated Mitchell for the delegacy. Two days earlier Sibley in Washington had offered himself as a candidate "without distinction of party." Goodhue, unwilling to wait for the Democrats to move, revealed in the *Pioneer* of August 8 that he was "requested to say that Henry H. Sibley will be a candidate." He followed this announcement with a strong editorial endorsing Sibley on August 15. Rice had selected Mitchell more for his connections with the Whig administration in Washington than for his popularity with Whigs in the territory, and local dislike for Mitchell resulted in a second "Territorial Convention," convened in St. Paul on August 10, by some of his Whig and Democratic adversaries. This group nominated as their candidate David Olmsted, a twenty-eight-year-old fur trader and Democratic politician who had recently been Rice's business partner in a federal contract to gather up the Winnebago Indians wandering off their reservation near Long Prairie.[11]

Olmsted, looking for support from the Whig-inclined *Chronicle and Register,* discovered that the paper was for sale. McLean had been appointed Indian subagent at Fort Snelling the preceding winter and was eager to get out of newspaper publishing. According to his partner, John P. Owens, the paper was sold to Olmsted in July. The trader proved both an indifferent publisher and an uncommitted candidate. Owens later wrote that "during the few months which Olmsted owned the establishment, the paper had different editors at different periods. Part of the time, we believe, it edited itself." As for Olmsted's candidacy, Rice quickly persuaded him to withdraw in favor of Mitchell by offering him full control of their partnership in the Winnebago removal.[12]

In the meantime, Goodhue, who had not yet been fully paid by Secretary Smith, continued to complain to Sibley about finances. "You know that I have worked at this press and my brother with me like galley slaves, for more than a year, my wife doing the work of two hired girls in keeping boarders; beside having the care of our little ones — that we have lived a life of wretched privation, unusual to us — in a shanty, unplastered, through the winter for want of my pay for the public printing — and that much of the small amount I have received from the Secretary, was in Soldiers warrants at $150. each, which were unavailable to me in the payment of debts, except at a ruinous sacrifice. . . . If I fail of receiving my pay, and the Secretary remains in office to harrass me with these ruinous delays, we have no remedy left but bankruptcy." Joseph R. Brown made a quick visit to Washington to confer with Sibley about the situation in the territory. Shortly after he returned, he wrote the delegate that "Goodhue is secured, and bound to support you in *any position* or under *any* and *all* circumstances." Because of the extended session of Congress, Sibley was unable to get back to the territory to campaign. Nonetheless, the voters on September 2, 1850, chose Sibley over Mitchell by a vote of 649 to 559.[13]

The campaign between the Rice and Sibley factions had been bitter. "The distinction between 'Whig' and 'Democrat' was supplanted by that between 'Fur' and 'Anti-fur' and the campaign degenerated into a rancorous squabble," commented William W. Folwell, Minnesota's respected historian. Fred B. Sibley, managing his brother's business at Mendota, wrote him that "The expenses of the election have I imagine some little exceeded One Thousand dollars, but not much." The Rice-Mitchell forces, he estimated, had spent three or four times as much. Goodhue wrote Sibley that the Rice interests "freely and openly" offered money for votes. Joe Brown, reporting that Judge David Cooper of the territorial supreme court was Mitchell's strongest supporter in Stillwater and St. Anthony, wrote that "It is said Rice *loaned* Cooper $400 and made him a *present* of a keg of Brandy, and it is a matter of debate *which* made him a Mitchell man."[14]

The bitterness hung on after the election, and a number of new developments disquieted the Sibley forces. Mitchell went to Washington for the apparent purpose of exerting influence with newly elected President Millard Fillmore, and rumors floated back that Mitchell men were to replace incumbents in certain Indian agencies. Daniel A. Robertson arrived from Ohio to establish a new newspaper, the *Minnesota Democrat,* which promptly urged formal party organization. The *Democrat* "will be a zealous, fearless and unwavering advocate of the principles and organization of the Democratic Party as promulged [*sic*] by the uncompromising school of Jefferson and Jackson," he declared in his salutatory on December 10, 1850. Olmsted sold the *Chronicle and Register* to Charles Henniss and that paper began to make similar noises on behalf of the Whigs. Dr. Potts wrote Sibley that Henniss paid Olmsted $1,000 in cash borrowed from Robertson and "the balance" in notes endorsed by Rice. The scheme, according to Potts, was that "if Henniss could get any or all of the [official] printing he was to divide with the Democrat." Late in 1850 when both papers moved into a new three-story brick building owned by Rice, Sibley's friends became convinced that Rice would control both self-appointed party organs.[15]

In the three-cornered battle for the official printing that was shaping up, the chance of a two-way split between *Democrat* and *Chronicle and Register* seemed likely. "This you will perceive leaves the 'Pioneer' *no where*," Joe Brown wrote Sibley, "and as it is, or will be a kind of hermaphrodite sheet, has no party, and can hope for nor receive support but from the Fur Company, it must naturally die and *then, then* the organs can grind finely, and both having the same great head [*Rice*] to direct their oppera- tions [*sic*], both parties *must* be brought to a co-operation with the views and plans of that head." In view of the threat that such a development posed to Sibley, Brown thought the delegate's friends of both parties in the legislature should be brought to- gether to save the printing for the *Pioneer*.[16]

On January 14, 1851, a combination of Sibley supporters and Whig followers of Ramsey in the legislature awarded the print- ing to the *Pioneer*, but the Whigs exacted their price. Goodhue was to share the printing with a projected paper that would represent the Whig party more reliably than Henniss's *Chronicle and Register*, which was reputedly kept alive by financial infu- sions from Democrat Rice. Goodhue's version of the deal was that the new Whig organ must be launched "within one hundred days" in order to share in the spoils. He was not disappointed when the paper did not materialize until September 17, 1851. Its name was the *Minnesotian;* its editor was John P. Owens, its publisher, George W. Moore. The *Chronicle and Register* had expired six months earlier in February, 1851.[17]

While these maneuvers were taking place, Sibley's supporters were further agitated by a campaign of the Rice-Mitchell forces to remove Aaron Goodrich, chief justice of the territorial su- preme court, and have him replaced by Judge Cooper. Goodrich was not highly respected as a jurist, and his relationship with the proprietress of the American House was a scandal in St. Paul, but he had supported Sibley in the late election, and Sibley's friends were grateful to him as well as bitter against Cooper.[18]

On January 14, 1851, the same day it was awarded the printing

contract by the legislature, the *Pioneer* appeared with a denunciation of Mitchell and Cooper that may well stand as the peak
of invective for the frontier press.[19] "While we regret the continued absence of a U.S. Marshal, and a judge of the 2d district,
from Minnesota, we would not be understood to lament the
absence of A. M. Mitchell and David Cooper, the incumbents
(oftener *recumbents*) of these two offices. It would be a blessing
if the absence of two such men were prolonged to eternity. In
the present scarcity and high price of whiskey, their absence may
be considered a blessing. . . . We never knew an instance of
a debt being paid by either of them, unless it were a gambling
debt — and we never knew an act performed by either of them,
which might not have been quite as well done by a fool or a
knave. . . .

"Since the organization of the Territory, Mitchell has not
been in it, long enough by a continued residence, to be entitled
to vote; yet he has been long enough here to be known as a man
utterly destitute of moral principle, manly bearing, or even
physical courage. . . .

"As for Judge Cooper, besides lacking a residence at Stillwater,
at least ever since last May, he has neither there nor any where
else, any attachable property, that the officers can find. . . . He
left Stillwater, owing a large amount of postage, owing stores,
groceries and tradesmen of every description. He is not only a
miserable drunkard, who habitually gets so drunk as to *feel
upward* for the ground, but he also spends days and nights and
Sunday, playing cards in groceries.[20] He is lost to all sense of
decency and self respect. *Off* the Bench he is a beast, and *on* the
Bench he is an ass, stuffed with arrogance, self conceit and a
ridiculous affectation of dignity. . . . On his passage up the
Minnesota river last summer, paying such attentions to a certain
California widow on board, as a sot well could pay, he not only
kept drunk, but when the boat returned to Fort Snelling, and
the news there met him, of the death of his wife in Pennsylvania,
he was so shamefully inebriated, that the awful intelligence
scarcely aroused him.

"Such is the man, aided by Mitchell, (whose least fault is
drunkenness, and whose very name is a bye word for contempt

in Minnesota,) these we say, are the men who are now attempting to make this Judge Cooper the Chief Justice of Minnesota! We did think that by the appointment of two such men to *any* office in Minnesota, we had drained the cup of degradation to its dregs. If any punishment deeper and more damned than this, awaits us, we can only say, may God have mercy upon Minnesota! . . .

"Feeling some resentment for the wrongs our territory has so long suffered by these men, pressing upon us like a dispensation of wrath, a judgment, a curse, a plague, unequalled since the hour when Egypt went lousy, we sat down to write this article with some bitterness; but our very gall is honey, to what they deserve."

Late the following wintry morning (January 15, 1851), as Goodhue and a friend were leaving a session of the legislature, Joseph Cooper, a younger brother of the judge, stopped them in the street. After demanding to know why Goodhue had written the article, Cooper attacked the editor with his fists. Goodhue drew a gun and so did Cooper. They were still threatening to blow each other's brains out when the sheriff — a man appropriately named Cornelius Lull — rushed up to enforce the peace. He had disarmed Cooper and was taking Goodhue's gun when Cooper again rushed at the editor. Goodhue drew a second pistol. Cooper threw a rock. By this time a crowd had gathered, some seeking to restrain Cooper, others shouting "Let him kill the son of a bitch." When one would-be peacemaker succeeded in pinioning Goodhue's arms, Cooper rushed him with a knife and stabbed him in the stomach. Goodhue fired. Cooper cried out that he had been hit, and stabbed Goodhue again, this time in the back. Thus injured, the two combatants were finally restrained and led or carried away for medical attention.[21]

The brawl set off a tumult in the town. Judge Cooper's friends called an indignation meeting that night at Mazourka Hall. Friends of Goodhue, alarmed by rumors that a mob would destroy his press, attended the meeting to ensure that no violence would grow out of it. The *Chronicle and Register* of January 20, 1851, published a prejudiced and inflammatory account of the affray. The *Pioneer* of January 23 countered with sworn affidavits of witnesses, including a minister, that Cooper was the assailant.

On February 6 it noted that a "Law and Order Meeting" was held at the Methodist Church and resolutions were passed "reprobating all attempts on the part of individuals to take the law in their own hands" and condemning attacks on private character in the press. In its account of this meeting, the *Pioneer* brazenly remarked: "We understand the last resolution to refer to the outrageous and abominable attack made by the Chronicle of last week, upon the private character of the editor of the Pioneer." Dr. Potts, as Goodhue's physician, was able to write Sibley a highly specific description of the editor's condition. "Both wounds bled a great deal and gave people the impression that he was mortally wounded, and indeed he was under that conviction himself even after I told him that neither of the wounds had penetrated any of the cavities. The morning after the affray he took a small dose of oil, and anxiously looked for the operation of it, to find out whether the communication had been cut off." [22]

Goodhue was able to resume his editorial duties after two weeks of convalescence. He pressed no formal charges against his assailant, but convinced that H. M. Rice was behind the assault (it was rumored that the pistol taken from Cooper belonged to Rice), he returned to the partisan wars more than ever committed to Sibley's camp.[23]

He at once resumed his vendetta with Secretary Smith. "After long trial and observation of the old scoundrel, C. K. Smith," he wrote Sibley in February, 1851, "I am satisfied that he ought to be instantly removed from office. He is a hypocritical, lying, dishonest old scoundrel. . . . If you could get his cursed old political head off, it would be your crowning political glory of the year." [24]

The removal of the secretary, when it was effected in October, 1851, was a triumph for Ramsey, however, rather than for Sibley. On a trip to Washington in May, the governor became convinced that he himself had been the object of some secretarial machinations. "The President, unless his trip to New York & the press of business may drive it out of his mind will remove him," Ramsey wrote on May 15, 1851, in "strictest confidence" to Sibley at Mendota.

Ironically, Goodhue did not have the satisfaction of reporting the news of Smith's removal. When it reached St. Paul, he was on a trip down the river, so the *Pioneer* of October 30, 1851, was content to remark that it was "a joyful occasion," "that every body was pleased," and that the ex-secretary was absent in Ohio.

The final chapter, however, was written by Goodhue, for Smith returned briefly to the territory in November, and the editor, recalling his prediction that the secretary would steal away, reported on November 20, 1851, that Smith "clandestinely left Minnesota, in the night, without paying his creditors" and was last seen by passengers on the steamboat "Excelsior" rowing down through Lake Pepin "with a jug by his side."

James M. Goodhue's career as Minnesota's first editor was not to continue much longer. Before Smith's departure Goodhue had accompanied the official party to Traverse des Sioux for the treaty making there in July, 1851. The following January he had to share the official printing with the new Whig organ, the *Minnesotian*. On August 27, 1852, he died of a fever probably contracted when he fell from the ferry he and his brother Isaac operated on the Mississippi at St. Paul's lower landing.[25]

A "gentleman of high and responsible position in this community" wrote the tribute to the territorial promoter published in the *Pioneer*, stating that "His most bitter opponents were convinced, whatever might be his course towards them, that he loved Minnesota with all his heart, and all his might." One of those opponents, Daniel Robertson of the *Minnesota Democrat*, wrote: "No editor could have done more than he did, to spread abroad a knowledge of the resources of the Territory, and to attract immigration hither." The *Express* reported that "The procession which followed him to the grave was the largest ever known in the Territory," and the *Minnesotian* of August 28 observed, "We have never seen a greater degree of dismay settle upon the countenances of any community than was visible in St. Paul on Wednesday, when it was announced that he was dying." [26]

Thus Sibley was deprived of his most articulate ally in a period when he was to come under attack for his part in the negotiation of the Sioux treaties. For several months after Goodhue's death, his brother Isaac carried on, but the fire wasn't there. In February, 1853, Joe Brown, one of the most colorful, influential, and able men in early Minnesota history, became the second editor of the *Pioneer.*

After having been apprenticed to a printer in Pennsylvania, Brown ran away, joined the army, and arrived at the future site of Fort Snelling in 1819 as a fourteen-year-old drummer boy. At twenty, honorably discharged from military service, he began his long career as one of the chief traders among the Sioux, and as lumberman, townsite promoter, and politician. In the 1840s he represented the area between the Mississippi and St. Croix rivers for two terms in the Wisconsin territorial legislature, served in seven sessions of the Minnesota territorial legislature (1849, 1851–55, 1857), and was a member of the constitutional convention in 1857. Brown County is named for him. An able but a much more temperate man than Goodhue and one whose manifold interests prevented the whole-souled attention that Goodhue had given the *Pioneer,* Brown remained its editor until 1854, when Earle S. Goodrich took over. With Brown's occupancy of the editorial chair at the *Pioneer,* the belt for partisan slugging in the territory passed from that paper to Robertson's *Democrat.*[27]

"Colonel" Robertson, in some respects, was a likely contender for the title. Thirty-eight years of age when he came to the territory in 1850, he was a large man of military bearing and commanding presence with none of the injured innocence of Goodhue's expression. In his adopted state of Ohio, Robertson had been an editor, a United States marshal under President James K. Polk, and a delegate to the Ohio constitutional convention of 1850, where he argued cogently, if in part unsuccessfully, for a unicameral legislature and the governor's right of veto. He was also a lawyer, a scholar who corresponded with leading European naturalists and archaeologists of the period, and the founder of the Minnesota Horticultural Society. He was to remain a citizen of Minnesota for the rest of his life.[28]

Sibley's friends assumed that the *Democrat* would promote Rice's interests, but this assumption was only partly justified. While the *Democrat* did indeed proclaim the Rice doctrine of formal party organization and unity of Democratic forces, Rob-

ertson had his own ambitions. They were soon to help propel
Sibley and Rice into uneasy alliance.

In its first two years, the *Democrat* directed intermittent vol-
leys at Ramsey and Sibley — the former for being a Whig, the
latter for not being enough of a Democrat. It was a little like
taking potshots at President Eisenhower a century later. Both
men were widely liked and trusted, irrespective of their party
affiliations. In the summer of 1851, Sibley's influence with the
Sioux was instrumental in successfully negotiating the longed-for
treaties of Traverse des Sioux and Mendota that opened southern
Minnesota to eager white settlers — negotiations conducted by
Ramsey and United States Indian Commissioner Luke Lea — and
the next year, his influence in Congress was an important factor
in getting the treaties ratified. Even the Rice-Sibley antipathy
abated when Rice agreed — for a sum — to use his influence with
the Indians to get their assent to treaty amendments required by
the Senate. When news of the treaties' ratification arrived at St.
Paul, it set off a celebration that would have done justice to the
announcement of an armistice in the twentieth century. Ramsey
and Sibley "were some" in the slang of the day. Robertson faced
huge odds in any effort to dislodge the two men from the esteem
of the territory.[29]

But the editor of the *Democrat* played to Washington rather
than to the territory. In November, 1852, Franklin Pierce, a
Democrat, was elected president. He could be expected to appoint a Democrat to succeed Ramsey as territorial governor. The
best-known Minnesota Democrat in Washington was Sibley, but
Sibley was known to have preferred General Lewis Cass of Michigan to Pierce for the Democratic nomination. Robertson could
dream.

He did more. On December 15, 1852, almost the entire second
page of the *Democrat* was devoted to an exposé of the Sioux
treaty "frauds." "A general impression prevails in this community, that there is something wrong in the conduct of Governor
Ramsey and others, in the disbursement of the large sum of
money appropriated by Congress for the payment of the Sioux
Indians for their lands," the article began. It noted that $275,000
was due the chiefs who had signed at Traverse des Sioux. "At the

time of the signing of this treaty, the names of the chiefs and braves signing the same, were, they have declared in national council, without their knowledge placed to a paper assigning the greater part of said sum to H. H. Sibley, our delegate in Congress, and those connected with him in trade. Respectable witnesses who were present state that Mr. J. R. Brown sat near the table occupied by the Commissioners, and after each chief had signed the treaty, asked him to touch a pen which he (Brown) held in his hand. The Indians, supposing it a part of the treaty, of course did not refuse, whereupon his name was immediately transferred to the assignment or obligation. The Indians, as appears, were never consulted in relation to that paper, and all of them affirm that none of them knew or suspected that they were signing anything but the treaty. This transaction took place in the presence of Luke Lea and Alex. Ramsey, and certainly with the knowledge of the latter."

The chiefs, the exposé continued, learned of the "fraud" a few months after the treaty had been signed and went to St. Paul seeking justice of Ramsey. He assured them the money would be paid according to the terms of the treaty. But when the time came to disburse the payments: "After some weeks spent in endeavoring to force the Indians to sign receipts for nearly the whole amount of the $275,000, and acknowledge the validity and justice of the fraudulent paper, during which time his Excellency had been employed in making new chiefs and deposing the old ones, they succeeded in getting a number of names to the necessary receipts, amongst which there was but one Indian recognised by the Indians as a chief." Most of the Sioux money, the *Democrat* charged, went to the traders, each of whom had deducted from his share 15 per cent for a bribery fund used to get the treaty ratified. Furthermore, said the *Democrat,* Ramsey made payments in bank paper, in violation of federal statutes regulating the disbursement of public moneys.

The article concluded: "The nefarious disbursement of the Sioux money, has exasperated the Indians, seriously impairing their confidence in the Government and its Agents; aroused the indignation of the half-breeds; dissatisfied many meritorious creditors, and shocked the moral sense of the moral portion of this community. Our fearless exposure of this iniquitous business will subject us to the furious, nay, savage assaults of the Sibley and Ramsey party, and all persons whom they can in any way enlist in their combination. Their reliance is upon their extensive combination and large amount of money, but we have an abiding confidence that TRUTH and JUSTICE will triumph over the most powerful and audacious iniquity."

Robertson did not have to engage in any investigative reporting in order to furnish his readers with this "fearless exposure." A man named Madison Sweetser had appeared in St. Paul in September, 1851, directly after the signing of the Sioux treaties. Sweetser was a brother-in-law of George W. and William G. Ewing, whose fur company, based at Fort Wayne, Indiana, was a rival of the American Fur Company. The Ewings' traders had been excluded from any share in the benefits of the treaties, and Sweetser was on the spot as an agent of the Ewings to do what he could to prevent implementation of the treaties. The co-operation of Robertson's *Democrat* was helpful.

J. P. Owens, editor of the *Minnesotian,* enjoyed trading blows with the *Democrat* and promptly came to Ramsey's defense. The more aloof *St. Anthony Express* joined in. Joe Brown, in the *Pioneer,* at first said that the characters of Ramsey and Sibley were too well known to need defense, then wrote a detailed defense anyway. In sum, the defense made much of these points: the people wanted the treaties; the Indians were reluctant to give up their lands and could be induced to treat only through the influence of the traders, of whom the most influential was Sibley; the traders would not use their influence unless they were assured of at least partial payment of debts owed them by the Indians; federal law prohibited such a provision in any treaty; the Indians had been willing to pay their debts and fully understood the significance of the "trader's paper" they signed at Traverse des Sioux; federal law did not apply to Ramsey's disbursements, and he had only used discretion in paying with New York bank drafts rather than with gold.[30]

The defense did not satisfy Robertson. Week after week the *Democrat* repeated and amplified the charges of fraud through column after column. In February, 1853, Sibley's friends in the legislature had to work to get a vote of eleven to seven for a resolution expressing appreciation of Sibley's services to the territory. In Congress Sibley demanded — and finally got — a special investigation of the charges.[31]

Weeks dragged by. Robertson left St. Paul for Washington by way of Ohio, where he solicited letters recommending him to President-elect Pierce for the governorship of Minnesota. Senator Augustus C. Dodge of Iowa, a Sibley intimate, urged Pierce to appoint Sibley. Pierce was inaugurated — and appointed Willis A. Gorman of Indiana. To Senator Dodge, who went to the White House to ask why Sibley had been passed over, the president explained that Sibley was too closely identified with the fur trade to serve ex officio, as the governor did, as superintendent of Indian affairs in the territory.[32]

Sibley and Ramsey had to wait a full year before the investigating committee appointed by the president made its report on the Sioux treaties. In the meantime, Robertson sold the Democrat to the ever available David Olmsted, whose name went up on its masthead in the issue of July 6, 1853. With Robertson out of the way and newly appointed Governor Gorman urging unity, the Democratic factions fused to elect Rice to succeed Sibley as territorial delegate in October, 1853. Pioneer and Democrat split the official printing for the legislative session of 1854. On January 24, 1854, Robertson wrote a letter of retraction to Ramsey: "I believe it to be but an act of simple justice to you and myself to say in an explicit manner . . . that the testimony in the late investigation of your official conduct in that regard, satisfies me that you have been fully acquitted of having been actuated in said treaties or payments by corrupt or fraudulent designs." He further expressed his intention to give a copy of the retraction to the New York Herald. Ramsey replied that "all resentments on my part towards you are at an end, and that every legal measure which I may have had in contemplation in doing justice to my own character are for the future abandoned."[33] The steam had gone out of the campaign against Ramsey and Sibley.

In February, 1854, the report of the investigating committee was accepted by the Senate, clearing Ramsey.[34] The Pioneer of March 23 commented: "A Democratic Senate has done itself honor by rendering justice to a political opponent," and then quoted the report in full. The *Minnesotian* of March 18 exulted: "Law and Justice Triumphant. We learn authentically from Washington that on the 23d of February, the Senate Committee on Indian Affairs unanimously adopted a report fully and entirely acquitting Gov. Ramsey from all 'imputation of impropriety' in the late Sioux payments." The *Democrat* of March 22 buried the news in three brief paragraphs at the end of a half column of miscellany from a correspondent at Washington: "Yesterday an event happened in the Senate, which has given great satisfaction to all Gov. Ramsey's friends here, and I hope will be read with pleasure and gratification by every citizen of the Territory."

As the Sioux treaty "fraud" ground to an end, newspapers in the territory were assuming more clearly partisan attitudes, and they were astir with the promise of innovation. A fifth weekly, and the second in what is now Minneapolis — the *North-Western Democrat* published at St. Anthony by Prescott and Jones — had been in the field since July, 1853. As early as December 7, 1853, the *Minnesota Democrat* declared that it would soon introduce a daily edition. Business in St. Paul promised to justify the step. The population of the territory was estimated at 30,000, of St. Paul about 4,000. Local advertising, plus notices of Galena, Dubuque, and St. Louis businesses, which had been confined to page four and a column or two on pages one and three, had crowded news from pages one and three in most issues of all five weeklies. The *Pioneer,* which probably led in circulation since it was the only one to boast, claimed on the fifth anniversary of its founding (April 13, 1854) that it went to "nearly a thousand subscribers within the Territory, and is also sent to almost every county in the different States of the Union." Circulation and advertising rates had remained unchanged throughout the five years. In the spring of 1854, it was time for a change. St. Paul and the territory seemed poised for new and more dramatic growth. Railroad fever was beginning to mount. One by one, the St. Paul weeklies declared their intention to publish daily editions, while the settlements up and down the rivers began to look to printers to bring them weeklies of their own.

The Dailies Take Over

"Earl[e] S. Goodrich a young man who I . . . believe wields as keen and much abler pen than Mr. Goodhue is going upon my recommendation to Minnesota to put himself under your control," Ben C. Eastman, Democratic politician, Wisconsin Congressman, and Sibley crony, wrote to the master of Mendota early in 1854. "He has nothing in the world . . . and therefore needs help . . . but you will never make a better investment — I think than by putting him at the head of a Newspaper in your Territory which shall be your organ."[1] Such was the sponsorship — and the fractured grammar — that introduced Earle Goodrich to the territory. As the *Pioneer's* third editor, he was to transform the capital's oldest weekly into its first daily and shift the paper's major emphasis from territorial promoter to Democratic partisan.

The period between the debut of the daily press in 1854 and the introduction of the telegraph in 1860 pulsed with the movement of rapid change. The territory reached out for closer ties to the Union in government and transportation; it achieved the first when Minnesota became a state in 1858 and fumbled the second when a series of railroad schemes failed. In both efforts the newspapers of the capital were rabidly, though not reliably, partisan in the political sphere and promotional in the economic. Partisanship itself underwent a change as the Whig party in Minnesota fell apart, disrupted by the Kansas-Nebraska Act, and yielded its adherents to the new Republican party, repeating on a smaller stage the action played out in the national arena.

The swiftness of change which the newspapers chronicled was

paralleled in their own development. Goodrich brought out the first issue of the *Daily Minnesota Pioneer* on the morning of May 1, 1854; the same evening the *St. Paul Daily Democrat* appeared; the *Daily Minnesotian* fell in line on May 11, and on May 15 a newcomer to the capital — the *St. Paul Daily Times* — bowed in. Thus a town of about four thousand inhabitants, to which publishing had been introduced only five years earlier, acquired four daily newspapers within fifteen days. None of them, however, could be considered a stable publishing operation. A fifth daily — the *St. Paul Daily Free Press* — was introduced in October, 1855, to give Willis A. Gorman (who had replaced Ramsey as territorial governor in 1853) his own particular Democratic mouthpiece, but it failed to gain a following and expired after six months. And before the period ended, hard times and political realignments were to reduce the original four dailies to three, and for a brief interval to two.[2]

Elsewhere in the state, Republican auspices were responsible for the two other dailies established in this period. William A. Croffut and Edwin Clark brought out the *Falls Evening News* at St. Anthony on September 28, 1857, because, they said, Republicans of that city lacked a daily organ. An aggressive sheet, lively in style, the *News* was Minneapolis' first daily, for it assured residents of the city across the river that it was their paper, too. "In fulfillment of our mission, one of the proprietors . . . will make Minneapolis his home, in order to become more thoroughly identified with her people, and to insure her a full modicum of our Editorial attention." Down the Mississippi, the *Winona Republican,* which began weekly publication in 1855, started a daily edition in 1859. Not entirely sure of its reception, however, the proprietors called the newspaper the *Winona Daily Review* in order not to endanger continued publication of the *Weekly Republican.* Not until a month later did it shed its disguise and emerge as the *Winona Daily Republican.*[3]

The appearance of four dailies in the capital in 1854 before weeklies had sprouted elsewhere in the territory — other than at St. Anthony, Stillwater, and Winona — suggests the condition of settlement. Goodhue had complained that the territory was getting a surfeit of tradespeople and professional men who settled in St. Paul, that what Minnesota needed was farmers. An inventory of St. Paul businesses published by the *Times* in December, 1855, reported twenty-two grocery stores (representing the largest aggregate capital investment, a total of $264,000), twelve clothing and dry goods stores, eight hardware, seven millinery, seven drug, six boot and shoe, and four book stores; nineteen saloons, thirteen hotels, six blacksmiths, five barber shops, three livery stables; four banks; forty-one lawyers, nineteen doctors, two dentists; nine warehouses, five sawmills, one gristmill, six furniture and cabinet factories, and four harness and saddle manufactories. But the increased number of steamboat arrivals reported by all the papers (from 310 in 1854 to 1,068 in 1858) brought farmers as well as goods, and many more settlers streamed into Minnesota over wagon trails. The population of the territory increased dramatically from 6,077 in 1850 to 172,023 in 1860, and the newcomers changed the predominant political cast of the area from Democratic to Republican. They poured westward into the Minnesota River Valley and pushed northward along the Mississippi River. And in their wake came townsite developers, encouraging printers to locate at their bases of speculation, or when encouragement was not enough, establishing weekly papers themselves to spread the lures of immigration. Boostering, which had been the principal justification for the capital's weeklies, now passed to the weeklies on the rim of settlement.[4]

For the new dailies in the capital, political auspices such as those which introduced Goodrich were the rule rather than the exception. David Olmsted, Robertson's successor at the *Democrat* and the man who launched the daily, became the first mayor of the city of St. Paul in 1854 and was again a candidate for territorial delegate to Congress in 1855. Other editors of the *Democrat* from September, 1854, to October, 1855, were Charles L. Emerson and the ubiquitous Joe Brown. Behind all three while they occupied the editor's post was the purse of Henry M. Rice.[5]

The two Whig (subsequently Republican) dailies — the *Minnesotian* and the *Times* — were edited by men who had personal and sometimes financial ties to party leaders. J. P. Owens, the original editor of the *Minnesotian,* was like his sponsor Alexander Ramsey so staunch a Whig that, according to a contemporary, "even after the Whig party had been dead and buried, Owens held on to the corpse."[6] More adaptable was Dr. Thomas Foster, who succeeded Owens as editor of the *Minnesotian* on October 1, 1857. A fellow newspaperman credited Foster with contributing "largely to the establishment of the Republican party in Minnesota." Foster had edited several papers in Pennsylvania before coming to the territory as Ramsey's private secretary, and he got the *Minnesotian* berth after appealing in vain to Ramsey to set him up in a drug and liquor business. Ramsey was apparently equally helpful to Thomas M. Newson, editor and publisher of the *Times,* who repeatedly requested the former governor to endorse his notes. Newson, a New Yorker who had edited a paper in Connecticut before migrating to St. Paul in 1853, brought out the *Times* less than two months before a group of antislavery men living in St. Anthony met to organize the Republican party in the territory on July 4, 1854. They delayed formal organization, however, until March, 1855, when they held a territorial convention at St. Anthony. The new Republican party rapidly became a force in territorial politics, and one of its staunchest adherents was Thomas Newson's *Daily Times.*[7]

The shift from weekly to daily publication led to various changes in the papers. For one thing, dailies demanded presses that could print more rapidly, and their owners soon acquired steam-powered presses.[8] For another, advertising and subscription rates, of course, increased. Among the dailies, the former were uniform: from seventy-five cents for a first insertion of twelve lines or less to a full column at an annual rate of sixty-five dollars. The *Daily Pioneer* and the *Daily Times* set annual subscriptions at six dollars, the *Daily Democrat* at eight dollars; the *Daily Minnesotian* announced no annual rate, but had instead a weekly rate of fifteen cents.

All four papers also continued to publish weekly editions at the old rate of two dollars a year, and in addition the *Minnesotian* issued a triweekly edition at four dollars. The weekly editions were, in effect, digests of the dailies. In them the news space was divided roughly into fifths, one fifth for each weekday. Under the appropriate weekday heading, the principal news and opinion items of local origin were republished from the paper's daily editions. A majority of the advertisements were the same as those in the daily paper.

Like the weeklies, the new dailies appeared in four pages of uniformly gray, solid text, set in single columns without illustrations and with only small label headlines. The most notable change was a reduction in page size from twenty by twenty-five inches to fifteen by twenty-one inches, and a consequent reduction in the number of columns from seven to six. The *Daily Times,* however, measured fourteen by twenty inches and carried only five columns.

Pages one and four, the last two columns of page two, and most of page three in all four dailies were solid with advertising. The rest of page two was devoted to local news, "telegraphic dispatches," items clipped from exchanges, or excerpts from short fiction lifted from magazines. The news hole on page three tended toward departmentalization. Here, for example, the *St. Paul Daily Democrat* placed news items from St. Anthony (clipped from the *North-Western Democrat*), while the *Daily Pioneer,* under a heading "Commercial," mentioned commodity markets in St. Paul, St. Louis, and Galena, or under "River News" reported steamboat arrivals and departures. The editors did not attempt to write editorials for each issue; several days might pass with the space under the masthead devoted to news items, both local and otherwise.

They were likely to be otherwise in the case of the *Pioneer.* This paper slipped badly in its early months as a daily, probably because editor Goodrich was in New York buying equipment. All three of its competitors carried more items about St. Paul, and an occasional descriptive article about the territory was more likely to be found in their pages than in those of the *Pioneer.* More importantly, some serious errors in judgment suggested that whoever Goodrich had left in charge was even less attuned to frontier town and country than he was. The *Daily Pioneer* was only a few weeks old when it attacked a homestead bill then pending before Congress. "Granting lands to the lazy landless, can never enhance the value of the public domain," the issue of May 17, 1854, declared. "No man is worth having in a new country, who lacks the energy to gather together the small pittance now demanded by the government for its public lands. There may be exceptions, occasioned by peculiar and continued misfortunes, but the rule in general will hold good. Such a course would bring upon the frontiers, where we want live, active workers, the curse of an idle population, willing to declare themselves paupers, and always to remain so. For, the able bodied man who would take a grant of land under the provisions of the contemplated Homestead Bill, when an acre costs no more than the price of a dozen tipples, has 'shiftless,' 'lazy,' 'pauper-by-nature' stamped on him as irremovably as if placed there by precept of fore-ordination. We want no such men here, to act as clogs and hindrances to the development of our glorious Northwest. Their presence would be an insult to our fruitful, generous soil."

The writer did not seem to know an insult when he wrote one. But his competitors did. Newson in the *Times* of the following day (May 18, 1854) wrote a column-long rebuttal that was temperate and well reasoned. On May 19 the *Pioneer* recanted. The criticism of the homestead bill was not the editor's at all, according to the explanation. It had been written as a letter to the paper and had been published as an editorial by mistake. Owens ridiculed the explanation in the *Daily Minnesotian* of May 20. After quoting the original article, which he called a "haughty and purse-proud insult to the poor and industrious landless," Owens wrote that *he* was willing to accept the explanation but that most people would wonder why the editor of the *Pioneer* permitted "an issue of his paper to intervene *between* the publication of the offensive article and the disavowal of its sentiments. . . . Finally, the more fault-finding among the disbelievers will say, right out, that the editor of the Pioneer got on the wrong side of a great and leading question, and not having the moral courage to own up manfully, he chose a very roundabout and bungling way to get out of the difficulty."

Less than a month later the *Daily Pioneer* looked ridiculous on another count. Wordiness in writing was a weakness not limited to that paper's columns, but it was more marked in the *Pioneer* because of its editors' fondness for fancy words, not all of which expressed the writer's meaning. On one such instance the *Daily Democrat* pounced with glee: "The concluding paragraph of the *Pioneer's* article [on territorial expansion] is devoted to Cuba. It says: 'We believe in Cuba — *annexed, enlightened, circumcised* and *free.*' Now we can comprehend how Cuba can be 'annexed' — practice makes perfect, and we are getting skillful at the business. About Cuba 'enlightened' we are not so clear, unless it is to be done by gas. But Cuba *'circumcised'* is a new quality in this connection which we never heard of before, and *how* the thing is to be done we confess utter ignorance."[9]

Sibley, concerned by the falling-off in the quality of the paper, wrote Goodrich from Mendota late in July, 1854: "There is great complaint on the part of the subscribers & friends of the Pioneer, that it is fast losing its influence and character as a newspaper, and that it is not delivered regularly in the City. Now that you have re-assumed your place, I hope these things will be remedied. And every thing brought down to a close, & systematic business standard. Otherwise, the enterprise must & will fail. It is due to you that you should be informed of what I hear . . . affecting the character of the paper. You must be as well aware as I am, that it is much easier to keep up the character of a paper, than it is to raise it when down." Goodrich did not need more than one such admonition. The *Pioneer* directly showed evidence of sounder, more careful editing.[10]

None of the papers at this time indicated an awareness of the technique of the interview. In October, 1854, for example, when Territorial Delegate Rice paid a brief visit to St. Paul, the *Daily Times* was apparently eager to hear from him on a number of issues. But instead of seeking him out to put the questions directly and report his answers, Newson wrote in the issue of October 30: "It was our intention to put several pertinent questions to Hon. H. M. Rice on his course on the Minnesota Land Bill, but the Pioneer of Saturday morning covered the ground so effectually that we shall now wait until the questions propounded by that journal have been satisfactorily answered, when, with the permission of our honorable Delegate, we shall crave his attention for a short time. . . . In common with the Pioneer, we have been waiting anxiously for our honorable Delegate to explain the charges brought against him, and we should regret his leaving the Territory without doing so. The columns of the Times are at his disposal." The offer went unacknowledged, and Newson apparently made no further effort to develop a news story.

Yet such initiative as these papers showed was displayed by Newson of the *Times*. Late in 1854 his paper started carrying a column of business news written by Charles H. Parker, whose business card elsewhere in the paper identified him as a banker, exchange broker, and attorney. Parker wrote about real estate and exchange rates and reported bank failures around the country, information doubtless gleaned from eastern exchanges.[11]

It was Newson, too, who took the community to task for social shortcomings in a way that had been missing from the capital's press since Goodhue's death. "For the first time we took a look into our jail yesterday, and were fairly disgusted with everything appertaining thereto," he wrote in the *Daily Times* of September 22, 1854. "Such a miserable, loathesome, pestilence-breeding establishment, is a disgrace to the city, to the county and to the Territory. The apartments for the prisoners are small, dirty, odious in the extreme; while the polluted air arising therefrom is enough to kill off a regiment of healthy men." Newson also gave editorial support to the temperance movement, inveighed against the use of tobacco, and deplored such theatrical offerings as came to town because they lacked moral tone. He was not, however, a mere scold — no scold could have won the respect and affection in which he was held by his contemporaries.

An exception to this regard, it should be noted, was voiced by his printers in the first dispute between a Minnesota editor and union labor of which a record has been found. The oldest union in Minnesota was organized by the printers of St. Paul on December 30, 1856. Soon after, Newson had some difficulties over the discharge of two printers from his shop. Two years later the St. Paul local received a charter from the National Typographical Union, and the following year eleven printers in St. Anthony and Minneapolis organized a second chapter. In 1858 Newson again clashed with the printers when he declared for a nonunion shop and refused to pay "a price and a half" for Sunday work and work done after nine o'clock at night. At a meeting on March 27, 1858, the twenty-two union members resolved that the *Times* office be labeled "as a 'Rat' and *unfair* Office," and that journeymen printers who did not leave it within a week were also "Rats." [12]

The resolution of the issue is not recorded, but by the end of the year Newson and his printers were united in the annual race to be first on the street with the full text of the president's message to Congress. Owens of the *Daily Minnesotian* told about it ruefully on December 13, 1858, in one of those rare newspaper pieces that allow the reader to look behind the printed page. Under the headline, "The Battle among the Printers," he wrote: "About five o'clock on that [Saturday] morning, Mr. ALLEN, of BURBANK & Co.'s stage line, roused all the printers in the city by arriving express with the message. Be assured, there was an immediate rousing of sleepers in all directions, as though Gabriel's trump was sounding. Gathering in hot haste to their respective offices, outside doors were locked and craftsmen commenced 'digging in' to the twelve column document, as though life and death were in the balance. The eight or nine hands in the MINNESOTIAN Office — though laboring under a disadvantage from the sickness and absence of their foreman — worked away, confident that their superior energy and vim would be rewarded, as in previous years, by a triumph over either of the other offices, and that the Minnesotian edition would be first in the field."

But it was not to be. "The *Times*' hands, it appears, deserted their own office, and with the editors and proprietor worked as journeymen in the office of the *Pioneer* — a fraternal feeling between Democratic and Republican organs delightful to behold!" Even so the *Times* and *Pioneer* — with a combined force of twenty hands — beat the *Minnesotian* by only one hour and fifteen minutes. President James Buchanan's message filled page one and more than half of page two in all three papers on December 13, 1858.

The defeat did not prevent Owens from praising the stagecoach company for expressing the message without additional charge. When winter closed the Mississippi to commerce, St. Paul was dependent for mail on the overland stage from down-river distributing points. This trip could take as long as five days, and complaints about the reliability of the drivers were common in St. Paul newspapers. Owens' tribute was as detailed as it was unusual. He reported that Mr. Allen of Burbank's had induced the railroad agent at La Crosse to request that a number of copies of the message be printed in Chicago for rapid transmittal to La Crosse. The packet of copies left Chicago by train at one o'clock Thursday afternoon, was transferred to another train at Milwaukee at six that evening, and arrived at La Crosse at six on Friday morning. "At thirty minutes past 8 o'clock," Owens continued, "Mr. Allen started with the stage, containing three passengers besides himself, and the full regular mail. At thirty minutes past four o'clock on Saturday morning, he reached St. Paul, and delivered the Message to each of the newspaper offices, and at six o'clock the press in St. Anthony were supplied. . . . The detentions were occasioned by changing horses ten times, and some difficulty in getting over the Zumbro river, from the unsafe character of the ice. The newspaper offices of Winona, Wabasha and Reed's [Read's] Landing, Lake City, Red Wing and Hastings were duly served by Mr. Allen with the Message as he came along. The whole time from Chicago to St. Paul, in-cluding all stoppages and detentions, was 40 1/2 hours; and from Washington City, where it was delivered to Congress at 40 minutes past 1 o'clock on Monday, the 6th, the time to St. Paul is 112 hours."

The co-operation demonstrated by the *Times* and the *Pioneer* in the printing of Buchanan's message was not typical of rela-tions among the newspapers of the period. Indeed, it seems remarkable in view of the way in which editors exchanged brick-bats. The invective Goodhue ordinarily reserved for political figures had become characteristic of all the editorial offices, and it was applied unsparingly to rival editors. Even the moral and humane Newson could be stung to fury by attacks from his fel-low-Republican Owens so that on one occasion he was moved to say of Owens: "You crawl over God's fair earth like the poisonous serpent, whose slimy body leaves pollution behind, but your toothless fangs are powerless. Unprincipled, unmanly, devoid of decency, a stranger to truth, an outcast from society, a low menial who does the bidding of his master, and receives in return a glass of whisky, whose very countenance has stamped upon it 'petty larceny' who delights in corruption and laughs at Virtue, who would undermine and destroy our free institutions for the paltry sum of one dollar — *you* have done more to corrupt society and keep it corrupted, than even the arch fiend of Pandemonium, in whose services you are engaged."[13] Charges of venality, in particular, were frequent and indeed they had some basis in fact. There was the glaring example of Earle Goodrich.

Sibley's financial support of Goodrich, the young man who had "nothing in the world," was generous but not unlimited, and in time it proved insufficient to keep the new editor of the *Pioneer* in line. The arrival in 1854 of the dapper young journalist from Genesee County, New York, had been well timed, for Joseph R. Brown, who edited the *Pioneer* after Goodhue's death, had other interests, not the least of which was his townsite at Henderson. As Eastman had foreseen, Goodrich, a facile writer with some training in law as well as in printing, was a welcome recruit to the Sibley wing of the Democratic party. Sibley set him up in partnership with Brown in publishing the *Pioneer*. "I have made arrangements, to Goodrich perfectly satisfactory, that will place him in charge of the Pioneer as a weekly now, but as a daily & weekly both after 1 May," Sibley wrote Eastman on March 12, 1854. "He goes on tomorrow [*to New York*] with the necessary means to purchase all the additional material, including a power press, that may be required."[14]

The necessary means, according to a letter from Sibley to Goodrich of the same date, was a sum not to exceed $1,500 for which arrangements had been made through the St. Paul banking firm of Borup and Oakes. The sum proved insufficient. From New York on April 7, 1854, Goodrich wrote Sibley of his difficulties in finding a proper power press. Fires had destroyed so many presses that factories were behind in their orders, he said, and it was only through the "opportune failure of a man" that he had got the promise of one in six weeks. "Its cost is

$2000 — This may stagger you — but time will show it to have been the cheapest. I have purchased type to the amount of $450 — and the assortment got will enable me to do as good work in St. Paul as is done in New York, and as cheaply. I shall purchase an engine of three horse power in Buffalo, which will cost between $300 and $400. I shall also get a card press there costing $50. I have bought ink to the amount of $67. I shall purchase paper, say $150 to $200, in Buffalo. So you see my bills will run up to some $3000. I have given Taylor & Co. Strachan & Scott's accpt. for $1100 — ninety days, in part payment for press; and Conner & Low, ditto $400 same time for type, paying them balance in cash. The funds I have left will buy the engine, card press, and paper; and I shall want some $900 more to pay up for the press. I fear you think me reckless — but I am satisfied the end will show otherwise. We start the Daily as much for its moral effect as profit — to give the Pioneer a commanding name and influence."

Sibley undoubtedly shared his editor's ambition for the paper, but there was a limit to his willingness to pay for it. On June 27, 1854, when he sent Goodrich a draft on a Galena bank for $300, it was accompanied by the comment: "I hope you will now be able to complete entirely the arrangements for the Pioneer office, and not be compelled to call for more funds hereafter, for I frankly confess to you that you have all I can advance for that establishment, without putting me to serious inconvenience."

Sibley hoped in vain. Goodrich continued to need additional capital. Early in October, 1854, the partnership of Brown and Goodrich was dissolved.[15] Brown withdrew temporarily from St. Paul journalism, leaving Goodrich in sole command of the *Pioneer.* The next summer Goodrich returned to New York in search of a partner who could supply both capital and printing experience.

It was not a good time for him to be absent from the territory. Party factions were again lining up behind their favorites for the post of territorial delegate to Congress. Late in July, 1855, the Sibley faction walked out of the Democrats' convention to caucus by themselves and nominate Olmsted. The residue nominated

Rice, and the Republicans chose William R. Marshall, a St. Paul banker.[16]

The subsequent three-cornered race was bitter, even without the vitriolic pen of Goodrich, who lingered in New York. On August 18, 1855, he wrote Sibley: "You have expected me in person at St. Paul before this, and have doubtless indulged in some unpleasantness of feeling at my unexpected delay." He went on to explain that he would "leave here about the middle of the week, accompanied, as I hope, by one of the most accomplished printers in the country. . . . He has some ready funds which he puts into the purchase of these [printing] materials.[17] I told him the office had cost me $10,000; that he could come in as a partner to the amount of one third on paying in $5,000." Only a brief paragraph mentioned politics, but it was significant: "I am in blissful ignorance as to what is going on politically in Minnesota. I merely know that Olmsted, Marshall, and Rice are on the course. May the 'home-stretch' show them occupying the positions in which I have written them down."

Back in St. Paul, the paper for which he was responsible was less detached, and its editorial stance became progressively more confusing. Throughout August, with David Olmsted's name riding high at their head, the editorial columns were devoted to attacking Rice day after day, criticizing him for Know-Nothingism, "self-interest," and lack of support for a northern Pacific railroad route. Early in September, after Goodrich returned from New York, there was no abatement in the *Pioneer's* campaign against Rice. As late as September 25, 1855, the paper castigated supporters of Rice in the Minnesota Valley — "a country which has never received a favor from Mr. H. M. RICE, but on the contrary has been cursed by his treasonable desertion of the interests of the Territory to promote his own."[18]

Then abruptly on October 1, eight days before the election, Olmsted's name disappeared from the editorial columns of the *Pioneer,* and Goodrich devoted two of those columns to an effort to justify its absence. He made the point that the anti-Rice faction in Ramsey County had bolted the Democratic county convention which had endorsed Rice in September. Airily skipping over the fact that his paper had approved just such a bolt from the party's territorial convention a few months earlier, Goodrich expressed regret that the bolters had "become leaders in the disastrous policy of party disorganization." Furthermore, he charged, the friends of Olmsted were snuggling up to the abolitionists. "We cannot follow our friends in their political vagaries; and feel compelled to withdraw THE PIONEER from any further participation in the present Delegate canvass."

But Goodrich did not maintain even this position for the brief duration of the campaign. On October 9 he advised his readers that "You can only give effect to the Democratic sentiment that is within you, by casting your vote for Henry M. Rice. Let every man prove himself one thing or the other to-day — Democrat or Abolitionist. On no account permit your personal prejudices to make of you an OLMSTED man." The reversal was complete.

The Goodrich switch inspired rumors of a merger of the *Pioneer* and *Democrat,* and by the end of October the rumors were confirmed. The first issue of the combined *Pioneer and Democrat* was published on November 1, 1855. The purse of Henry M. Rice had unified the organs of the two Democratic factions, even though his election failed to do so for the groups they had represented. Subsequently, Newson's *Times* alleged that Olmsted's friends had wearied of subsidizing Goodrich's taste for high living and clamped down, forcing the editor into an alliance with Rice. Goodrich snorted "stale libel," but his parting from Sibley was not amicable. Ben Eastman, the man who had brought them together, commented on the split in a letter to Sibley. "When I recommended Goodrich to you I did so more because I thought he could serve you than because I desired you to serve him," Eastman wrote. "Immediately I learned that he might serve himself instead of you I wrote you by way of caution. Since he has been treacherous to you I hope the devil will catch him and take him to his hottest hell and there keep him in a warm corner." [19]

Although shifting personal antagonisms at the local level continued to underlie the partisanship of the St. Paul dailies throughout this period, the emergence of the Republican party and differences between the parties at the national level began to stiffen the papers' editorial stances as the territory moved toward statehood. Before their merger, both the *Pioneer* and the *Democrat* repeated the familiar Goodhue argument that as long as the territory had no vote in Congress, it was folly to engage in controversy on national issues. The *Minnesotian* and the *Times,* trying to outshout each other as voices of Republicanism, conceded no such restraints. Newson particularly, as puritan and humanitarian, as well as the only Minnesotan to attend the first national Republican convention at Pittsburgh in February, 1856, saw slavery as a moral question as well as a political issue.[20] In the face of attacks on the national administration by both *Minnesotian* and *Times,* the united *Pioneer and Democrat* found it increasingly difficult to maintain a position above the battle.

It was the issue of slavery, of course, that ultimately drew all these stripling dailies into the national arena — slavery moving into Kansas, a territory like Minnesota approaching statehood. On other national issues the papers had little to say. In an election year, it is true, they deplored Know-Nothingism and tried to smear their opponents with the offensive label, but they said surprisingly little about national land policies or the tariff.

Slavery was different. All the St. Paul dailies considered the institution a curse and a blight; all expressed opposition to its extension. But unanimity ended there. The *Times* and the *Minnesotian* sympathized with the abolitionist cause, but "abolitionist" was a dirty word in the columns of the *Pioneer* and later in the *Pioneer and Democrat.*[21] While Northerners oppose slavery, the *Daily Pioneer* of July 3, 1855, declared, they remember that "the obligations of the Constitution . . . preclude them from in any wise interfering with the 'peculiar institution' where it exists by virtue of State legislation."

The antislavery convictions of the *Times* and the *Minnesotian,* exacerbated by the Kansas-Nebraska Act and the turmoil in Kansas, boiled into demands for armed resistance and, ultimately, to proposals for an armed solution to the North-South conflict. As early as May 14, 1855, before blood had been shed in Kansas, the *Times* was urging Northerners to go to Kansas "prepared to resist to the death the threats of the banditti." The *Minnesotian* of May 22, 1855, calling for a Republican territorial convention in Minnesota, was even more inflammatory. "Republicans of Minnesota!" the paper exhorted. "Think of the wrongs and outrages perpetrated upon your brethren of Kansas. The heel of the Slave-driver is upon their breasts, and his knife at their throats. Think of these things, and be up and doing while there is yet time for the accomplishment of good works; for the day and the hour has certainly arrived, when if you would preserve the Freedom of this land, you must buckle on your armor and prepare for the contest."

When the Kansas legislature passed a law requiring voters to swear their support of the Kansas-Nebraska Act, the *Daily Times* of September 10, 1855, exploded: "Talk of the oppression of King George — it is nothing in comparison to this infernal, damnable . . . iniquity. And yet we must not say anything — must not raise our voice! Why, forsooth? — Because the Union is in danger! Such outrageous proceedings almost justify civil war." The following day the *Times* raged on: "Let the Slave Oligarchy continue its course in Kansas, and if the Federal Government does not interfere, civil war will follow. The whole power of the North will be brought to bear against this den of iniquity."

In December, 1855, came news of mob violence in Kansas, followed by the death of an antislavery settler and the calling out of the militia. "We have anticipated blood-shed for some time past," the *Times* said in an understatement published on December 10, "and if the difficulty stops here, we shall be greatly disappointed. The Free men of Kansas are determined to defend their rights, even at the muzzle of the musket, and if they don't do it they are unworthy of the name they bear. If it *must* come to this, let it come. The South has gone far enough. Let the North now act."

When further violence erupted late in May, 1856 ("Civil War in Kansas! Lawrence Destroyed/Free State Blood Spilt"), the *Minnesotian* of May 30 intoned: "The war between Freedom and Slavery has commenced." The *Times'* reaction was equally inflammatory, and the *Pioneer and Democrat* of May 31 was incensed at both of them. They were, it said, taking their cues from "that despicable wretch" William Lloyd Garrison, and were making "appeals worthy in every respect except in imbecility, of their newly-acknowledged political guide."

The *Pioneer and Democrat's* own guide — indeed its hero — was Stephen A. Douglas, and his doctrine of popular sovereignty was the paper's creed. Texts of Douglas speeches — and he made many — were published complete in the *Pioneer and Democrat.* In August, 1857, the Little Giant paid a brief visit to St. Paul, and the paper did not overlook a detail of the triumphant arrival, the dinner in his honor, the procession to the Rice residence where he was a guest, the serenade, the introduction by Rice, the welcome by ex-Governor Gorman, and, of course, the Douglas response "in a happy manner." When the Democratic party split over the Lecompton constitution for Kansas, the *Pioneer and Democrat* was predictably in the Douglas corner, condemning the instrument not only because it permitted slavery but also because it violated the principle of popular sovereignty. The first of the debates between Lincoln and Douglas also got full treatment. The *Minnesotian* of August 26, 1858, claimed "The Dred Scott Champion Pulverized," while the *Pioneer and Democrat* of the same day asserted that "DOUGLAS completely demolished LINCOLN." Douglas' triumph in the Illinois election was hailed by the *Pioneer and Democrat* of November 9, 1858, with a woodcut of a spread eagle on the masthead, proclaiming "Great Democratic Triumph!" The presidency, it seems, would have been anticlimactic.[22]

Such national partisanship fused with local prejudices in the dailies during the transition from territory to statehood. The effort to present the Union with a new state stamped with a definitive Republican or Democratic party label became more marked in 1857 as a constitutional convention got under way. But the constitutional battle was prefaced by a related controversy that caused the St. Paul papers briefly to close ranks against a common enemy — those who proposed to remove the capital from St. Paul to St. Peter.

When possible boundaries of the new state had first been discussed, the *Daily Pioneer and Democrat* of February 18, 1856, called for an east-west line from the St. Croix to the Missouri no farther north than the forty-sixth parallel. But six months later on August 9 it was urging the adoption of a north-south line running along the Red River Valley and south to Iowa, a boundary consistently favored by the *Minnesotian* on the grounds that it would give the new state varied resources of lakes, minerals, and lumbering, as well as agriculture. The *Pioneer and Democrat* shifted ground when it became clear that support for the east-west boundary centered in a group of St. Peter townsite promoters — among whom Governor Gorman was the most prominent — who hoped to make that town the capital. An east-west boundary would strengthen their argument that St. Peter would be more centrally located than St. Paul. In February, 1857, a bill for removal of the capital to St. Peter was introduced in the territorial legislature. The *Daily Pioneer and Democrat* reacted immediately. On February 7 it said that members who voted for the bill, and Governor Gorman, if he approved it, would find "that for the infamy which must attach, St. Peter stock will fail to compensate them, or time to obliterate the mark of disgrace which will fasten on their names."

Supporters of removal were willing to risk it, and the bill passed the Council (Senate) on February 12. Six days later both the *Times* and the *Pioneer and Democrat* published the text of Attorney General Lafayette Emmett's opinion that removal of the capital by legislative action rather than by popular vote violated the Organic Act of the territory. The same day the House passed the bill by a vote of 20 to 17. All three papers expressed outrage. The legislative majority had exhibited "not only a degree of scoundrelism which was atrocious, but the most audacious impudence," the *Pioneer and Democrat* shrilled on February 24. All three papers charged bribery. All three expected Governor Gorman to sign the bill. St. Paul seemed powerless to protect its own.[23]

Then on March 2 the *Pioneer and Democrat* hinted at a desperate measure that might save St. Paul: "The Territorial Council has been in session thirty-six hours, from Saturday morning up to the time of our going to press last night; with a fair prospect of continuing so during the remaining six days of the session. Cause: Absence of a member — call of the Council — and inability to suspend the call." The absent member was Pembina's Joseph Rolette, chairman of the committee on enrolled bills, and absent with him was the essential enrolled copy of the removal bill. The Council was unable to proceed with any business until the call could be suspended, and the necessary two-thirds vote for suspension could not be mustered. Council members settled down in the chamber for the duration.

On March 4 the *Minnesotian* reported: "We Editors being of the privileged class who can enter the Council room during the pendency of the call, our readers may want to know how things appear inside. The members all look in good health and spirits. Some of them appear somewhat careworn and anxious, particularly some of the older sinners of the majority. . . . The best that the hotels afford is sent to them at the proper hour, and they have plenty of beds and bedding to render them comfortable at night. Their friends outside may rest assured that they are taking most excellent care of themselves." Friends outside did not need the reassurance. "The only ones who are especially exercised about the matter," according to the *Pioneer and Democrat* of March 3, "are Gov. Gorman, and the balance who are interested in the Capital outrage. The Governor has become insane on the subject, and spends most of his time in the public streets and hotels, swearing with all the profanity, though with little of the delicacy of a fishwoman."

According to all three papers, Rolette and the engrossed copy of the removal bill were still missing when the session expired at midnight on March 7, 1857. St. Paul's appreciation was obliquely tendered by the *Pioneer and Democrat* of March 24, when it reported Rolette's subsequent departure for Pembina: "by his fidelity to the true interests of the Territory, his loyalty and zeal in the cause of right and justice, [he] earned hundreds of warm friends and admirers."

But when Rolette departed, harmony among the capital's newspapers went with him. Early in June, 1857, the people of the territory elected delegates to a convention to draft a constitution for Minnesota's admission to the Union as a state, and before the month was out the *Minnesotian* was charging Democratic skulduggery. The convention was to open in St. Paul on July 13, but, according to the *Minnesotian,* the Democratic delegates planned to arrive in advance of that date. "It is evident some high-handed outrage upon the rights of the people is contem-

plated," the *Daily Minnesotian* warned on June 30, as it urged
Republicans to be on hand not later than July 10. The next day
the *Pioneer and Democrat* promptly denied any plot and coun-
tercharged: "The game of the Republicans is to organize the
Convention on a Republican basis, with the aid of the bogus
delegates from St. Anthony." But on the eve of the convention
on July 12 the paper hoped that "all preliminary questions will
be met by the Convention in a friendly spirit . . . and decided
justly."

The hope was short-lived, for both political parties wished to
represent the new state when it entered the Union. The papers
of July 14 were largely devoted to accounts of the disruptive
events at the Capitol, reported with partisan pens. Depending
on which paper you read: Territorial Secretary Charles L. Chase
(Democrat), as the responsible officer, had called the convention
to order; Delegate John W. North (Republican), responding to
a request from a majority of delegates in advance of the convention, had called it to order; on a motion of ex-Governor Gorman
(Democrat) the convention had voted a twenty-four-hour adjournment; the adjournment motion had lacked a majority;
Democratic delegates had withdrawn on adjournment, leaving
a Republican mob insufficient for a quorum; a Democratic minority, hirelings of the national administration, had pulled out
and the Republican majority had proceeded to organize the
body.[24]

The *Pioneer and Democrat* of July 14, 1857, was both pleased
and prophetic. "The action of the Democratic Delegates yesterday, meets our cordial approval. It was timely, expedient, and
right. If two Conventions are held, and two Constitutions submitted to the voters, let the blame fall upon those who would
disfranchise a portion of the people of the Territory, because
they committed the great crime of sending Delegates to the Convention opposed to Negro Equality and Nullification. We glory
in the spirit displayed by the Democratic members."

With such support, the Democratic delegates settled down to
business at one end of the Capitol, while the Republicans—
similarly championed by the *Minnesotian* and the *Times*—set
about constitution making at the other. At first the *Pioneer and*

Democrat and the *Minnesotian* seemed disposed to report the proceedings of both groups, each claiming for its own the legitimate title of constitutional convention. But after a couple of days of this, the *Pioneer and Democrat* declared on July 17, 1857: "We find on perusing the report of the Republican gathering, prepared for our paper, so many glaring and mendacious misrepresentations, that we do not think our duty as a journalist would justify us in giving further currency to their slanderous lies." The *Minnesotian* said nothing about lies; it simply dropped the Democratic proceedings from its columns.

Of the two accounts of the conventions, the *Minnesotian's* gave readers the better insight into the making of a constitution in the weeks that followed, perhaps because Thomas Foster, the editor of the paper, was a member of the Republican body. Proceedings of the Republican convention showed it quickly settling into a routine of committee reports and floor debate of draft provisions. The Democrats, on the contrary, appeared to be convening only to recess or to hear self-justifying speeches which were dutifully reported in full by the *Pioneer and Democrat*.

Near the end of July the eastern exchanges carrying reports of the dual conventions started arriving in the territory, and the St. Paul editors suddenly became aware of how ridiculous the situation looked to outsiders. The *Pioneer and Democrat* of July 21 blamed the unfavorable picture on what it regarded as Republican control of the telegraph, which had inched its way as far west as Galena under the auspices of privately subscribed stock. The *Minnesotian* was more realistic. Early in August it quoted an editorial from the *Minnesota Advertiser* urging delegates of both parties to make concessions. On August 8 Democratic Delegate Moses Sherburne proposed a conference committee to work out "some plan by which the two bodies can unite upon a single Constitution."[25]

The *Pioneer and Democrat* of August 9 reported the Sherburne resolution — and its indefinite postponement — without comment, but the *Minnesotian* of August 10 remarked: "Notwithstanding this apparent defeat of a measure so anxiously hoped for by every true citizen of Minnesota, of whatever party, we are assured by leading and influential Democrats that it will yet be accomplished. We are certain there is nothing in the way of such a desirable end on the Republican side of the Capitol; and we must say that Judge SHERBURNE deserves the cordial thanks of his constituents — both Democrats and Republicans — for having the manliness and nerve to be the first to lead off in preparing the way for a compromise upon one Constitution."

From that point until a conference committee actually succeeded in working out a single draft late in the month, the *Minnesotian* supported the efforts of the compromisers, while the *Pioneer and Democrat* was stiff-necked and offensive. Its preference was to submit both constitutions to the voters. The *Minnesotian* of August 20 opposed such a course, commenting that "this question . . . has passed out of the line of politics, and has assumed the shape of a plain, practical business matter. Our only safety from anarchy and unforeseen distress and ruin in all of our business interests, is in submitting but one Constitution to the people."

Of differences separating the two partisan bodies, the question of apportionment of representatives in the legislature was the thorniest, but no clear exposition of the conflicting proposals on this point emerged in the reports of the newspapers. The *Pioneer and Democrat* preferred to emphasize a more emotional issue — the right of franchise, which it sometimes referred to as "Negro equality" or "Nigger suffrage." Although Republicans themselves were split on this issue, the *Pioneer and Democrat* painted them all "Black Republicans." The *Minnesotian* of July 31 reported that the committee on elective franchise in the Republican convention had specified the right to vote for "every white male inhabitant over 21 years of age," and that committee member John W. North of St. Anthony concurred in the report but objected to the inclusion of the limitation "white." Subsequently the *Minnesotian* carried a letter from North declaring his position "in favor of equal suffrage regardless of complexion." The *Minnesotian* itself refrained from taking a position on the issue. The compromise solution — retention of the restrictive word "white" in the constitution and submission of the issue to a separate referendum — the *Pioneer and Democrat* of September 2 dismissed as "a miserable expedient." The *Minnesotian* explained on September 14 that supporters of Negro suffrage had accepted the compromise because they had become convinced that the issue might defeat the constitution and that time was needed to prepare the voters for its acceptance.[26]

A compromise draft of the two constitutions was worked out by a conference committee and adopted by large majorities of both conventions on August 28. Even then the bickering did not end. Members of the two groups refused to sign the same document, and copyists worked late into the night to produce two copies of the compromise document so that each group might sign separately.

Nine anxious months passed before Congress approved the constitution and granted statehood. The obstacle was the South's insistence than Kansas be given prior consideration in the expectation of maintaining the North-South balance in the United States Senate. The people of Minnesota chose Sibley over Ramsey to be the first governor of the state, sent Rice and James Shields to Washington as its first senators, and elected three representatives before Southerners in Congress would acknowledge that it was entitled to more than one. Early in April, 1858, the *Pioneer and Democrat* published column after column of debate in the Senate over admission, then hinted darkly at a Republican conspiracy as the cause of the delay: "Who are these men, who thus work malignantly in the dark, and dare not show their hands? We are justified in believing that they are composed of the clique of spoilsmen of which the *Minnesotian* is the fit representative." The *Minnesotian* countered by pointing out that the Democrats had a majority in both houses of Congress.[27]

After such a long wait, the two-day interval between final Congressional action in May, 1858, and the arrival of its announcement in the territory was inconsequential. The *Daily Minnesotian* of May 14 exulted: "Under our latest news head, we give the proceedings in Congress on the 11th inst., obtained from the Dubuque *Express and Herald,* brought by the Grey Eagle yesterday afternoon. They confirm the news previously brought at 6 o'clock, A.M., by the Steamer Milwaukee, that Minnesota was on Tuesday last formally admitted into the Federal Union by a vote of 157 to 38! . . . Let everybody rejoice with exceeding great joy." Another article in the same issue, head-lined "How the News was Announced," reported that "The news of the admission of Minnesota into the Union spread throughout the city yesterday morning with the celerity that fire runs over a dry prairie in a gale of wind. The *Pioneer* issued an extra, which it scattered through town, and the *Minnesotian Office*, a large sheet handbill, in which was displayed in six inch letters, 'MINNESOTA IS ADMITTED INTO THE UNION.'" And the paper added, "Everybody seemed satisfied, that we were at last out of that '*snarl*,' and everybody said to everybody, as each drew a long breath, 'Well! what next? Good times, eh?'"[28]

CHAPTER 4

The Weeklies Disperse

WHILE ST. PAUL'S DAILIES were grappling with the politics of transition to statehood, another segment of the press was intent on acquiring the muscle needed by the new body politic. The capital's dailies had come on with a rush in 1854, and in the next three years the same vitality brought a surge of new weekly newspapers along the rivers that provided access to the wilderness. A few of these weekly enterprises were to prove more or less direct ancestors of papers still published today at Minneapolis, Chatfield, Hastings, Mankato, Mantorville, Red Wing, St. Cloud, Wabasha, and Winona; many more were to be casualties of the hard times following the Panic of 1857. Some talked in the golden tones of immigration promoters, others with the raucous voices of political belligerents; a few spoke in foreign tongues; and at least one was so strident a voice of abolition that violent men attempted to throttle it. The effort was in vain. The editor was a woman.

Before 1854 only two weeklies had appeared outside St. Paul, both of them in St. Anthony — the *Express* in 1851 and the *North-Western Democrat* in 1853. The year of the dailies, 1854, saw the first weekly at Stillwater, the *St. Croix Union,* and at Winona, the *Winona Argus,* as well as three more weeklies in the two printing centers: the *St. Paul Financial & Real Estate Advertiser,* the *Minnesota Weekly Times* at St. Paul, and the *Minnesota Republican* at St. Anthony. The pattern of outstate concentration and extension continued. In 1855 Stillwater got another paper, *Rube's Advocate;* Winona got two more papers — the short-lived *Winona Weekly Express* and the *Winona Repub-*

lican, which lives today in the *Winona Daily News* — while St. Peter, Sauk Rapids, Brownsville, Red Wing, and Shakopee joined the townsites that boasted printers and papers. (It is interesting to note that United States land offices were located at all these towns except Shakopee at the time their papers came into being. The presence of a land office would, of course, offer additional revenue to a local paper in the form of both official and incidental printing.) In 1856 a third paper was established at Stillwater, second papers were established at Red Wing and Shakopee, and papers were introduced at Carimona and Chatfield (two each); as well as at Henderson, Hastings, Faribault, Preston, Owatonna, Cannon Falls, Read's Landing, Watab, Monticello, Oronoco, and Nininger. Ironically, 1857 — the year of the severe panic that was to choke off most of these new voices — was also the year of greatest expansion. Twenty-seven English and foreign-language weeklies were launched, eleven of them in towns that had not previously known a newspaper. The numbers, of course, reflect the condition of settlement. All of them were located at townsites — some of which no longer exist — on the Mississippi, St. Croix, Minnesota, Crow Wing, Cannon, and Zumbro rivers. In all, about a hundred English-language weeklies were started outside St. Paul and St. Anthony between 1854 and 1860.[1]

Foreign-language weeklies also appeared in St. Paul and elsewhere.[2] Friedrich Orthwein, a transplanted Milwaukeean, was responsible for three of these, all in German and all short-lived: *Die Minnesota Deutsche Zeitung* launched in St. Paul in 1855;[3] *Minnesota Thalboten* begun in Chaska in 1857; and the *Minnesota National Demokrat* issued in St. Paul in 1857. The latter year also saw the publication of the first Swedish paper, *Minnesota Posten,* established at Red Wing by Eric Norelius, a Lutheran clergyman born in Sweden.[4] In 1858 the first Norwegian paper, *Folkets Röst* (Voice of the People), was published by Ole Nelson and Company from the *Pioneer and Democrat* plant in St. Paul, and the German-language paper, the *Neu-Ulm Pionier* began in that southern Minnesota city on January 1, 1858.[5]

The political patronage so important to the founding of many Minnesota newspapers was of special significance to the third weekly established at St. Anthony and the second one in the genealogy of today's *Minneapolis Tribune*. (See the diagram on page 132 below.) This was the *Minnesota Republican* initially issued on October 5, 1854. It was the first newspaper in the Northwest and perhaps in the country to carry the name of the emerging political party. The same antislavery leaders who had met at St. Anthony three months earlier to form a new party — John W. North, William R. Marshall, and Dr. Vickers Fell — passed the hat among fifty like-minded pioneers. They raised $1,200 and with it put together a printing office. Installed as editor was the Reverend Charles G. Ames, a Baptist minister who had arrived in the territory in 1851. "I did not become a journalist from malice prepense," Ames later recalled, "but only incidentally and by the way, as it were; for I somehow made myself think of it as an extension of my minister work. In a small way I was somewhat notorious as an advocate of radical reforms, and was especially hot against intemperance and slavery."[6]

The heat was reflected in the paper's salutatory, which declared that "the editor . . . is under no other pledge than 'to serve the interests of Liberty and Temperance according to his own discretion.'" These reform objectives were coupled repeatedly throughout the pages of the new weekly. Minnesota, it said, on October 5, 1854, should enter the Union "as a *Free State* — free alike from a system of grog-shops, and from a corrupt public sentiment, which will lend voluntary sanction or support to oppression. . . . let the young and vigorous Republican party move forward to the conflict, bearing on its banners, 'LIBERTY AND TEMPERANCE!'" Ames exhorted his readers.

That the ardent reformer was not without a sense of humor is proved by his recollections of the *Republican's* first days. He recalled that "By spells, I was printer and publisher, as well as editor. . . . Sometimes the editorials were first composed in the composing stick; often I picked up my own locals, reported proceedings of meetings, collected bills due for advertising and job work — when I could. . . . I must have officiated now and then as roller-boy for I have recently amused myself by looking over a few surviving numbers of the *Republican,* and muddier printing I never saw! Once our supply of ink gave out, and we used some of our own making. . . . At the door of Friend [W. W.] Wales's book store was hung out a placard, '*Minnesota Republican* for sale here; price 5 cents,' under which I saw penciled the discriminating judgment, 'Not worth a damn.' Several people, however, thought it worth just that much, and I could depend on a steady income of that kind, if no other."[7]

Ames edited the *Republican* until he was elected register of deeds for Hennepin County in 1857, when the paper passed to Croffut and Clark of the *Falls Evening News*. The events of the next few years suggest that newspaper publishing in the frontier community was as turbulent as the waterfall that drew settlers to the townsite. In 1859 the sometime daily *Falls Evening News* was reduced to publishing only three evenings a week, and the name of the *Republican* was changed to the *Minnesota State News* to conform to the title of the triweekly. On December 10, 1860, the *Evening News* resumed daily publication, only to suspend entirely on April 13 of the next year. The *State News* struggled on, moving to the Minneapolis side of the river in March, 1863, and leaving St. Anthony without a printing office. Nine months later it collapsed from malnutrition. The paper "cannot be made a paying concern," the *State Atlas* of November 11, 1863, observed.[8]

The *Atlas* itself had cause to reflect on the transient nature of newspaper enterprises. Founded as a weekly in 1859 by William S. King, an ardent Republican, it succeeded St. Anthony's *North-Western Democrat* (1853–56) and three short-lived papers — the *Minnesota Democrat* of Minneapolis (1856), the *Minneapolis Gazette* (1858), and the *Minneapolis Journal* (also 1858). For a time in 1860 the *Atlas* also issued a daily, but it was as a weekly that it endured as long as it had the field to itself. After Tom Foster showed up in 1866 as the editor of a competitor, the *Minneapolis Chronicle,* neither paper prospered. A merger was arranged by King and flour millers William D. Washburn and Dorilus Morrison. The new paper was called the *Minneapolis Daily Tribune;* volume 1, number 1, bore the date May 25, 1867.[9]

Despite the instability indicated by the frequent changes at St. Anthony and Minneapolis, the papers of the new state were numerous enough by 1858 to make their first attempt at formal association, if not concerned enough to sustain it. On June 3 of that year thirteen men representing twelve newspapers met in St. Paul for the first convention of Minnesota editors and publishers. Styled a preliminary meeting of the Editorial Fraternity of Minnesota, the group set about organization. Columbus Stebbins, editor of the *Hastings Independent,* was elected president; Frederick Somers of the *St. Paul Pioneer and Democrat* and Andrew J. Van Vorhes of the *Stillwater Messenger,* vice-presidents; David Blakely of the *Bancroft Pioneer,* and Daniel S. B. Johnston of the *St. Anthony Express,* secretaries. Others who attended were James Mills of the *Pioneer and Democrat,* Thomas Foster of the *Minnesotian,* William A. Croffut of the *Falls Evening News,* Thomas Newson of the *St. Paul Times,* J. Ketchum Averill of the *Winona Times,* W. C. Dodge of the *Minnesota Free Press* (St. Peter), Marshall Robinson of the *Glencoe Register,* Charles Brown of the *Southern Minnesota Herald* (Brownsville), and C. B. Hensley of the *Mankato Independent.*[10]

The first resolution passed by the group declared that "it is expedient to organize an Editorial Association for the Stc.e of Minnesota, for the cultivation of more intimate and friendly relations, and for the mutual advancement of the publishing interests throughout the State." Van Vorhes, Newson, and Mills were appointed to draft a constitution for the association. Other resolutions urged publication of the general laws in all Minnesota newspapers, establishment of paper manufactories in the state, consideration by "the editorial fraternity" of uniform rates for subscriptions and advertising, and changes in compensation by the legislature for the publication of legal advertising to correspond with "the usual rates of advertising" in the St. Paul newspapers.

The group also resolved "That the next annual meeting of this Association be held in St. Paul, on the anniversary of the birth of BENJAMIN FRANKLIN; and that an Executive Committee of three be appointed, who shall make all necessary arrangements for such meeting, and shall also select suitable persons to deliver an Oration and read a Poem on that occasion." But the effort proved abortive. Franklin's birthday in 1859 passed without a convention, let alone oratory and poetry. "I did not think of it and it is doubtful if any of the other Minnesota editors did," Johnston, one of the two secretaries, later confessed.[11]

The reader of the period who was accustomed to the St. Paul papers found few surprises in the out-state journals. In appearance, content, advertising, and subscription rates, they resembled their territorial predecessors with few and not marked exceptions. The major fault of too many of them was their failure to report the news of their communities, and this failure did not go unremarked by the capital's dailies. The *Daily Minnesotian* of November 13, 1857, commented astringently about a "class of country papers of which it has been truly said, 'that were it not for the heading, no one could tell from the matter, whether it were published in Timbuctoo, or the Western Country.'" The *Daily Pioneer and Democrat* of May 8, 1859, praised the *Glencoe Register* but referred scathingly to "the ordinary 'run' of our country exchanges in the matter of local news and local facts . . . the mass of sheets that come to us now from all quarters weekly without a word about crops, without a suggestion about tillage . . . it requires genius to edit a country paper properly."

A country editor's indulgence in sentimentality as a substitute for "hard" news was held up to ridicule by the *Daily Pioneer and Democrat* of November 13, 1858. "Some body down in Prescott [Wisconsin], on the pining edge of puberty, is suffering dreadfully from an over dose of the New York *Ledger,* moonlight and bad pastry. He wants a 'friend to greet—a bosom to harbor him.' . . . He says he is 'alone.' . . . He wants a bosom, does he? In heaven's name then why don't he get the article, and get all the consolation he can out of it without troubling the public with his caterwauling. Or does he expect the bosom to come to him? . . . Bosoms, indeed! Why, learn to Polka, man, and use your eyes."

Such excesses aside, the St. Paul critics overlooked the fact that their own papers had been vulnerable to the same charge of insufficient attention to local news in an earlier period. In any case, the similarities among the weekly papers were to be expected, for they were established for the familiar purposes of promoting settlement and serving as political party spokesmen—the emphasis varying with the individual journal. Pre-eminent among the boosters was the *Emigrant Aid Journal*, established by Ignatius Donnelly and others to attract settlers to Nininger City. An extreme partisan was the *Chatfield Democrat*. A successful blending of the two functions was achieved by the *Winona Republican*.

Donnelly and a partner, Philip Rohr, launched the *Emigrant Aid Journal* on December 1, 1856, from Philadelphia, where Donnelly practiced law before he moved to Minnesota Territory. Its distinction was suggested by the larger size of its page — twenty by twenty-six inches — by its last two pages printed in German, and by its elaborate logotype — six and a half inches deep, hand-lettered amid festoons that framed scenes of a waterfall, steamboats plying a river, wagon trains plodding, and a railroad train streaking across wide prairies. Under all these icons of westward movement was printed the arresting legend: " 'DOST THOU KNOW HOW TO PLAY THE FIDDLE?' 'NO,' ANSWERED THEMISTOCLES, 'BUT I UNDERSTAND THE ART OF RAISING A LITTLE VILLAGE INTO A GREAT CITY.' " The great city of Donnelly's dream was Nininger, located on the Mississippi near present-day Hastings and named for John Nininger, one of the townsite's proprietors who was a brother-in-law of former Governor Ramsey.

According to the prospectus which appeared in the first issue of the *Emigrant Aid Journal* on December 1, 1856, the paper was to be published monthly until May, after which it was to appear every two weeks. "Some slight intermission may occur between this number and the next," but following the opening of navigation "both the editors of the paper will be permanently located in Nininger." This plan went awry. Donnelly reached Minnesota about four weeks after the first issue was published, but Rohr remained in Philadelphia. The next issue did not appear until June 20, 1857, and by that time Donnelly and Rohr had turned over the editorial direction to A. W. MacDonald. They recruited him from the staff of *Scientific American* with the promise of a salary of $2,000 the first year, plus $3,500 for the support of the paper to be raised by assessing each townsite proprietor one dollar a lot.[12]

"A newspaper in the West is the voice by which the new town makes its merits and its claims known to the surrounding world," the *Journal's* prospectus proclaimed on December 1. "It is the voice by which those afar off are attracted towards it, and once interested, by which their business, their interests and their success are made public. . . . Publicity, in this country, is the one great necessity for success — and publicity we need for our town's sake and our paper's success."

The *Journal,* according to the prospectus, was to be "the representative of the great 'Emigrant Aid Society of Minnesota,'" which was described in detail in another article in that first issue. The society would be chartered to aid emigrants who lacked the capital for removal to Minnesota. Yeoman or mechanic could buy a share of stock through weekly payments; a share would pay for his transportation, a year's provisions, and the implements needed to put in a crop. Land was available at $1.25 an acre under the terms of the Pre-emption Act, which was explained in another article on the page. The society offered an unexampled opportunity, the *Journal* boasted; no other territory or state provided anything like it for the emigrant. "In Illinois he will be met by the Illinois Central railroad, the fever and the ague. In Iowa, by land speculators who infest the State like a famine."

Nearby states were further needled in the second issue on June 20, 1857, which contained the text of an address on Minnesota given by Donnelly at the Broadway House in New York City on March 27. In describing the topography of the territory, Donnelly commented on the bluffs along the Mississippi. "The land had spirit enough to get up a little, instead of lying stretched out in the Illinois fashion, as if laboring under a chronic fever and ague," he said. The wit is reminiscent of Goodhue, as is the exuberant rhetoric of another passage: "Then when I rode out upon the high, clear, sunny, breezy prairies and breathed in that delightful, that exhilarating atmosphere, than which there is nothing purer or sweeter in all God's created world; and when I looked around me at that beautiful diversity of field, wood, and water, rounded lake and crystal stream, I said to myself this surely is earth's Paradise: Eureka! I have found it."

Neither Donnelly nor editor MacDonald, however, had Goodhue's enduring qualities as observer and reporter of the frontier, and gradually the paper lost its distinction. The Emigrant Aid Society did not long remain solvent, and many other grand schemes for Nininger went down in the Panic of 1857. By March, 1858, some months before the last known issue of the *Journal* was published on May 5, 1858, the content of page one had become no different from that clipped by other frontier weeklies from eastern papers and magazines. The issue of March 17 contained pieces on "Curiosities of Science — No. 2," "African Productions and Discoveries," "Modern Jerusalem," "Boys out at Night," "The Sea Serpent Caught," "Cheating the Devil," "How it feels to be Hanged," and "The Drunkard's Cure." The imagination that saw Minnesota's land imbued with "spirit enough to get up a little" had been caught by other projects. The next paper established at Nininger — the *Dakota Sentinel* — was to be Republican, antislavery, and devoted to furthering Donnelly's future in politics.[13]

The major interest of the *Chatfield Democrat* was never anything but politics. It was the second paper of that name, the first having been published briefly in 1856. From its inception the *Democrat* had to compete for readers with its equally partisan opposite number, the *Chatfield Republican*.[14] Editor and publisher of the second *Democrat* was C. C. Hemphill, and a single-minded man was he. From September 11, 1857, when he brought out his first issue, until December 10, 1859, when he wrote his valedictory and turned the enterprise over to Judson W. Bishop, Hemphill gave short shrift to nonpolitical material. When a letter describing the resources of the Chatfield area did succeed in penetrating the columns of the *Democrat*, it was set in agate type. Otherwise settlement was left to muddle along unsung.

Hemphill devoted most of his space to criticizing the Republicans, whom he described as "a party whose whole cry is nigger, nigger — and nothing else."[15] Most of page two was devoted to news and opinion favorable to Democrats in Fillmore County, in Minnesota, or in the nation; the balance of the paper was largely made up of items unfavorable to Republicans, who were virtually always called "Black Republicans" or "Woolies" because of the party's stand on slavery and Negro suffrage. The news, as in most politically oriented frontier papers, might be rewritten or taken directly from exchanges, but the comment was usually the editor's. In a typical editorial addressed to "Democrats of Fillmore County" on September 11, 1857, Hemphill accused the "Black Republicans and the Know Nothings" of preparing "for another sneaking and underhanded contest. . . . Black Republicanism is made up of impudence and barefaced assertions, and we call upon the democrats every where to meet them as they deserve, by hurling back into their teeth, the thousand lies that will be met before the close of the coming election."

The best-known public figure in the *Democrat's* columns was the Honorable James Michael Cavanaugh, one of the state's first representatives in Congress. He had settled at Chatfield and, of course, he was a Democrat. "We feel a pride, a gratification, in thus belonging as we ever have, to the great national democratic party, whose beneficent influences are wide spread as the Union itself," Hemphill wrote in his salutatory on September 11, 1857, "and in the dissemination and advocacy of those principles, we trust our patrons will ever find us, so long as we shall be found in our present position." He never went back on his promise.

The newspaper that struck the best balance between partisanship and promotion was the *Winona Republican*, volume 1, number 1, of which appeared on November 20, 1855. Its publishers may have learned a lesson from the two papers that preceded it in Winona. The *Winona Argus*, which began publication in October, 1854, was lively in its praise of the territory but unemotional in its support of the Democratic party. It attracted adequate backing from advertisers and subscribers until the Panic of 1857 tightened the community's purse strings, causing the *Argus* to fold. The *Winona Weekly Express* was established on August 14, 1855, to support David Olmsted's bid for territorial delegate to Congress. When Rice defeated Olmsted, the *Express* of October 16, 1855, turned column rules to dress page two in mourning black and announced that "Henry M. Rice, whose past career has been that of a selfish, grasping Shylock, has, by the aid of the Almighty Dollar and Official pimps, been elected as Delegate to Congress." The headline for this outburst read "Hung be the Heavens in Black." That was the end of the *Express*.

The accounts and equipment of the *Express* were taken over by a joint stock company — King, Foster, Dye and Company — who brought out the *Republican*. "The time has come for the establishment of a newspaper, published in our midst, not *wholly* devoted to Politics, and the absurd and uninteresting recriminations which so often sully the columns of such papers," the *Republican* declared in its prospectus on November 20, 1855.

To edit the paper, the proprietors hired Captain Sam Whiting, one of the most colorful characters in Minnesota journalism. Whiting seemed ever torn between newspapering and the sea. Born in Hempstead, New York, in 1816, he had gone to sea at sixteen, sailed for thirteen years with the London and Liverpool Packet Line, then for nine years in the China and East India trade. He is said to have founded the first newspaper in Panama, and he rose to the command of his own ship before deciding to forsake the sea for the frontier. Arriving in Winona in 1854, he became assistant editor to William Ashley Jones at the *Argus,* but resigned after a few months to join a polar expedition in search of a missing arctic explorer, Dr. Elisha K. Kane. The successful cruise had lasted nearly six months, at the end of which Whiting returned to Minnesota Territory in time to help launch the *Republican.* Through several of the early issues of the paper, Whiting published his "Journal of a Polar Cruise in Search of Dr. Kane," an exotic report to find its way into the columns of a midwestern frontier weekly.[16]

In the first issue on November 20, Whiting also described his pleasure in returning to Winona, and his account of the changes that had occurred in his absence constituted some of the most effective promotional writing since Goodhue's. "Now, on the spot so lately one unbroken field of green, neat cottages and spacious stores are standing; a mammoth Hotel is rapidly progressing towards completion — and all around are seen abundant signs of a thriving and most prosperous community. The towering pipe of a steam mill which is also in process of erection, promises ere long to facilitate the means of building, by a reduction in the price of lumber."

Whiting did not limit himself to prose in glorifying the virtues of the territory; he was a man "who frequently rushed into verse where poets might have feared to tread."[17] The December 4, 1855, issue of the *Republican* carried an example under the title "Voice from Minnesota":

There is a land of pure delight, upon Earth's sunny sphere,
Where patient industry will thrive; where health and wealth
    will cheer;
It is a land in glorious hues by bounteous Nature drest,
Where MINNESOTA's prairie flowers adorn the charming WEST.

Come from the crowded city's noise, from dusty, gay Broadway,
Where MAMMON's heartless votaries spend their lives in vain
    display;
Come with good faith, and stalwart arm, and help us to improve
These EDENS of the glorious WEST, sweet scenes of peace and
        love. . . .

Competition for settlers was increasing among the townsites, and in the spring of 1856 the *Republican* found it necessary to refute a nasty rumor. "Very many who have arrived here during the past week have been agreeably disappointed in finding us still fifteen feet above high water mark," the issue of May 6, 1856, declared, "and inform us that a certain class of individuals commonly known as 'sharks' get aboard of every steamer, and by exaggeration and false statements endeavor to have them stop at *their city*. . . . The current news ringing in the ear of every emigrant who has heard of Winona and is travelling thither, is, that the Mississippi is over her streets! we answer once and for all time to come, that it is a willful and malicious falsehood and we envy not the miserable creature that utters it — we only wish the waters might for a time cover him sufficient to wash out every stain from his depraved character."

Whiting gave color to the *Republican*, but the stability that ensured its continuation was provided by its third editor, Daniel Sinclair.[18] A native of Scotland, Sinclair came to the United States and settled in Pennsylvania when he was sixteen. He had served an apprenticeship to a printer and had been married for one year when he went to Winona in 1856 at the age of twenty-three. Through five changes of proprietorship in the next year,

Sinclair was the constant. With Walter G. Dye, one of the original proprietors, he bought out Alfred P. Foster, E. L. King, "and others" in June, 1857; in September Sinclair and Dye became D. Sinclair and Company; in November it became Sinclair and (W. C.) Dodge; three months later it was D. Sinclair and Company again; in May, 1857, Dye was back as a partner, although the name of the firm remained unchanged. Sinclair was to be the editor and publisher for fifty years, and in 1867 the respect he had earned among his fellow editors was signalized by his election as first president of the Minnesota Editors and Publishers Association.[19]

Yet another noteworthy weekly started its career as a townsite promoter, then acquired a new editor, a new name, and a change of objective that made it the most controversial paper in the new state. This was St. Cloud's *Minnesota Advertiser,* subsequently the *St. Cloud Visiter* edited by Jane Grey Swisshelm.

George F. Brott, one of the townsite proprietors at St. Cloud, had bought a press and an assortment of bad type and induced a man named Henry C. Cowles to edit a newspaper. The *Minnesota Advertiser,* launched in January, 1857, was not a publication likely to lure immigrants or gladden the hearts of settlers already on the spot. The illegibility of bad type was compounded by the frequency of typographical errors, even in display advertising, and Cowles was more inclined to dwell on the determination and perseverance needed for emigration that on its benefits and rewards. For one innovation, however, the *Advertiser* should be credited: all of page four was devoted to a large map of Minnesota Territory showing a number of trails and projected rail lines converging on St. Cloud. But in preparing the first long paragraph of text to run under the map, the imagination of the editor obviously deserted him, for it was devoted not to "Saint Cloud — Her Resources and Prospects," as the heading proclaimed, but to a garbled version of the history of the original Saint Cloud, the seat of French kings, for which the townsite was named.

Cowles' leading article in the issue of August 27, 1857, was a boring lecture on "The Press" that concluded: "It is a useful thing in a community to have a well conducted paper. To bring it

JAMES M. GOODHUE *published the first newspaper in Minnesota Territory, the* Minnesota Pioneer. *The first issue appeared in St. Paul on April 28, 1849, less than two months after the creation of the territory. From that time until his death in August, 1852, Goodhue successfully promoted the attractions of the area in the columns of his paper. A colorful and outspoken writer, he dominated territorial journalism during his brief career. This portrait is a daguerreotype taken about 1850.*

THIS WASHINGTON HAND PRESS *in the museum of the Minnesota Historical Society may be the one upon which Goodhue printed the first issue of the* Minnesota Pioneer. *Used in the* Pioneer *office, it was given to the society by the Pioneer Press Company in 1905.*

THIS ISSUE of the Minnesota Pioneer, dated April 28, 1849, was the first newspaper printed in Minnesota. It published the text of the Congressional act creating Minnesota Territory. Although Congress approved the bill on March 3, 1849, news of it did not reach the frontier settlement of St. Paul until April 9 when a steamboat arrived from downriver.

PRINTERS *in Goodhue's shop and in those of other territorial papers set type from chest-high cases like that shown at right in an engraving which appeared in the St. Paul city directory of 1859. When printing began in Minnesota, all type was set by hand, and it continued to be until after the invention of the linotype in the 1880s.*

A SMALL LOG BUILDING *at Third and Wabasha streets in St. Paul was Goodhue's first residence in 1849. A year later it was enlarged and used as the* Pioneer *office. The newspaper had previously been printed at two other locations on Third Street. Sketch by Robert O. Sweeny, 1852.*

JUDGE DAVID COOPER *of the territorial supreme court (below) and Charles K. Smith, first secretary of Minnesota Territory, provoked Goodhue's wrath. The editor was physically assaulted for his denunciation of Cooper, and he saw Smith removed from his job after a feud that lasted over two years. The engraving of Cooper and the drawing of Smith by Carl Bohnen were made about 1850.*

THE MEN *pictured below were the territory's leading political figures. Henry H. Sibley (left) and Henry M. Rice (right) led opposing factions of the Democratic party. Alexander Ramsey (center), first territorial governor, was a Whig and later a Republican. All three were deeply involved in the ownership of early papers. Sibley photograph courtesy Sibley House Association, Minnesota Daughters of American Revolution; Ramsey photograph taken about 1860; Rice photograph taken about 1858.*

ST. PAUL, *the capital of Minnesota Territory, looked like this in 1851 when the Whig newspaper, the* Minnesotian, *appeared. In that year Goodhue described the young village "springing up fresh and vigorous, like the skeleton of a great city, where but yesterday stood a forest, filled with wild Indians." Water color by Jean Baptist Wengler, 1851; courtesy Landesmuseum, Linz, Austria.*

JOHN P. OWENS *had the longest career of any territorial editor — from 1849 to 1857. A staunch Whig, he became editor of the* Minnesota Register *in 1849. Later he served on the combined* Chronicle *and* Register *and the* Minnesotian.

NATHANIEL MCLEAN *was the second owner of the* Register. *It is sometimes called Minnesota's first newspaper, but the first issue was actually printed in Ohio. McLean was for a time associated with Owens in the publication of the* Register.

DANIEL A. ROBERTSON, *editor, lawyer, and naturalist, founded the* Minnesota Democrat *of St. Paul in 1850 as the first strongly partisan spokesman of the Democratic party in the area. To embarrass Governor Ramsey, the* Democrat *initiated an exposé of the so-called Sioux treaty frauds in 1852. A portion of the first issue of the paper is shown.*

LIKE MANY *territorial politicians, Democrat David Olmsted was also involved in newspaper publishing. Olmsted, who was a candidate for territorial delegate in 1850 and later mayor of St. Paul, owned the* Chronicle and Register *for a brief time. Later he bought the* Democrat *from Robertson and launched the* St. Paul Daily Democrat *in 1854. Photograph taken in 1861.*

JOSEPH R. BROWN, *one of the ablest and most versatile men in early Minnesota history, became editor of the* Pioneer *in 1853 after Goodhue's death. Later he edited the* St. Paul Daily Democrat, *and he also founded and published the* Henderson Democrat *in 1856. Daguerreotype taken in the 1850s.*

EARLE S. GOODRICH, *a young journalist from New York, succeeded Joe Brown as editor of the* Minnesota Pioneer. *Under his direction the first daily paper in Minnesota — the* Daily Pioneer — *was issued on May 1, 1854. The New Yorker continued to edit the paper until 1865. Engraving from A. T. Andreas,* An Illustrated Historical Atlas of the State of Minnesota *(1874).*

WITHIN FIFTEEN DAYS *in May, 1854, four daily newspapers appeared in St. Paul. Thomas M. Newson was editor of one of them, the* St. Paul Daily Times, *which became the first Republican paper in the capital. Newson remained with the* Times *until it merged with the* St. Paul Press *in 1861. Photograph taken in the 1860s.*

Saint Paul Daily Times.

NEWSON, MITCHELL & CO.   ST. PAUL, MONDAY, MAY 15, 1854.   VOL. 1, NO. 1.

SEVERAL INNOVATIONS *in Minnesota's territorial press were introduced by Newson. One of them was the regular appearance of a business column written by Charles H. Parker, a St. Paul banker and attorney. The Parker column at right appeared in the* Daily Times *of December 2, 1854.*

COMMERCIAL MATTERS.
From Messrs. BORUP & OAKES, Bankers and Exchange
Dealers.   Nov. 10, 1854
Exchange on New York...................1¼ ₱ cent.
  "   "   St. Louis,.....................1¼ ₱   "
  "   "   Chicago,......................1   "   "
We refuse for the present all Ohio money except State Banks.
  "   "   "   " Indiana except   "   "
  "   "   "   " Virginia.
  "   "   "   " Tennessee.
  "   "   "   " Kentucky except Bank Ky.
  "   "   "   " District Columbia.
  "   "   "   " Georgia except Atlanta.

BANKING HOUSE OF C. H. PARKER.—Rates of Exchange,
Eastern.........................¼ per cent. premium.
Southern.......................¼ per cent. premium.

EDITED BY C. H. PARKER.

MONETARY.
Nothing of interest has transpired in this city, with reference to money matters, within the past week. There is undoubtedly no great financial pressure upon the masses, particularly upon our business men. The panic about Atlanta and Macon money here has ended in *smoke, as to Atlanta* and repudiation as to Macon. The former is received as usual by Messrs. Borup & Oakes, while the latter is no longer taken by Messrs. Mackubin and Egerton the reputed correspondents of the owner of said money.
The rates of interest, are unchanged 2 1-2 per cent are ... on Real Estate ... ... on ...

NEWSON *was also the first newspaper editor known to have clashed with the typographical union organized by St. Paul printers in December, 1856. The oldest union in Minnesota, the St. Paul local received its charter two years later, and in 1859 the charter pictured at right was issued to a second chapter at St. Anthony and Minneapolis. The document is preserved in the collections of the Minnesota Historical Society.*

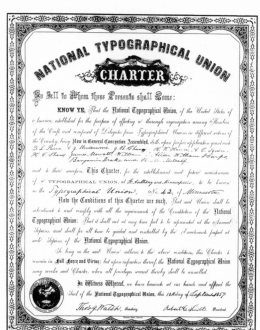

DR. THOMAS FOSTER *was sketched "in Duluth on a breezy day" by an unknown artist. A physician, Foster had a varied career. He went to the territory as Governor Ramsey's secretary in 1849. With Ramsey, he was influential in establishing the state's Republican party. In 1857 he took over the editorship of* the Daily Minnesotian *of St. Paul, and later he was associated with the* Minneapolis Chronicle *and the* St. Paul Dispatch. *Foster also founded Duluth's first paper, the* Minnesotian, *in 1869.*

AN 1857 VIEW *of Main Street in St. Anthony (now part of Minneapolis) shows the office (right) where the* St. Anthony Express *was published in 1851 and the building across the street in which the* Minnesota Republican *was printed. At left is the Winslow Hotel.*

THE FIRST THREE *weekly newspapers to be published in what is now Minneapolis were issued at St. Anthony, the community on the east bank of the Mississippi that became part of Minneapolis in 1872. The earliest was the* St. Anthony Express *of May 31, 1851.*

THE NORTH-WESTERN DEMOCRAT *and the* Minnesota Republican *were the other weekly newspapers published at St. Anthony before one appeared in Minneapolis. First issues of the* North-Western Democrat *(July 13, 1853) and of the* Republican *(October 5, 1854) are shown in part. These two papers are among the earliest in the genealogy of today's* Minneapolis Tribune.

ISAAC ATWATER *edited the* St. Anthony Express *during most of its existence from 1851 to 1859. Atwater, a lawyer, also wrote a history of Minneapolis. Engraving from* Magazine of Western History, July, *1888.*

WILLIAM A. CROFFUT *was a founder in 1857 of the* Falls Evening News *of St. Anthony, the first daily outside of St. Paul. He later worked for the* New York Tribune *and edited the* Washington Daily Post. *Engraving from* Andreas, Illustrated Historical Atlas.

EDWIN CLARK *was Croffut's partner in the* Falls Evening News. *Clark was publisher and business manager, and Croffut served as editor. Described as a "stirring, energetic man" by a fellow newspaperman, Clark was eighty-seven years of age when this photograph was taken in 1921.*

THIS *1857 photograph of Minneapolis, St. Anthony's youthful rival, shows the office of the* second Minnesota Democrat. *The newspaper began publication in 1856 and is the third paper in the ancestry of the present* Minneapolis Tribune.

STOVES!

COMPETITION DEFIED

At the Cheap

Stove Store.

On Third, between Roberts and Jackson streets.

ADVERTISEMENTS and "cards" in territorial newspapers were often sweeping in their claims but usually were typographically sedate. Unusual for its large type and engravings is the ad above from the Weekly Minnesotian (St. Paul) of October 29, 1851. The one below is reproduced from the North-Western Democrat, July 28, 1855; the others (top to bottom) are from the Minnesota Register, August 11, 1849; Chronicle and Register, August 12, 1850; Minnesota Chronicle, August 2, 1849; Minnesota Pioneer, July 26, 1849; St. Anthony Express, May 31, 1851.

THE BOMB SHELL.

THE EARTH'S A SHELL, THROWN, FROM OLD NATURES MORTAR.

TERMS. 50 CENTS PER ANNUM FORT RIPLEY, M.T. JULY 26 · 1854.

R. POLLOCK BOMBARDIER. H. NUGENT GUNNER. C. HERMAN POWD-MONKEY

PROSPECTUS.

The appearance of the BOMB-SHELL before the Public, may be as unexpected and to some as unwelcome, as that of its Proto-type in its design in to the centre of a just few square, or behind the bre'st-works of a foe; its prospe-... appearance our Shell will be as harmless the Egg of the Turtle Dove, and except in defence of the innocent, will never be charged with extensive mat-er some have insis-uated that its inven-tion has emenated from the eternal regions; we deny the... climate. For his own amusement, and pas time, he has cut from wood the type from which this impress i on was taken.

The shell will pre mise nothing, which it can not perform; though in appearance you will naturally expect it roughly handled. Nothing of...

PROSPECTUS
OF THE
MINNESOTA POSTEN.

MINNESOTA POSTEN,
A New Paper to be Published every other Week at Cannon Falls, M. T., in the Swedish Language.

This paper is now being started under fair auspices. The want of a Swedish Newspaper has long been felt in this Territory and adjacent States. Thousands of Swedes, who have left their Native Land and Relations on the other side of the Ocean, have came to this Territory and made it their permanent home, and expect to live and die here,—while, for the most part, unconversant with the language of their adopted country, but yet desirous to make themselves acquainted with the land in which they live, it is but natural that a paper in their own language is a thing much needed.

The want felt is both of a religious and political nature. The Swedes, like other foreigners, are strangers in a new land, scattered like sheep having no shepard. They need encouragement and enlightenment on the subject of Religion; they need an organ to advocate their cause and by means of which they may set themselves in communication with each other, and ways and means be discussed that will best promote their spiritual welfare. Politically, they need a true understanding of the laws and institutions of this country so that they may be able to do their duty as citizens and enjoy the privileges afforded. They need, moreover, to be enlightened on the political questions of the day, so as not to become the tools of every party politician to further his own selfish interests as the case has often been heretofore. These wants the paper contemplated will attend to.

In matters of Religion, it will advocate the principles of the Evangelical Lutheran Church, yet without bigotry and sectarian jealousy. In politics it will advocate no certain party; it wishes to be independent. It will advocate the cause of truth and justice wherever it is found, but on the contrary, rebuke wrong, injustice, tyrany and oppression.

If we succeed, by this undertaking, in leading a portion of our inhabitants into the way of virtue, religion and justice, we believe that we will confer a blessing upon our community at large, and would deserve the approbation and good will of all our fellow citizens.

If sufficient encouragement is extended to warrant the undertaking, we will issue the first number of the MINNESOTA POS-TEN early in June. Its size will be the same as the Cannon Falls GAZETTE, and will be issued regularly every other week at one dollar per annum, invariably in advance.

It will be a good opportunity for merchants and business men to spread their advertisements before the Swedish public through this paper as it is the only one of the kind in Minnesota.

All communications having reference to the paper should be directed to the editor,

REV. E. NORELIUS,
Cannon Falls, Goodhue Co., M. T.

ONE of the most unusual newspapers published in Minnesota Territory is shown above. The Bomb Shell was printed at Fort Ripley from type carved by a soldier. The only known copy of the prospectus, dated July 26, 1854, is in the Minnesota Historical Society's collections. A prospectus, declaring editorial goals and inviting subscriptions, usually preceded the publication of a pioneer newspaper. At left is that issued by Minnesota Posten, a Swedish-language newspaper established at Red Wing in 1857.

THE ELABORATE LOGOTYPE *above, depicting the symbols of westward movement, appeared on the* Emigrant Aid Journal *launched by Ignatius Donnelly and Philip Rohr in 1856. The newspaper, which died in 1858, boosted the town of Nininger City, located on the Mississippi River near present-day Hastings.*

IGNATIUS DONNELLY, *an Irishman who was a prolific author and a fiery orator, later held several state offices, served in Congress, and became a nationally known leader of the Farmers' Alliance movement and the Populist party. Photograph taken about 1850, courtesy National Archives, Washington, D.C.*

THE DREAM *of a chain of railroads linking Minnesota to the rest of the nation was a major topic in the 1850s. In April, 1858, the* Pioneer and Democrat *published the extra shown above urging passage of a $5,000,000 railroad loan bill. Edmund Rice, shown at left in an engraving made about 1880, was a director of the territory's first railroad company — the subject of another long editorial war.*

THE OFFICE *of the* Pioneer and Democrat *at Third and Jackson streets, St. Paul, is pictured as it looked about 1856. The area's first paper, the* Minnesota Pioneer, *and an early competitor, the* Minnesota Democrat, *merged in 1855.*

FOR THE FIRST FEW YEARS, *territorial news-papers were concerned largely with the promotion of the area. In the 1850s slavery was the issue that drew their interest to the national scene. This item in the* Pioneer and Democrat *of November 9, 1858, hailed Stephen A. Douglas' triumph over Abraham Lincoln for a seat in the United States Senate.*

JOB PRINTING *has been called "the meat and potatoes" on the newspaper printer's table. Subscriptions and public printing contracts were not enough to sustain the early papers. Commercial printing revenues allowed them to expand their selection of types and helped pay for better presses. This advertisement appeared in the first St. Paul city directory, published in 1857.*

In the territory's *first Capitol, built in 1853, the 1857 legislature approved a bill to make St. Peter rather than St. Paul the capital. The structure at Tenth and Wabasha streets was destroyed by fire in 1881. Photograph taken before 1872.*

Willis A. Gorman, *the first Democratic governor of Minnesota Territory (1853–57), figured in the scheme to remove the capital to St. Peter. A bill to do so was supported in 1857 by a group of St. Peter townsite promoters, among whom was the governor. This photograph was taken about 1866.*

Joseph Rolette, *a fur trader from Pembina in the extreme northwestern corner of the territory and a Democratic member of the 1857 legislature, saved the capital for St. Paul. He did so by disappearing for 123 hours with the enrolled copy of the capital removal bill. Without that essential copy, the measure was not technically approved. The pastel portrait at left shows Rolette in the modified voyageur garb he wore in the legislature.*

By *1858 there were enough newspapers in Minnesota to warrant a convention of editors and publishers. Columbus Stebbins (left), shown in an oil portrait by an unknown artist, was editor of the* Hastings Independent. *Stebbins was elected president by the convention. Andrew J. Van Vorhes (center) was named one of the two vice-presidents. As editor, owner, or both, he was associated with the* Stillwater Messenger *from its beginning in 1856 until it was sold in 1868. The photograph was taken about 1867. One of the two secretaries was Daniel S. B. Johnston (right) of the* St. Anthony Express. *Johnston is shown as he looked in 1875.*

Congress *at last admitted Minnesota to the Union as a full-fledged state in 1858. The* Winona Times *of May 15 celebrated the event with headlines large for the day and the rare device of a line drawing (shown actual size). The eight-inch-long story proclaimed, "The prospects of the infant State are flattering in the highest degree."*

BRING OUT THE BIG GUN

GLORIOUS NEWS!!

MINNESOTA A STATE!!!

100 GUNS FIRED AT WINONA:

GENERAL REJOICING,

JANE GREY SWISSHELM, *the fighting editor of the*
St. Cloud Visiter *and the* St. Cloud Democrat
from 1857 to 1863, was the most outspoken Min-
nesota abolitionist of her day. In her lifetime, she
was one of the best known women in the United
States. When she died in 1884 a fellow editor re-
marked, "In her time she was a tiger." This por-
trait is from a daguerreotype made in 1852.

WILLIAM B. MITCHELL, *Mrs. Swiss-*
helm's nephew and assistant edi-
tor, took over the Democrat *after*
her departure for Washington,
D.C. A temperate and able news-
paperman, he edited the Democrat
and later the St. Cloud Journal
and Journal-Press *until his retire-*
ment in 1892.

MRS. SWISSHELM *started the* St. Cloud Democrat *in August, 1858, after vandals destroyed the press of the* St. Cloud Visiter. *She continued to publish the* Democrat, *which reflected the "sharp corners" of her opinions on many topics, until she left St. Cloud in 1863. Her office is shown above.*

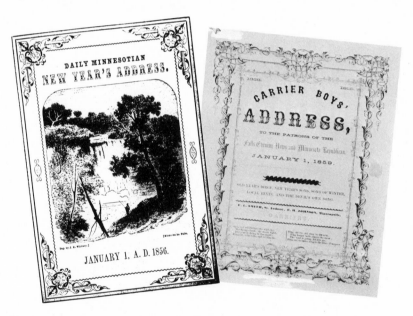

FOR MANY YEARS *newsboys distributed humorous greetings to their customers on New Year's Day. In exchange, the carriers were rewarded with coins and cookies. The* Daily Minnesotian's *"New Year's Address" of 1856 reflected the slavery issue in rhyme: "Republicans agree, That all new states come in the Union — FREE." The "Carrier Boys' Address" given out by the* Falls Evening News *and the* Minnesota Republican *in 1859 featured verses by Tennyson on its cover.*

WINONA, *one of the first towns beyond the capital area to have a newspaper, looked like this in 1861. In 1855 it had three papers: the* Argus, *the* Weekly Express, *and the* Weekly Republican.

DANIEL SINCLAIR *settled at Winona in 1856. He soon became a partner in the* Republican, *with which he was associated for fifty years. In 1867 he was elected president of the Minnesota Editors and Publishers Association. Photograph taken in 1867.*

THIS *advertisement touting the* Winona Republican *appeared in a booklet published by the newspaper to promote Winona's prospects in 1858.*

LATEST NEWS.

TELEGRAPHIC!

BY

Winslow's Line to St. Anthony.

REPORTED FOR THE NEWS.

WASHINGTON NEWS.

CONFERENCE OF SOUTHERN SEN-ATORS.

No More Troops to Fort Moultrie.

EXPEDIENT FOR REPLENISHING THE U. S. TREASURY.

New Pacific Railroad Route.

SELECT COMMITTEE TO MEET NEXT WEEK.

PROBABLE CHANGE IN THE CAB-INET.

PIONEER JOURNALISM *in Minnesota ended with the coming of the telegraph in August, 1860. After the Civil War, the state's press developed along the natonal pattern; the twentieth century saw the rise of large metropolitan dailies. The headlines above are from the* Falls Evening News, *December 10, 1860.*

WILLIAM J. MURPHY, *for whom Murphy Hall on the University of Minnesota Campus is named, owned the* Minneapolis Tribune *from 1891 to 1918. In that period the* Tribune's *circulation became the largest in the state.*

HERSCHEL V. JONES *owned the* Minneapolis Journal *from 1908 until 1928. John Cowles later purchased the* Tribune, *the* Journal, *and the* Minneapolis Star *to form the present* Tribune *and* Star.

JOSEPH A. WHEELOCK *presided over the evolution of today's* St. Paul Pioneer Press, *which traces its lineage back to the territory's first paper, Goodhue's* Minnesota Pioneer. *As editor of the* St. Paul Daily Press, *Wheelock merged it with the* Pioneer *in 1875, and it was he who made the* Pioneer Press *the state's leading paper in the years before his death in 1906. This photograph of Wheelock, whose Minnesota career began in 1850, was taken about 1865.*

WILLIAM R. MARSHALL, *a Republican who became governor of the state in 1866, was a founder and the first editor of the* St. Paul Daily Press *in 1861. When he volunteered for Civil War duty, Wheelock became editor. Marshall photo taken about 1865.*

FREDERICK DRISCOLL *bought a half interest in the* Daily Press *in 1863. As business manager, he worked with Wheelock to make the* Pioneer Press *the state's leading paper in the early years of the twentieth century. Photograph taken about 1889.*

to the proper standard of usefulness the public should take some pains to keep it on a good foundation. A word to the wise is sufficient." The wise must have nodded in assent and withdrawn their subscriptions and advertising in the hope of speeding the end of the poorly conducted enterprise. That was the last issue of the *Advertiser*.

Its demise left Brott with a press on his hands. After some reflection, he paid a call on Mrs. Swisshelm, sister-in-law and member of the household of Henry Z. Mitchell. "I stated to him, as preliminary," Mrs. Swisshelm wrote later, "that I was an out and out Abolitionist, and could not edit a paper in which I had not full liberty to express my sentiments on any question. He replied that he was a Democrat, but that all Democrats recognised a lady's right to talk any kind of politics she had a mind to; that the object of a press here, was to advertise the town and surrounding country, to make the public acquainted with its advantages so as to induce immigration. This object my reason and conscience fully approved."[20]

The statement suggests a fighting editor. Jane Grey Cannon Swisshelm did not look like a fighter. She did not even look like an editor. On the frontier and elsewhere newspaper editors were men, yet this woman, fragile and feminine enough to be likened in appearance to Jenny Lind, "the Swedish Nightingale," had a reputation as an editor that preceded her to the territory. Her arrival in St. Paul had been accordingly noted by the *Daily Pioneer and Democrat* on June 23, 1857: "MRS. SWISSHELM, a lady of considerable fame as a writer, and for a number of years the *editor* of the Pittsburgh Saturday Visiter, a fearless but now defunct Freesoil paper, was in this city yesterday; and intends to make her residence in this territory for one year, in the vicinity of Saint Cloud."

Jane Swisshelm was not merely a woman, she was a woman in retreat from a disastrous marriage, a woman whose only companion was a six-year-old daughter. She had gone to St. Cloud because her sister's family had migrated there the previous year and because Pittsburgh had become untenable. Her husband, who early in their marriage had been unable to leave his mother for her, had developed into a petty despot. Trying to run a newspaper and salvage a marriage had brought her low; when she recovered, she determined to abandon both. Minnesota was her escape valve.[21]

Her first issue of the *St. Cloud Visiter* on December 10, 1857, sounded as if the experience had unhinged her. The salutatory which marked the first number of a newspaper in those days usually ran from a short paragraph to a half column, rarely a full column. Mrs. Swisshelm's, significantly entitled "Personal," ran two and a half columns, and rarely has such a wandering effusion appeared in a newspaper. Beginning with a reference to her physical collapse in the middle of composing an editorial for the *Pittsburgh Saturday Visiter* a year earlier, the writer progressed to her arrival in the territory, to the grasshopper plague, to Indian outbreaks, to the Fort Ripley garrison's duty in Kansas, to the rigors of Minnesota winters, and finally to the cheerfulness of all hands in the face of such trials. There was a point to all this, the reader must have been relieved to discover. Because of such equanimity, the writer had decided to stay in St. Cloud. She must do something, and since she had had more experience than anyone else there in writing for the press, she would edit the newspaper.

The *Advertiser* had been "decidedly conservative," she noted, and she begged "forbearance for the many sharp corners on our opinions." These were not immediately apparent in the prospectus which she published in the issue of December 24. The *Visiter* would not be "the organ of any party or sect," she wrote, but its columns would be open to members thereof. The paper intended to deal fairly with opinions differing from its own, "but the editorial department will never represent anything but the convictions of the editor."

Some of those convictions were then spelled out, and they reflected the influences that had operated on the writer. "1st. The Divine law is the Supreme law in all lands created by its author." Jane Grey Cannon had been born to Scotch-Irish parents and brought up on strict Presbyterian theology. When she joined the church after great soul-searching, she "was assured, to her satisfaction, that she 'should be a thistle-digger in the vineyard.' "[22] The easy tasks had little attraction for her.

"2nd. All men are created free; and equal in the right to life, liberty and the pursuit of happiness." In Louisville, Kentucky, where James Swisshelm had taken his wife in an effort to escape from his mother, Jane's direct observation of slavery strongly reinforced her revulsion against that institution. Her efforts to supplement her husband's small income by conducting a school for Negro children brought threats to burn their home.

"3d. The Bible, and the Constitution of the United States are antislavery; and human chattledom is unconstitutional in any association professing to receive either as fundamental law." As a schoolteacher, Mrs. Swisshelm had written articles on slavery and women's rights for a Pittsburgh antislavery paper, the *Spirit of Liberty*. After it and yet another abolitionist paper, the *Albatross*, suspended publication, Mrs. Swisshelm launched the *Saturday Visiter* in order that Pittsburgh should not be without an abolitionist press.

"4th. Paying taxes is as unwomanly as voting; and is a privilege which should be exclusively confined to 'white male citizens, of this and other countries.' " The satirical tone may have been inappropriate, but it expressed the writer's indignation at the status of her sex. Twice she had been especially humiliated by women's inferior status at law: when her husband had threatened to sue her mother's estate for her services as a nurse during her mother's terminal cancer illness, and again when she separated from her husband and had to establish her property rights in court. As an ardent feminist, she took pains to sprinkle her historical allusions with references to foremothers as well as forefathers.

The "sharp corners" were more apparent in Mrs. Swisshelm's comments on a wide variety of topics in subsequent issues of the *Visiter*. Governor Samuel Medary's annual message to the legislature ("we do not remember ever seeing a better message from the governor of any place"); President Buchanan's message to Congress ("this dark, dark blot upon our national escutcheon"); kissing games ("this disgusting absurdity"); the Reverend T. E. Inman's strictures on dancing ("With all due deference, we must say that such assertions are simply absurd."). On behalf of Minnesota womanhood, Mrs. Swisshelm petitioned the territorial legislature in February, 1858, to include in a homestead bill a protection of woman's equity in a homestead. And in June she took issue with those who cried havoc because of the grasshopper plague. Times were hard, she did not deny, but she had seen no evidence of great destitution in Stearns County. In July she remarked that there was no destitution as long as there was a potato crop, and she urged subscribers who lacked cash to bring in their produce.[23]

The financial position of the paper was, in fact, precarious. Mrs. Swisshelm estimated that the *Advertiser* and the *Visiter* together must have cost Brott $2,500, plus his original investment of $800 for press and equipment. By the spring of 1858, the two papers had brought in only $462.55.[24] The editor thought it unfair that Brott should have to carry the burden alone when the other townsite proprietors benefited as much as he did from the *Visiter's* publication. Most benefited, she figured, because his holdings were largest, was Sylvanus B. Lowry, a former partner of Henry M. Rice in the fur trade and a potent figure in local Democratic politics. But Lowry, a native of Tennessee and a Democrat of Buchanan persuasion, strongly disapproved of the *Visiter's* abolitionist position and its editor's disregard for the Democratic establishment. He told her as much when she went to him seeking financial support for the *Visiter*.

Readers must have done a double-take when they saw the issue of February 18, 1858, for it announced Mrs. Swisshelm's intention to "make the Visiter an Administration organ, to support Mr. Buchanan's measures and advocate his re-election." The explanation followed immediately. Mrs. Swisshelm was recommending Buchanan as a suitable candidate for 1260 rather than 1860. After an extended review of moral progress since the birth of Christ, Mrs. Swisshelm concluded that Buchanan and the Democrats would be about right for the middle of the thirteenth century "when kingcraft and priestcraft shall be triumphant, and the masses shall be provided with masters to exact their labor and furnish them with their peck of corn each week."

Lowry was annoyed and other readers must have awaited the next issue with varying degrees of anticipation. They had to wait until March 4 because, as the editor explained, an agent had forgotten to forward paper. "As that article is now enormously high, business very dull, and one of our best typesetters has joined the Red River Company, we have concluded to issue but once in two weeks until navigation opens."

For the doubled interval, she gave Lowry something to think about. "Some of our old friends think it very odd that we should, 'all of a sudden' have become a staunch Buchanan Democrat, but they never were in Stearns county," she wrote. "Follow-my-leader Democracy is the manifest destiny of this region, not that there is anything in the air unfavorable to freedom of individual opinions, but that the first settler here is a Southern gentleman, one who possesses in a high degree the qualities which have enabled 300,000 slaveholders to govern 25,000,000 of men, who by the Declaration of Independence ought to have been their political equals. These qualities are, the habit of command, the indomitable will and confirmed self-esteem, gained by the exercise, from infancy, of irresponsible power. To these are added, in this instance, a mind of more than ordinary vigor, highly cultivated taste, great geniality of disposition; and the candor and frankness which to such a character become matters of course. Well, a majority of our people are German Catholic and no free people on earth are so trained to habits of veneration and obedience, except the small fry of northern office seekers who worship before commissions even more devoutly than a catholic does at the symbol of the cross."

Mrs. Swisshelm went on to say that many Stearns County newcomers who had been Republicans or Douglas Democrats in their home states had become Buchanan Democrats when they understood how "our oldest inhabitant" controlled political appointments and removals. "Their knees double up and their back bones double down like the fibers of a green cabbage blade held over the escape pipe of a steam engine. . . . Well, this being the case what was the use of our keeping up a 'factious opposition' like the little stick trying to turn the course of a great river. It is nice for women to be gentle and yielding, especially if there is money to be made by it. Our publisher assured us Mr. ——— never would patronize the Visiter if it opposed the administration. Self interest suggested that our fortune would be

about made if we could support Mr. Buchanan. We thought the
matter over five minutes and concluded that maybe we *could* if
we tried. . . . Our last issue was the result; and with all deference, to our brethren of the press we are willing to maintain that
that number of the St. Cloud Visiter is the best Administration
organ ever published in Minnesota; and the only one which
frankly avows and maintains the real objects of the Buchanan
Democracy."

Lowry must have wondered if there were not some way of shut-
ting off the torrent. He should have been warned that the lecture
hall would not be an effective means in view of Mrs. Swisshelm's
comment on a recent lecturer in the town. "Mr. [Henry C.] Wait,
the Republican Democratic member of the Constitutional Convention of Minnesota, delivered a lecture at Wilson's Hall, on
Wednesday evening, the 17th ult. Subject — 'Our Gentlemen.'
We admire Mr. Wait's modesty and total want of egotism in the
choice of a subject. No other topic could possibly lead him farther
from self, unless he had chosen to discuss 'Our Honest Men.' " [25]

Lowry and his lieutenants were not warned. James C. Shepley,
Lowry's lawyer, followed Wait in the lecture series, addressing
himself to the subject of "Women." The categories under which
he discussed the topic were not formed entirely by the times.
After disposing of coquettes, flirts, and old maids, he turned his
attention to the advocates of women's rights, especially those
whose advocacy led them to write for newspapers. "His ideas on
this point presented nothing new, except that high flavoring of
double distilled extract of gall, one might expect from a bilious
man," Mrs. Swisshelm reported in her account of the lecture on
March 18, 1858. But he had overlooked several varieties, the editor noted, and she directed his attention to one of them: "the
large, thick-skinned, coarse, sensual-featured, loud-mouthed
double-fisted dames, whose entrance into a room appears to take
one's breath, whose conversational tones are audible at the fur-
thest side of the next square, whose guffahs resound across a mile
wide river, and who talk with an energy which makes the saliva
fly like — showers of melted pearls. They deck their portly persons in coarse prints of bed-spread patterns and rainbow hues,
made into fousy ruffles and many frumples, as they stand to per-

form their office as high priestess at the shrine of Euchre."
There was a great deal more, including the suggestion that this
card-playing type was dedicated to snaring spouses for unmarried
female relatives.

The "type," it seemed, was too readily recognizable in the
person of Mrs. James C. Shepley. Early on the morning of
March 24 the office of the *Visiter* was broken into, the press
destroyed, and the type thrown into the street and into the Mississippi River. The vandals left a message for the editor which said:
"The citizens of St[.] Cloud have determined to abate the nuisance of which you have made the *'Visiter'* a striking specimen.

"They have decided that it is fit only for the inmates of
brothels, and you seem to have had some experience of the tastes
of such persons.

"You will never have the opportunity to repeat the offence in
this town, without paying a more serious penalty than you do
now.

"By order of the Committee of Vigilance."[26]

Poor vigilantes! How sadly they underestimated the editor!
That night the Stearns House was "filled to suffocation" with
an indignation meeting. Chairman Charles T. Stearns called
Mrs. Swisshelm to the platform to give her account of the affair,
and she complied in great detail. The handwriting of the Vigilance Committee threat, she said, had been identified as Lowry's
by "Four disinterested men." She concluded her address by saying, "If you think gentlemen, that it will be for the honor of
St. Cloud, that I should die here, and in this cause, God's will be
done! my will is made, my pledge will be redeemed, my vow
fulfilled, and my life given in the cause of God's suffering poor."

After that, committees were appointed to draft resolutions
and to devise means to ensure the speedy resumption of publication by the *Visiter*. The resolutions might have been edited
by Mrs. Swisshelm herself. *"Resolved,* By the citizens of St[.]
Cloud in meeting assembled, that we consider the act as a das-
tardly, mean, and contemptible crime, entitling the perpetrators,
aiders and abettors, whomsoever they may be, to a home in the
penitentiary, and that we regard them as beings — *we will not
say men* — capable of stooping to any meanness and fit subjects

(no matter what their professions) to associate with convicts and felons.

"*Resolved,* That this attempt to stifle free speech and to break down an independent press, because it refused to be controlled at the mere *dictate* of a certain clique, meets with our most hearty disapprobation, our strongest condemnation, and our utter detestation.

"*Resolved,* That the St. Cloud *Visiter shall be sustained.*

"*Resolved,* That we will sustain it."

Another resolution expressed confidence in the *Visiter's* "talented and distinguished" editor.

The *Visiter* was not able to resume regular publication until May 13, but the interval was hardly a respite for the vigilantes. Newspapers throughout Minnesota and in the East reported the outrage and condemned it. Shepley wrote a letter to the *St. Paul Pioneer and Democrat,* protesting that the destruction of the press was not politically motivated but was rather intended to prevent another libelous attack on his wife. "The proprietor of the paper is in Washington, and there was no one to control her [*Mrs. Swisshelm*], and I knowing her character, had reason to expect another libelous attack worse than the first, and destroyed the type to prevent it, always intending to pay Mr. BROTT, the owner, on his return."[27]

In the June 17 issue of the *Visiter,* Mrs. Swisshelm published an extended and unflattering description of a pair of women who lived in a Louisville boardinghouse where she had stayed briefly; in them she had observed the demoralizing influence that card-playing can exert. Readers must have wondered if Mrs. Swisshelm were not retreating from recrimination into reminiscence. But such was not the case. The sketch of the female card players was no mere digression. The June 24 issue of the *Visiter* reported that Shepley had filed a libel suit for $10,000 against the St. Cloud Printing Company. "The stockholders have resolved to defend, to the utmost, this bogus slander suit, and give the burglars as much law as will satisfy them," Mrs. Swisshelm reported. She also insisted that it was not Mrs. Shepley but rather the two women of her boardinghouse sketch who had served as models for her description of the Euchre priestess. A further defensive tactic was disclosed in the July 22 issue which announced that the *Visiter's* stockholders had presented the paper to Mrs. Swisshelm.

But their resolution wavered. The judge who would hear the libel suit was a friend of Lowry, and the chances of getting an unprejudiced jury seemed poor. Mrs. Swisshelm urged the former stockholders to settle out of court, especially when Shepley agreed not to press the suit if they would give him the assurance that Mrs. Swisshelm would never again refer to the vigilante raid in the *Visiter*. Mrs. Swisshelm gave her promise.

She discontinued the *Visiter* with the July 29 issue. On August 5 the *St. Cloud Democrat* appeared in its place. "When we authorized the Printing Company to pledge The St. Cloud *Visiter* to silence on 'the subject' of the destruction of our office, we did so, simply to get our friends out of our way; and to circumvent three lawyers," Mrs. Swisshelm wrote in the first issue on August 5, 1858. "The men pledged *their* honor that the *Visiter* should not 'discuss *the subject*.' *We* have pledged *our* honor that the paper we edit will discuss any subject we have a mind. As we are about the only democrat in this county, we conclude to quit *visiting;* and go to work to proclaim the doctrine of the old Jefferson school — 'liberty throughout all the land; and to all the inhabitants thereof.['] If these fellows destroy our office again, as they now threaten to do, we will go down to Hennepin County; and publish the St. Cloud *Democrat* there."

The little woman had won. Mrs. Swisshelm continued to publish the *Democrat*, its corners as sharp as ever, until 1863. Then a lecture tour — ironically, urging more severe punishment for the Indians who engaged in the Sioux Uprising — took her to Washington. An appointment to a clerkship in the War Department by her friend Secretary Edwin M. Stanton kept her there. She sold the *Democrat*, but it continued under the direction of her nephew and former assistant editor, William B. Mitchell. As *Visiter* and *Democrat*, she had made her point that violence should not prevail against the press, and the community, as well as the press of the state and the nation, had supported her.[28]

CHAPTER 5

Conflict:
From Railroads to Prize Ring

LAND GRANT FRAUD EXPOSED!
DENOUNCE RAILROAD LOAN SWINDLE
BANKS FAIL BUT NO ALARM FELT HERE
FRONTIER DECLARED SAFE AS INDIANS RISE AGAINST SETTLERS
MURDERESS EXECUTED
HEENAN-SAYERS FIGHT A DRAW IN FORTY-SECOND ROUND

THE ABOVE MULTIDECK, multitopic headline is fictitious, but it suggests how major news stories of 1854 to 1860 might have been displayed in the small type of St. Paul dailies near the end of the period. The papers intermittently urged the extension of the telegraph to St. Paul, and as the desired link with the East approached, they copied telegraphic dispatches from La Crosse and Dubuque papers, ran them all in one column, and headed the assortment with a succession of labels proclaiming the variety of items that followed. The effect was not unlike a newscast on a teenage "top-ten" radio station a century later.

Although the politics of transition from territory to statehood dominated the St. Paul press through 1858, the dailies did not entirely forsake the role of booster. Promotional efforts, however, underwent a marked change. Praise of the garden gave way to demands for the iron horse as a means of increasing immigration. Long articles extolling the natural riches of the land yielded to long speculations on the advantages to be gained by the building of railroads. Events that might be expected to discourage immigration — bank failures or an outbreak of Indian violence, for

92

example — were played down by some of the papers. In addition to promoting new transportation and communication ties to the rest of the Union, the St. Paul dailies made some notable innovations in the technique of news gathering and in appealing to readers' interests: an interview and sports stories appeared for the first time in Minnesota newspapers.

The impact of the railroad on the thinking of Minnesotans is suggested by two articles that found their way into the columns of St. Paul dailies — one a fantasy by a St. Paul druggist, the other a sermon by a St. Paul minister. Both druggist and cleric were inspired by events that aroused hopes for early railroad construction, and both invested the object of their hopes with the dominant concepts of the age — faith in democratic political institutions as a means of social progress and in evangelical Protestantism as the road to human redemption from sin.[1]

In the spring of 1853, a government-sponsored expedition led by Isaac I. Stevens set out from St. Paul to explore a northern route for a railroad to the Pacific. John Wesley Bond, a druggist much given to reading and reverie, outdistanced explorer Stevens. A wave of patriotic fervor swept him ahead to the Fourth of July, 1876, to witness in imagination the arrival at St. Paul of the first train from San Francisco and its meeting there with trains from New York, New Orleans, Lake Superior — and Pembina. In an article entitled "A Vision," published in the *Pioneer* of April 28, 1853, Bond evoked the imaginary scene as an extravaganza that anticipated the best efforts of Cecil B. de Mille.

Bond's dream train was propelled by two locomotives, one bearing the legend "Atlantic," the other labeled "Pacific," and it was loaded with every symbol in the patriotic catalogue. Two bands on board the first and last cars played "Hail Columbia" and "The Star Spangled Banner." Above them towered two white columns about thirty feet high, representing the Union and the Constitution and supporting an arch engraved "E Pluribus Unum." Surmounting this was "an immense spread eagle . . . holding in his beak a likeness of 'The Father of his Country,' in a plain gold setting, enwreathed with laurel; while high above, and over all floated the 'Star Spangled Banner.' " Under the arch was a white altar engraved "Freedom" and bearing a gold vase filled with water from the Pacific. It was guarded by two beautiful young women representing Peace and Commerce.

The final tableau was composed of an array of fifty more beautiful young ladies draped in white and standing on pedestals, one for each state of the Union, "which included the Canadas on the North to the Isthmus of Darien on the South, and from Cuba, in the South East to the Russian Settlements in the North West, from the Equator to the Frozen Regions." While cannon roared and thousands cheered, the train came to a halt on a bridge over the Mississippi, and Peace and Commerce tipped the golden vase, joining the waters of the Pacific to those of the great inland river. So loud was the outburst in praise of God and freedom that it reverberated around the world, inspiring Russians in the "last and only home of the despot" to rise and throw off their chains. Only then did the train pass on and the dreamer awake.

The railroad envisioned by the clergyman was equally freighted with the concept of manifest destiny and with patriotic ideology, but in addition it carried a heavy shipment of evangelical Protestantism. The sermon describing it, however, was preached in observance of a real, rather than an imagined, civic occasion.

Early in June, 1854, the Chicago and Rock Island Railroad Company celebrated the opening of the first line to reach the Mississippi by inviting a party of more than a thousand prominent Americans to travel in "the cars" over the line. At Rock Island the party was transferred to seven steamboats which churned up the river in a gala flotilla to St. Paul. The distinguished company included ex-President Millard Fillmore, historian George Bancroft, novelist Catherine M. Sedgwick, and about forty newsmen, the best known of whom were Samuel Bowles of the *Springfield Republican* and Charles A. Dana then of the *New York Tribune*.[2]

St. Paul boomers were not about to miss this opportunity to promote the glories of the territory. Committees were hastily appointed to arrange an elaborate ball, to escort guests to the Capitol, and to provide carriages and wagons for side trips to Fort Snelling. "Let the most be made of this occasion to demonstrate before a host of witnesses, that we are not behind more eastern latitudes, in the courtesies and amenities of social life," the *Pioneer* of June 8, 1854, urged its readers. Unfortunately the excursion party arrived a day ahead of schedule, and the courtesies and amenities didn't get a chance to achieve the full bloom of eastern latitudes. Nonetheless, after the guests had departed, the *Pioneer* expressed satisfaction. "More will be known about Minnesota in the Eastern and Middle States, within the next ninety days through this instrumentality, than would otherwise have been in ten years," the editor commented on June 10, 1854.

Another spokesman for the community was more impressed by the occasion's meaning for the realm of the spirit. On June 11, 1854, the Sunday after the visit of the excursionists, Reverend Edward Neill addressed his congregation on "Railways in their Higher Aspects." Choosing his text from Isaiah 40:3, "Prepare ye the way of the Lord, make straight in the desert a highway for our God," Neill envisioned railroads decreasing idleness, expanding "the mind of the nation," producing "great general intelligence," serving as "aids to contentment," and helping to overcome "sectional prejudices." But most important of all, he said, "They are invaluable aids in the promotion of *pure and undefiled religion. . . .* the laborer in Christ's cause . . . is enabled to advance along with, or before the wave of emigration, and commence turning the wilderness into the garden of the Lord, before the rank weeds of error have taken deep root." The minister concluded by reminding his hearers "that this world is a great station-house, in which we are awaiting the approach of the cars that lead to 'that bourne from whence no traveler returns,' but through which every traveler passes to regions of bliss or despair.[3]

"My hearers! some of you have tickets that will lead you to Hell. The car of death is hastening on swifter than an eagle hasteneth to its prey. . . . Before it appears we urge you to change that ticket. Christ is always in his office. He says, 'If any man knocketh, the door shall be opened.' If any man asketh, he will change his ticket. . . . Hasten before it is too late. Now, now, now, 'is the accepted time, and now is the day of salvation.' "

While druggist and cleric used the railroad to symbolize two dominant themes of mid-nineteenth century American thought, most writing about railroads in the newspapers of the 1850s was on a less elevated plane. It was largely concerned with the practical problems of who was going to build the roads and how they were to be financed. Two federal land grants in this period complicated both problems. Neither accomplished the longed-for introduction of the iron horse, which did not see regular service in Minnesota until 1862.[4] The first grant was repealed by Congress because of charges of fraud in its enactment; the effect of the second was dissipated by the acute depression following the Panic of 1857, but not before a bitter fight was waged over the issuing of state bonds to help finance railroad companies. Leading figures of the period were involved in both crises, and some of the political animus which has been described in earlier chapters carried over into the economic conflict, shaping it into strange alignments. The newspapers of the day not only mirrored these events but were also caught up in the battle.

The first federal land grant in aid of railroad construction in Minnesota was passed by Congress late in June, 1854. The original bill was carefully designed to exclude from its benefits any company which had been "constituted or organized" before passage of the act. It also entrusted the disposition of about a million acres of land to a "future legislature" of the territory. This wording supposedly eliminated from consideration the Minnesota and North Western Railroad Company, which the 1854 legislature had chartered four months earlier with the sweeping promise that the firm would receive any railroad lands granted by the federal government to the territory in the future. After the federal act was passed, two small but significant changes of wording mysteriously appeared in its text: the limiting term "future" before legislature had been deleted, and the phrase "constituted or organized" had been changed to "constituted and organized." On July 1, 1854, two days after the president approved the land grant bill, stockholders of the Minnesota and North Western met in New York, organized the company, and prepared to stake a claim to the newly granted lands.[5]

The major political figures of the territory were involved in these matters. Henry M. Rice, the territorial delegate, had been influential in getting support for the grant in Congress. His brother Edmund, Alexander Ramsey, and Lyman Dayton had been chosen as the Minnesota directors of the company. But former Delegate Sibley and Governor Gorman had been instrumental in inserting the prohibitions against the company in the original draft of the Congressional grant. Thus Sibley and Ramsey, who were usually to be found aligned against Rice, were in this case on opposite sides, and Ramsey and Rice were allies.

As soon as the events became known, cries of fraud echoed from St. Paul to Washington and back again. Congress promptly repealed the grant, then proceeded to conduct a special investigation which absolved all parties. The railroad company sought a court test of the repeal. Two successive Minnesota legislatures granted time extensions to the firm; the first was vetoed by Gorman and repassed over his veto, and the second was vetoed, modified by compromise, and reluctantly signed by the governor.

The land grant war raged for two years, and it was heatedly fought in the pages of the St. Paul daily papers. The battle lines were both incongruous and fluid. At the outset only the Republican *Daily Minnesotian* was in the railroad company's camp. The daily editions of the *Democrat, Pioneer,* and *Times* chorused fraud in an unprecedented three-part harmony. Then a change in editorship swung the *Democrat* over to the railroad company, and when that paper merged with the *Pioneer* under Rice auspices in 1855, it was the *Democrat's* support of the firm that prevailed. Finally, after two years of savage attacks against the company, Newson's *Daily Times* also capitulated. By that time the Minnesota and North Western had won all the battles but lost the war.

The *Times,* ever pure in heart, had almost a vested interest in the cause because the changes in the wording of the land grant bill first came to light when that paper published the original text of the measure on July 11, 1854. The *Minnesotian* of July 14 carried the revised version of the bill and claimed the *Times* was in error. Editor Newson appealed to Governor Gorman, and that gentleman dispatched J. Travis Rosser, secretary of the territory, to Washington to find out what had happened and why. There the matter rested for a couple of weeks. Then the *Demo-*

crat, which was edited at this time by David Olmsted, quoted on July 31 a dispatch from the *Galena Jeffersonian* charging that "the bill was fraudulently altered after its introduction — not by any amendment either of the House or Senate, not by the Member who originally introduced the bill, but by some hireling clerk, or venal member whose honesty was no proof against the gold or golden promises of a band of sharpers whose practice it is to accomplish their ends if necessary by bribery."

Throughout August and into September, 1854, the *Democrat* vied with the *Pioneer* and the *Times* in denouncing Wall Street swindlers. Then, abruptly, Charles L. Emerson, a newly arrived surveyor-turned-newspaperman and an ambitious Democrat, replaced Olmsted as publisher of the *Democrat* on September 8, 1854; the following day the paper altered its tone to call for a burying of differences in order to get some tracks under construction. On September 25 it published a letter signed by twenty-one prominent Minnesotans, including Ramsey and Dayton, addressed to members of Congress and asking for information about the role of Delegate Rice in the passage of the land grant bill. Answers from a number of Congressmen testifying to the delegate's industry and integrity appeared in both the *Democrat* and the *Minnesotian* late in September.[6]

During this period, the *Times* and the *Pioneer* also published the proceedings of the House committee investigating the alterations in the land grant bill. When Congressman Hestor L. Stevens of Michigan testified that he had directed a clerk to make the alterations without realizing their significance, the *Times* of September 5 railed: "How *could* a man with the intelligence of Mr. Stevens make such an alteration without knowing the effect it would have? . . . A more bare-faced, shameful perversion of justice, was never enacted." When Delegate Rice testified that the alteration was done without his knowledge, the *Pioneer* of September 7, 1854, fumed: "But the crowning shame and mortification to which the people of Minnesota have been subjected, throughout the whole of these transactions, is to be found in the fact that . . . while the halls of the Senate and of the House of Representatives rung with denunciations of villainy and fraud . . . not a single lisp was heard from Mr. Rice in defence of himself and of his constituents. . . . Minnesota was left without a defender." The *Minnesotian* of the following day dismissed these comments of its competitors as "gaseous scribblings" which "have no more effect than would a pair of pop-guns." After John C. Breckinridge of Kentucky, chairman of the House investigating committee, was quoted as saying that Rice was not to blame for the repeal of the land grant by Congress, the *Times* of September 29 quoted "a gentleman of unimpeachable character who was present during the investigation" as declaring that it "was a whitewashing affair. . . . Breckinridge . . . . is one of Rice's men."

In October a new phase of the dispute got under way as the railroad company, hoping to test Congress' repeal of the land grant in the courts, cut timber along the proposed route in Goodhue County. The federal district attorney obligingly sued the firm for trespass. Although the case was of great interest and importance and the site of the trial in the district court in Goodhue County was considerably closer to St. Paul than to Dubuque, all the St. Paul dailies, instead of covering the trial, reprinted accounts from the *Dubuque Daily Express and Herald*. Their comments on the proceedings, however, were their own.

The *Times* criticized John E. Warren, the United States district attorney, for failing to cite the fraudulent alteration of the grant bill in his prosecution, and after the court ruled in favor of the company, the paper implied that there had been collusion in bringing the suit. The *Pioneer* criticized Warren's "unaccountable stupidity, or still more unaccountable corruption" after the attorney appealed to the territorial supreme court. The *Minnesotian* joined the fray by publishing a letter from state's attorney John B. Brisbin which defended the conduct of the prosecution on the grounds that the alteration of the grant act was irrelevant to the issue in the trespass case. The *Democrat* published a letter from District Attorney Warren protesting that the only purpose of the suit was to restore the land grant to the territory, which could then act as it wished on the company's claim to the lands. To which the *Times* replied: "The Attorney has dug his own grave, and a decent respect for the community he has outraged should induce him to rest quietly in it and not render himself offensive by putrid exhalations from the loathesome charnel house wherein he has deposited his moral and political character." On December 8, 1854, the territorial supreme court upheld the verdict of the district court. The zealous Warren, without consulting his superior, appealed the case to the United States Supreme Court, and thereby lost his job.[7]

The next year (1855) brought the convening of a new legislature and with it additional legislation on the issue. Friends of Sibley, who was now a member of the Minnesota House of Representatives, supported a resolution asking Congress to disapprove the Minnesota and North Western's charter and restore the land grant to the territory on the terms of the original bill. The House failed to approve the measure, much to the disgust of the *Times* and the relief of the *Minnesotian*. Instead the legislature reenacted the railroad company's charter, amending it to extend for eight months the period during which the firm was required to begin construction. Governor Gorman vetoed the extension; the *Times* cheered and the *Minnesotian* scolded. The legislature passed the extension over Gorman's veto; the *Minnesotian* cheered and the *Times* scolded. "Corruption, bribery and drunkenness, have triumphed!" the latter proclaimed.[8]

While all this was going on, eastern papers reported that the national House of Representatives had acted to annul the Minnesota and North Western's charter. The *Times* of February 13, 1855, exulted: "From the very inception of the fraud, we were the first to expose it, and have ever since fought desperately to roll back the tide of iniquity which we plainly saw was destined to overwhelm us." A month later it was the *Minnesotian's* turn to gloat over the report that the Senate had defeated the charter annulment.[9] The *Democrat* thought the occasion deserved a "general Illumination." On March 23 it hoped "that every citizen will feel interest enough in this matter, to buy a few candles and let their light shine forth a beacon of hope and faith in the development of our great and glorious Territory." The *Times* of March 19 was subdued in admitting defeat: "Now as the question of annulment or non-annulment has been settled, we hope the Railroad Company will commence operations and push matters to a happy termination. If they do this, they will do more than we expect."

The *Times* did not really reverse itself for almost a full year. In the meantime, another election was held in October, 1855, in which Rice, the incumbent territorial delegate, was challenged by Republican William R. Marshall and Sibley-Democrat Olmsted.[10] Early in October the papers reported the appearance in the territory of railroad surveyors. The *Times* of October 5 was ready with an explanation: "Surveyors are sent here just on the edge of winter with no expectations of surveying the road, but merely to gull you, and when the company and its aiders and abettors *have* gulled you and received your votes, then they will turn round and laugh at you for your foolishness." The *Minnesotian* of October 13 expressed dismay that railroad money should be used on Rice's behalf, declaring that this was unfair to Republican friends of the railroad, of whom Marshall had been one of the most important. Three days later Edmund Rice, president of the Minnesota and North Western, wrote Owens of the *Minnesotian* denying that railroad influence or money had been used on behalf of his brother. He maintained that the surveyors had been hired to do a technical job and were without political instruction. Owens commented in the same issue that he was glad to have the letter, but it was still true that such Rice lieutenants as Charles Emerson and Joe Brown had said "the *only hope* of consummating the enterprise was H. M. Rice's election to Congress."

In the wake of the delegate election, merger of the *Pioneer* and the *Democrat* on November 1, 1855, left the *Times* alone in its opposition to the Minnesota and North Western. When the company applied to the new legislature in 1856 for another extension of time, the *Times*, too, capitulated. Everyone, it conceded, wanted a railroad. Congress had repealed the land grant to kill the company but had hurt the territory instead. "We believe the Company have some influence in procuring the grant, and that they still have some influence and friends in Congress," opined the *Times* of February 18, 1856. "If then it is designed or hoped to get Congress to repeal the act repealing the grant and thus right the wrong done the Territory and end litigation, the best thing we could do was to conciliate the Company by giving an extension of time and thus secure its aid."

So ended newspaper opposition to the first great scheme to secure railroads in Minnesota Territory. Governor Gorman did not hold out much longer than the *Times*. After vetoing the bill for the second extension of time, he signed a compromise measure. The *Pioneer and Democrat* of March 3, 1856, reported: "The lobby of the House was crowded with persons, anxiously awaiting the announcement of the Governor's determination in reference to the bill. The first sentence announcing the approval of the Executive, was barely read by the Clerk, when the feelings of the assemblage found utterance in enthusiastic and prolonged cheering." A week later the *Minnesotian* of March 10 noted the withdrawal in the United States Supreme Court of the trespass suit against the Minnesota and North Western company. The iron horse had too strong a hold on the imagination of the people of the territory to brook opposition from either press or governor.

It was to be expected that further efforts would be made to get another grant of land from the federal government. On August 26, 1856, the *Pioneer and Democrat* reported Edmund Rice's return from Washington with the news that a land grant bill had died in committee. Five months later the same paper reported another land bill in Congress, and an official of the Minnesota and North Western felt called upon to issue a statement to the effect that the company "is in no way concerned in the passage of the proposed bill." In March, 1857, the papers reported that the act, granting 1,300,000 acres of land, had passed both houses of Congress. Immediately there was talk of holding a suitable celebration, but the movers concluded that with a constitutional convention in the offing, it might be wiser to avoid letting anyone make political capital out of such a fete and to hold off until some railroad building had been accomplished. A celebration in any case might have distracted attention from the more important business of parceling out the land to railroad companies organized to share in the dispensation.[11]

The Minnesota and North Western did not share in the bounty. The 1857 and 1858 legislatures failed to revive its charter, and in a second case dealing with the repeal of the original land grant, Edmund Rice instituted for the firm an appeal which was carried to the United States Supreme Court. There in 1862 the company lost, and it was not heard from again. After at least one false start, the legislature divided the lands among four companies, each of which was charged with construction of one of the four lines specified in the Congressional grant. "All the roads are taxed at the same rate — three per cent on their gross earnings," the *Pioneer and Democrat* noted on May 21, 1857.[12]

The press approved of the omnibus railroad act and urged the companies to get on with construction, but for the next several months after the Panic of 1857 hit with force, there was no money in the territory and silence enveloped the subject.[13] Then on January 22, 1858, the *Minnesotian* carried a letter, signed "Old Citizen," asking the newspaper to oppose a measure in the legislature which would issue *"from four to five millions of dollars in State Bonds* to be handed over to sundry irresponsible *Rail Road Companies* under the specious pretence and double purpose of giving a currency to the people and building their roads." That was the first press notice of what was to become known as the Five Million Dollar Loan Bill. But it was not the last. The battle over the railroad loan was to be as protracted as that over the first land grant. In the ensuing debate, however, it was the *Minnesotian* that opposed the measure, while an unnatural alliance of the *Pioneer and Democrat* and the *Times* supported it.

At issue was a bill to amend the constitution to permit the future state to issue up to five million dollars' worth of bonds to aid the land grant railroad companies in starting construction. "Soulless, pennyless corporations are always eager and grasping in their demands upon the public treasury," the *Minnesotian* warned on February 4, 1858, "but it is seldom that demands as enormous as the present one, have ever been made by companies so entirely destitute of means." The lead editorial went on to list the editor's objections: a constitutional provision would remove the matter from legislative control; credit of the state would be committed before one mile of railroad was built; the proposed security was inadequate; none of the lines could be completed on the proceeds of five million, so they would not be able to earn revenue. And the editorial concluded: "We hope the Legislature will look well into this matter, and *not involve the tax payers of the State in an embarrassment from which it will take them a long time to extricate themselves.*" An opposition meeting — "a crowded affair" — was held in mid-February, with Gorman, Colonel Robertson, and Judges Cooper and Goodrich as principal speakers. Some legislators favoring the loan canceled their subscriptions to the *Minnesotian,* but the paper boasted that it would be able to continue publishing without them.[14]

The *Pioneer and Democrat* self-righteously refrained from commenting on the bill while it was under consideration in the legislature, but from March 5, when it passed both houses, until April 15, when it was submitted to referendum, Earle Goodrich's paper argued for the loan amendment. Its favorite theme was summed up in a subhead of an article on March 21: "Speedy Railroad Construction the best Possible Emigration Agency." Under the heading, it discussed what it came to refer to as "the law of railroad progress." Citing as authority a writer in *Railroad Record,* the *Pioneer and Democrat* affirmed that "one mile of road to a thousand of population, is the ratio in the United States. Carry this out, and in 1866, if Minnesota then has four-fifths of her land grant railroad lines in operation, she will have 1,200,000 of population — or 2,000,000 in 1870." Progress by economic law was as simple as that.[15]

On the eve of the referendum, both the *Pioneer and Democrat* and the *Minnesotian* issued extras on the proposed constitutional amendment. "To Expose the Infamy of the $5,000,000 Swindle," shrieked the *Minnesotian.* "Down with Fogyism! Minnesota must go Ahead," asserted the *Pioneer and Democrat.* Both four-page extras reprinted articles that had been previously published in regular editions, but true to its more progressive outlook, the *Pioneer and Democrat's* was printed on bright yellow paper and embellished by that then rare device, a cut of a railroad train streaking across the entire top of page one. Also prominently displayed was a pledge by some legislators to "vote against any proposition to levy a tax either for the interest or principal of the proposed loan of State credit." (No one pointed out that the pledge was hardly binding on future legislatures.) An article in

the *Minnesotian's* extra listed the territory's newspapers according to their partisan persuasions and their stands on the loan.
The score against the loan stood at fourteen Republican, one
Democratic, one nonpartisan, total sixteen; for the loan, six Republican, seven Democratic, two nonpartisan, total fifteen. Six
papers were listed as not having taken a stand.[16]

The Republican papers listed as being against the loan were:
Minnesotian, Die Minnesota Deutsche Zeitung (St. Paul), *Falls
Evening News* and *Minnesota Republican* of St. Anthony, *Still-
water Messenger, Hastings Independent, Red Wing Republican,
Minnesota Posten* (Red Wing), *Lake City Tribune, Wabashaw
County Herald* (Read's Landing), *Chatfield Republican, Ban-
croft Pioneer, Mankato Independent,* and *Cannon Falls Bulletin.*
Republican papers said to be for the loan were: *St. Paul Times,
Minneapolis Gazette, Winona Republican, Rochester Free Press,
Faribault Herald,* and *Mantorville Express.*

The sole Democratic paper given as against the loan was the
Red Wing Sentinel. Democratic papers for the loan were: *St.
Paul Pioneer, Minnesota National Demokrat* (St. Paul), *St. An-
thony Express, Rochester Democrat, Sauk Rapids Frontierman,
Wasioja Gazette,* and *Belle Plaine Enquirer.*

One nonpartisan paper, the *Neu-Ulm Pionier,* was listed as
being against the loan. Two were listed as being for it: the *St.
Paul Advertiser* and the *Shakopee Reporter.*

The newspapers may have been equally divided on the issue,
but the vote of the people in the referendum was substantially
in favor of the loan — yeas 25,023, nays 6,733. The *Minnesotian's*
chagrin almost got lost in a scrambled metaphor. After noting
that neither immigration nor the influx of capital was up to expectations for the season, it bobbled ". . . in the desperation, occasioned by the cry, 'we must *do something*,' all hands opened
their mouths and blindly shut their eyes and took the panacea
which the Railroad officials offered as an infallible cure for the
'hard times.' "[17]

The loan controversy, however, did not end with the referendum. Hard times doubtless raised obstacles for newly elected
Governor Sibley when he went to New York later in the year to
negotiate the sale of the state's bonds. But the *Pioneer and Demo-*

crat of January 20, 1859, in reporting his lack of success, blamed the *Minnesotian,* then edited by Thomas Foster. In a burst of purple rhetoric, it likened the failure of negotiations to "a poison, swift, and sure, and fatal, which turns the gilded chalice of our overflowing future into an urn — arid and ghastly with the ashes it entombs." And the editorial went on to ask: "Who dropped — what arch-fiend, poured the deadly drop of 'cursed hebenon' into the transparent draught. What traitor set the match to the magnificent pile which it cost years of public legislation and private toil to rear. Where is the snake whose fangs have bit into the marrow of our life — and turned the healthy currents of our blood to swift messengers of death. Citizens of St. Paul! When Gov. SIBLEY went to DUNCAN & SHERMAN, on the day appointed for their final decision, they put into his hands for answer, *a copy of the St. Paul Minnesotian,* which openly denied that the faith of the State was pledged for the redemption of the bonds, and *boldly advocated repudiation.* They could not take the bonds of a State, which supported a newspaper openly pledged to repudiation. There, gentlemen, is the poison — the traitor — the snake."

Foster was not at all abashed by the onslaught. In the *Minnesotian* of the following day, he replied that it seemed much more likely that the reluctant capitalists had looked at copies of the *Pioneer and Democrat* of November 23, 1858, which reported that the state "had absolutely 'No TANGIBLE SECURITIES' to defend itself from loss" in case the railroad companies defaulted — a fact, said Foster, which "doubtless had its effect in deterring from investment in the bonds."

More threatening than the *Pioneer and Democrat's* bark was the bite of a resolution introduced in the St. Paul Common Council on March 2, 1859, condemning the *Minnesotian* for "its unwise and suicidal policy." Since that paper was the official printer for the city at this time, the pressure was unmistakable. Issues of the *Minnesotian* from March 2 through 8 are missing from the historical society's files, but Thomas Foster was not a man to take such pressure supinely. Unfortunately, both Goodrich and Newson set partisanship ahead of principle and failed to support their colleague of the press against intimidation by government. "It is a matter of supreme indifference to us," the *Times* commented, while the *Pioneer and Democrat* asserted that the resolution was "designed to guard the people of St. Paul *against* the persecutions of the infamous set of brokers and rotten politicians, who own and control the *Minnesotian*."[18]

The council laid the resolution over for a week. When it was brought up at the next meeting, Alderman William Branch introduced a substitute motion: "WHEREAS, We the twelve tyrants of the city of St. Paul . . . did . . . appoint . . . the *Minnesotian* as our official organ, *And whereas*, said Press having neglected to advocate our special interests . . . *And Whereas* a paper called the *Pioneer and Democrat*, having published other seditious articles . . . *And Whereas* . . . the *Times* . . . might, we are fearful, publish something which may prove detrimental to our interests . . . *Therefore*, We have resolved and decreed that the aforesaid three presses be demolished, as we are about to establish one press only . . . which shall advocate our views only and the people are commanded to read, and believe, all the doctrines advocated therein, under the penalty of perpetual banishment, and to be placed at hard labor in the gold mines of the Zumbro." The council president was not amused and ruled the substitute motion out of order. The original motion was then passed by "a strict party vote" of five to four, according to the *Minnesotian*, which appeared not at all intimidated by the action.[19]

The *Pioneer and Democrat* could blame the *Minnesotian*, and the latter could blame "the swindlers" in extravagant expenditures of space and vituperation, but neither said much about the local aspects of economic stagnation that were the real reasons why the railroad projects failed to materialize. If support for railroad schemes was one type of territorial promotion, the silent treatment of less attractive conditions was another. The papers occasionally acknowledged reports of "hard times" elsewhere in the country, but they usually reported them with an air of "it can't happen here." On June 2, 1857, the *Minnesotian* had reprinted a prophetic article from the *Chicago Tribune*, warning the West against "that fever of speculation by which three-fourths, if not nine-tenths of her citizens are possessed," and the

Pioneer and Democrat of June 11 carried New York reports of unemployment in that city and of a "general disposition to croak."

Nine days later the *Minnesotian* rejected such pessimism. "Some of the Eastern journals are growing very nervous about the speculations in land in the Western country, and are predicting our ruin in emphatic and positive terms. Poor people! We hope they won't allow their grief at our impending ruin to interfere with their health." The article went on to give a happy example of western speculation involving an Illinois settler from Massachusetts who bought a quarter section for five dollars an acre and made a cash income of thirty-three dollars an acre the first year. Let the croakers try to discourage settlers from coming west, the article taunted; in the meantime, "hundreds are emigrants emigrating and *ruining* themselves by just such *speculations* as we quote above." The only crash heard in the West, according to a long article reprinted from the *Chicago Real Estate Register* in the *Minnesotian* of July 17, was the crash of carpenters' hammers, of wagons loaded with goods, of arriving trains and departing steamboats. "Fear not, ye wise men of the East," the paper advised. "The West will take care of herself, and, in spite of your crisis and your crash, will come out all right."

The excellent harvest of that year was especially reassuring. The *Minnesotian* reported on August 22 that all the territorial papers with which it exchanged issues "are crowded with long notices of the unprecedented crops, and glorious harvest. Nothing of the kind has been ever witnessed in the North-west before. . . . With full harvest, always follow prosperous times, and active business seasons. Croakers have about disappeared now, and it will doubtless be long before we will be troubled with their complaints of 'hard times' again."

The croakers, however, had not disappeared. On September 1, 1857, the *Pioneer and Democrat* carried a report on the "Commercial Crisis in the East" clipped from the *New York Herald*. The article stressed the mounting uneasiness on Wall Street as a result of several business failures and rumors of the precarious positions of some banks. Four days later the same paper's New York letter reported that business had "resumed its wonted tranquillity," but by September 20 the *Pioneer and Democrat* noted the "thirty-first failure of the week" in New York City, remarking "If money does not grow plenty before the beginning of next month, half the business men of New York will be obliged to cave in."

The *Minnesotian* carried less news about the eastern economic crisis than did the *Pioneer and Democrat,* and neither said much about local distress until late in September, 1857. Even then the *Minnesotian* was reassuring. On September 22 it commented: "In this city, confidence seems to be gradually gaining ground, and the entire tone of the business community seems to be decidedly more cheerful. The panic makers are making themselves scarce, and though many of our leading mercantile and banking firms were almost paralysed by the money panic at the East, financial and business matters will soon resume their wonted buoyancy. It tested their strength severely, but all of them will undoubtedly come out of the furnace unscathed." A day later the same paper cheerfully pointed to the bright side of the picture, saying that prices and rents were lower, crops were abundant, and the economy would be strengthened by the weeding out of speculators and weaklings. "Let no one then, feel any despondency, or listen to the dismal predictions of croakers," it advised. " 'Learn to labor and to hope,' and all difficulties will be overcome. The crash will still be as distant as ever, not merely postponed, but forever averted." On September 25 the *Pioneer and Democrat* reported the failures of more banks and dry goods houses in New York, Philadelphia, Boston, Indianapolis, and Dubuque, but the *Minnesotian* offered yet another denunciation of croaking quoted from the *Chicago Daily Press:* "It has now become evident, we trust, to the most hypochondriac intellect, that the late disturbance was a sheer, unfounded panic."

Finally on September 29 the *Pioneer and Democrat* conceded that the crisis in the East might have consequences for the West. After reporting more eastern business failures and the fact that the Bank of Pennsylvania had suspended specie payment, the article turned homeward: "So far the west has suffered comparatively little; but the end is not over. Every hour of financial disturbance in the east is fraught with incalculable troubles throughout the west. There has been a bountiful harvest gathered, and on the moving forward of that harvest to the east immediately depends the financial salvation of the west." On October 1 the *Minnesotian,* too, admitted the gravity of the situation when it stated: "The West cannot escape, and it will be wise to prepare as best we may for coming waves." The writer saw the West's principal problem as the marketing of its crops and advised those with surplus to sell at reduced prices rather than "winter over" their grain. On the causes of the crisis, the writer reflected that "Wanton extravagance, swindling speculation, and laziness, have brought all this disgrace and ruin upon us! Money enough has been sunk in this Territory, in crazy, fictitious 'corner-lot' speculation within two years to have more than doubled our pecuniary resources. . . . *Speculation, extravagance, idleness* — these have ripened into fruit, and we all must eat it. . . . Every man and every woman will see where improvement must begin. *Produce* and *save* — that is the law of prosperity."

The changed tone of the papers came none too soon. On October 3 they carried the announcement that the local banking house of Marshall and Company had closed its doors. Two days later they printed the card of Truman M. Smith, St. Paul banker, who announced that "the pressure of the money market and news received from the east, and the run on me yesterday, through a false report that I had closed my doors, has compelled me to suspend payment until I can collect or negotiate for some funds." [20]

Nonetheless, a review of "Monetary Matters" prepared for the *Daily Minnesotian* by J. Jay Knox and Company, St. Paul bankers, took a determinedly optimistic view on October 9. After commenting on the closing of Marshall and Company, the writer proceeded myopically: "With $80,000 of their depositors' money in their possession it was feared that excitement might follow, and a 'run' created on the other bankers in town. But such was not the case. On the other hand, deposits were made as usual, and our own, and, we doubt not, the deposits of other bankers, have daily increased. Never have we seen such cheerful depositors." The reader might have wondered about their cheerfulness when he reached the next paragraph, which noted Smith's closing and added, "His deposits remaining on hand were small, and will be returned to depositors before many days, we doubt not."

Myopia was mixed with anti-Eastern bias in the comment of the *Pioneer and Democrat* on October 17: "Read the telegraph news this morning, and you will find that the boasted New York system of banking has had to go down in the general crash." Myopia was mixed with spite in the *Minnesotian's* earlier comment on October 6 regarding news of the suspension of the New York banking house of Pierre Chouteau, Jr., and Company: "This firm owns all the Fur Company property in St. Paul and elsewhere in Minnesota. No damage done here, except perhaps, to SIBLEY — the sole fossil remnant of that old concern." How wrong the newspapers were was proved before the month was out. Borup and Oakes, the oldest bank in St. Paul and one which derived much of its prestige from Borup's former association with Sibley and the house of Chouteau, closed its doors on October 20.

For once the *Minnesotian* saw no note to cheer — or delude — its readers. The incontrovertible evidence was to be seen in its advertising columns, where notices of sheriff's sales had increased from two or three in early August to an average of a dozen a day by early November, 1857. The number of such notices continued to mount throughout the summer of 1858, reaching a peak of thirty-two in the *Pioneer and Democrat* of August 28. By October 20, 1859, after another summer of disappointed expectations, the *Pioneer and Democrat* went so far as to say that "of all the States in the Western slope of the Mississippi valley, Minnesota is decidedly, in some respects at least, in the worst condition. There is no use denying the fact, or attempting to cover it up. A large majority of the active business men of 1857 are bankrupt, while a few money-lenders have grown rich upon the ruin of whole communities of creditors. And with these bankrupt men in whom was lodged the marrow of the public spirit, all the superb enterprises and splendid hopes of their golden age, have gone down with them to a common grave." The croakers against whom the paper had inveighed could not have sounded more despondent.

Another ordeal, but one of shorter duration, that tried the editors as promoters was the Indian depredation that became known as the Spirit Lake massacre. In March, 1857, a party of renegade Sioux, led by a chief named Inkpaduta, murdered some thirty settlers in the vicinity of Lake Okoboji in northern Iowa, then moved across the Minnesota line and camped at Heron Lake in what is now Jackson County. There on March 26 they killed seven settlers. Accounts published in St. Paul newspapers varied in all the important details — the stated number of settlers killed ranged from five to fifty-three; one story said the attack was set off when a settler's dog bit an Indian who killed it, another said the dog was owned by the Indians and bit a settler who killed it; the size of the marauding band ranged from a handful to thousands; the area of its depredations was confined to the Iowa borderland or extended to the banks of the Watonwan River twenty miles from Mankato. The discrepancies are understandable, but the principal problem that agitated the editors was whether or not they should publish unverified reports discouraging to immigration. As usual, there was no agreement. Newson of the *Times* got out an extra on April 13, 1857, for which he was roundly denounced by Owens of the *Minnesotian,* while Goodrich of the *Pioneer and Democrat* published what he could get and sniped at both of his competitors.[21]

The *Times'* initial report on April 13 was alarming and, as it turned out, garbled enough. Under the heading "Savages on our Frontier! SETTLERS MURDERED! ! !" the story first made clear its source: "We lose no time in laying before our readers in an Extra, the following startling information just received from a gentleman who came through from St. Peter, and who assures us that the information is reliable. Our informant is Mr. H. B. NELSON, who states that the citizens of St. Peter were startled by the rumor that the Sioux Indians had been murdering the whites at Blue Earth, and pillaging and burning the dwellings, and were moving down upon Mankato with the determination of destroying the lives of all the whites." The details that followed were justified in an editorial on April 15. "Deeming Truth far preferable to a garbled and exaggerated statement, we lay before our readers this morning all the particulars we can gather concerning the late Sioux outrages at Blue Earth, the news of which reached us on the night of Monday last, and was issued in an Extra. We are aware that there are some who consider the suppression of these reports as paramount to every other consideration, but we are not of that class. If our friends on the frontier are in danger, we should not stop to ask whether it will injure our property or retard the growth of our Territory, but whether we can save them from the scalping knife and tomahawk of the savage."

The *Minnesotian* of the same date, on the authority of Governor Gorman, said that the *Times* report did not deal with new Indian depredations but was "a confirmation of the Spirit Lake massacre, the news of which we had three weeks ago," and concluded: "Immigrants may come on with safety. The purported Indian war is about as great a humbug as excited mortals in Minnesota were ever known to invent." The next day (April 16, 1857) the *Times* carried a letter "from Mr. Hezlep of St. Peter, to Mr. Howes now in this city," describing frightened settlers flocking into St. Peter and asking for ammunition, arms, and provisions without delay. But the *Minnesotian* of April 16 also had a letter from a settler at Traverse des Sioux to his son in St. Paul, expressing the view that the accounts of Indians approaching Mankato were doubtless greatly exaggerated.

The *Pioneer and Democrat* of April 18 had a new angle; it admitted that seven settlers had been killed at Heron Lake but denied that any had been molested within eighty miles of Mankato, and concluded with the information that "the Indians in the vicinity of Traverse des Sioux and Mankato, consisting of the bands of RED IRON and SLEEPY EYES, are very much alarmed at the excitement existing among the settlers, and are fleeing to Fort Ridgely to[o] for protection." The *Minnesotian* of the same date declared that the real danger was that Captain William B. Dodd, who had raised a company of volunteers at St. Peter, might recklessly shoot a lot of peaceable Indians "and thereby cause more serious trouble than has yet occurred." Indian agent Charles E. Flandrau, in his official report published in the *Pioneer and Democrat* of April 21, was unable to fix the exact number of persons killed but concluded reassuringly: "Persons coming into the Territory need feel no more apprehensions from the Sioux Indians than if this unfortunate affair had not occurred."

After the appearance of the agent's report the *Times* of April 27 was willing to close the file, but not without a final justification of its own course. Newson noted that his paper had "not published a single rumor without giving the author's name . . . we could do no more to prove their authenticity, and no less than to give it to the world as it came to us. . . . So far from 'retarding emigration' hither, every separate step which has been taken to send immediate assistance and to repel the invasions of the Red Man, (whether real or imaginary,) — has tended to inspire the coming thousands with a more vigorous confidence in our Territory and our people. And this is the action we shall always urge in similar emergencies, in spite of the . . . croaking of the money-getters who have bartered away their humanity for corner-lots. We are glad to believe that these number only a dozen or a score, but from them the grumbling newspapers take their cue. Some of them have suggested that the Press 'ought to be muzzled' for speaking what would injure Real Estate (we would like to see them do it!)"

The self-righteousness of the *Times* could be trying, but its record on matters of principle was better than that of either the *Minnesotian* or the *Pioneer and Democrat*. Unfortunately for Newson, principle was not enough to ensure economic health in a period of depression. In the legislature that convened in December, 1859, Republicans had enough muscle to throw the official printing to a Republican press. The problem was which one — the *Minnesotian* or the *Times*? Both Foster and Newson must have concluded that the patronage was essential to survival. Nothing else could account for the astonishing merger of the two papers in mid-December, a step which made the Republican legislators' decision easy but proved intolerable for the two strong-minded editors. The union lasted exactly six months. The *Pioneer and Democrat* of December 15, 1859, noted that in the new publishing firm of Newson, Moore, and Foster, the first and last named would be "responsible for the thunder," while the business office would get Moore's attention. "And in these days, the business office needs attention." Otherwise the rival daily was satisfied to "congratulate our neighbors on the consummation of a very wise stroke of political and financial policy."[22]

While the merger lasted, two heads did not prove better than one so far as editorial innovations were concerned. Goodrich eyed the combined circulation of his opposition and apparently concluded that more than political regularity was needed to hold his readers. As a result, the *Pioneer and Democrat* not only introduced what was probably the first formal interview to appear in a Minnesota newspaper, but also led in the attention which the dailies began to give to news of sports.[23]

The interview story had been introduced to journalism by James Gordon Bennett as early as 1836, but it was not widely adopted until after the Civil War.[24] The *Pioneer and Democrat* had more immediate models for the form, one of which appeared in its issue of September 21, 1859. Clipped from the *Home Journal* magazine, it was an interview with artist Rosa Bonheur in her Paris studio. The writer described the room and quoted Miss Bonheur's views on art and life. The artist doubtless impressed St. Paul readers as exotic, but she was as bland as tapioca compared to the first interviewee of the *Pioneer and Democrat* — a condemned murderess.

In March, 1859, one Stanislaus Bilansky, a St. Paul resident for over a decade, had died after an illness of nine days. The wake was interrupted by a coroner's inquest, provoked by neighbors' gossip. Bilansky's wife, attractive and younger than the deceased (she was reputed to be his fourth mate), had shopped for arsenic shortly before his illness and had reportedly refused to call a doctor in spite of his incessant nausea. Moreover, according to the subsequent testimony of her maid, she had been having an affair with a young Adonis named John Walker, who may or may not have been her nephew and who made his home with the Bilanskys. The coroner's jury, in a superficial examination, found nothing amiss and Bilansky was buried. But gossip was not. The body was exhumed, chemical tests were performed, and Ann Bilansky was arrested, tried, and convicted of murder. The punishment under Minnesota law at the time was hanging. Opponents of capital punishment and many other worthy citizens were aroused at the idea of hanging a woman. A jailer was careless and Ann Bilansky escaped. Posses concentrated on the Lake Como area, where after several days she was apprehended in flight with John Walker. On March 23, 1860, after much delay, she was hanged, the first person and the only woman in Minnesota's history to be so punished.[25]

The *Pioneer and Democrat* had been fairly restrained in reporting the story as it unfolded, but its issue of March 24 devoted six of the seven columns on page three to the case.[26] The first three columns reviewed events leading up to the trial and prosecution testimony at the trial, but it ignored defense testimony in a display of prejudice that was outrageous despite the fact that a verdict had been reached. "The defense was very slight," the paper explained, "and we deem it unnecessary to recapitulate it, as all can judge whether the evidence for the prosecution was sufficient to warrant a conviction."

Then came the interview. "Thursday afternoon, by the kindness of Mr. Hoffman, the jailor, we were permitted to have an interview with Mrs. Bilansky. We sought this, not on our personal account, but that we might be enabled to gratify, to some extent, public curiosity.

"She was seated in her cell, upon a narrow bed, and rose and shook hands. She looked very pale and thin, with dark circles around her eyes, as if occasioned by incessant weeping, but at that time she appeared perfectly composed. She soon commenced the old story of her trial, and the manner in which she deemed herself to have been wronged during its progress. She recapitulated all the evidence, the conduct of judge and lawyers and jurors, and all connected with it, and continually asserted that if she had had a new trial she could have cleared herself. She insisted on our taking down in writing what she said of this matter. It was strongly denunciatory, and as we believe it was groundless, and has been repeated to all who have visited her, we shall not publish it." The writer, however, did quote Mrs. Bilansky in one striking admonition that has been echoed in criticism of newspaper coverage of crime up to the present:

" 'Printers should never state before a man or woman's trial comes off, what the facts are — always let the witnesses come up and tell the tale before it is published. You might have to answer for character and life for a few words you put in before.' "

From the interview, the writer passed to a detailed account of the death march, the dialogue at the gallows, and a description of the crowd inside (about 100) and outside (1,500 to 2,000) the enclosure. Considering the excesses of much writing of the period, the article was restrained in tone, and it concluded on a note of social criticism. "We noticed half a dozen Sioux women, with their children. They were evidently interested in the manner the whites dealt out justice to murderers. We are doubtful if it impressed them with a very forcible idea of our superior civilization." If the writer was aware of the inconsistency between this criticism of his society and his earlier justification for seeking the interview, he gave no indication. Earle Goodrich's *Pioneer and Democrat* was not above admonishing its readers even as it pandered to them.

Another innovation by which the *Pioneer and Democrat* appealed to a widening reader interest was its handling of the first sports event which received extensive coverage in the Minnesota press. This was the world championship boxing match of 1860 between John C. Heenan and Tom Sayers. According to the *Minnesotian and Times,* it was a fairly humdrum encounter, but the *Pioneer and Democrat* invested it with airs of clandestine activity and international rivalry in addition to making the most of the plain "gut appeal" of physical combat.

Sports news had been introduced by eastern newspapers in the 1830s.[27] It began to shoulder its way into the columns of St. Paul dailies in 1856 when the *Pioneer and Democrat* reported the last race of the season at the St. Paul Trotting Park. A bay mare named Lilly Belle won a purse of $2,000 in three heats, and the paper commented on November 17, 1856, that "Upwards of $20,000 changed hands on this race. Sundry of our sporting men were pretty well 'cleaned out.' " Subsequently, a rare short item of a sports nature was limited to horse racing or race horses until the spring of 1860 when an American boxer named John Heen-

an — known to American fight fanciers as "the Benicia Boy" —
went to England to challenge Tom Sayers, the British ring champion, for the possession of a gem-studded belt and the title of
world champion.

As preparations for the fight got under way, the London correspondent of the *New York Times* and George Wilkes, editor
of *Wilkes' Spirit of the Times,* sent back extended dispatches
with a pro-Heenan bias, while London papers favored Sayers at
even greater length. A story from the *London Times* reprinted
in the *New York Herald* might be reprinted yet again in the
Pioneer and Democrat fully two weeks later. The interest attached to reports from the fighters' training camps was height-
ened by threats of government interference that forced the
fighters to move their training camps from place to place with
great secrecy. Both fighters were, in fact, arrested for disturbing
the peace but were almost immediately released on bail. The
promoters thought it best to change the date of the fight "with
the intention of bringing off the 'event' at an earlier and unexpected date; the place and time of meeting to be confided to a
limited number of 'amateurs' of pugilism the evening previous
to the day fixed for the contest."[28]

The suspense of uncertainty was compounded for St. Paul
readers. Not merely was it difficult to say when papers reporting
the fight would be delivered in St. Paul; it was impossible to say
when the fight would take place. Finally, the *Minnesotian and
Times* of May 1, 1860, carried the headline: "The Great Prize
Fight / Sayers Knocked Dumb and Heenan Blind / A Drawn
Battle / Heenan 'the Best Man.'" Beneath was a half-column
summary of the fight from "Liverpool dates to the 18th," followed by a brief round-by-round resumé.[29]

But for a really vivid account, St. Paul had to wait for the
Pioneer and Democrat of May 5. It offered not one, but three,
stories, as if today's *Minneapolis Tribune* were to publish in
succession in the same issue accounts of the same event by the
Associated Press, United Press International, and the New York
Times Service. First was a column and a half from the *London
Times,* then a half column from *Bell's Life,* and finally another
half column from *Wilkes' Spirit of the Times.*

That of the *London Times* was the most graphic. Sayers, the smaller of the two combatants (5'8" to Heenan's 6'2"; weights were not reported), had set out to blind Heenan and had fairly well succeeded by the twentieth round, but Sayers' right arm had been "put out of commission." Still they fought on. "In all the closes Heenan's immense strength prevailed, and he threw the champion easily, till in both the 21st and 22d rounds, Sayers was knocked off his legs. Still he came up gaily, though carefully, and generally managed in most of the struggles to give one or more of his heaviest blows on Heenan's left eye, which was now almost gone like the other.

"The scene gradually became one of the most intense and brutal excitement. There were shouts to Heenan to keep his antagonist in the sun — to close with him and smash him, as he had only one arm, while the friends of Sayers called to him to take his time, as the American was fast blinding, and must give in. . . . At this time several policemen came upon the scene, and did their best to force their way into the ring, but the crowd which now amounted to some 3,000, kept them back by rushing on the ropes, shouting and cheering the combatants to the utmost. During all this, the men fought on with varying success, the heavy 'thuds' upon the face of one or the other being heard clear above all the din. Sayers seemed to be getting weaker each time he was knocked off his legs, and Heenan more and more blind. It appeared all a chance whether the English champion would be struck senseless or Heenan remain sightless and at his mercy. Sayers now tried getting away and leading his opponent around the ring. In one of these runs he got a heavy blow on the neck, which enabled his antagonist to overtake him, when they closed and Sayers fell, Heenan striking him a heavy blow on the head while on the ground. An appeal of foul play was made, but it was overruled, as the blow was supposed to be struck in the heat of fighting, and Heenan, it was truly said, could scarcely see whether his antagonist was up or down. . . .

"In the thirty-eighth round Heenan got Sayers' head under his left arm, and, supporting himself by the stake with his right, held his opponent bent down, as if he meant to strangle him. Sayers could no more free himself than if a mountain was on him. At last he got his left arm free, and gave Heenan two dreadful blows on the face, covering them both with blood, but Heenan, without relaxing his hold, turned himself so as to get his antagonist's neck over the rope, and then leant on it with all his force. Sayers rapidly turned black in the face, and would have been strangled on the spot but that the rules of the ring provide for what would otherwise be fatal contingencies, and both the umpires called simultaneously to cut the rope. This was done at once, and both men fell heavily to the ground, Sayers nearly half strangled. The police now made a determined effort to interfere, which those present seemed equally determined to prevent, and the ropes of the ring having been cut the enclosure itself was inundated by a dense crowd, which scarcely left the combatants six square feet to fight in. Umpires, referees, and all were overwhelmed, and the whole thing became a mere close mob round the two men fighting."

Nonetheless, the fight continued for four more rounds before the police were able to stop it in the forty-second. The *London Times* account concluded: "How the fight would have terminated but for the interference of the police it is now literally quite impossible to say or even speculate." The reporter for *Bell's Life* was unable to see the final action, but a man from his office reported that Heenan floored both Sayers' seconds and kicked them, then closed with Sayers. Wilkes' account accused "ruffians" of making the police an excuse for stopping the proceedings and depriving Heenan of his well-earned victory.

Frustration at the inconclusive outcome simmered for weeks in London, according to sporadic reports published by the *Pioneer and Democrat*. And one London item noted that the sale of newspapers reporting the fight "surpassed anything ever known. During all the terrible excitement of the Crimean and Indian war no such sale was ever reached." The effect on newspaper sales in Minnesota is not recorded, but it is safe to say that the *Pioneer and Democrat's* account was relished by more readers than the prosaic treatment in the *Minnesotian and Times*.[30]

Had the fight been delayed for four more months, accounts of it might have arrived more promptly in St. Paul by telegraph. On August 29, 1860, the line from Dubuque to St. Paul was completed, and the first message was dispatched from the St. Paul office. For several years the St. Paul newspapers had urged that public subscriptions be taken to supply the necessary funds, but they never pushed the idea with the commitment they accorded the railroad. Although the territory's railroad schemes had gone awry, now at least a telegraphic link to the East had been forged. The service was erratic, and the newspapers were not infrequently embarrassed by lack of telegraphic news because of storms or sudden changes of temperature which snapped the wire. In one instance, service was cut off by "some mysterious influence of moonbeams on the electric current."[31] Nonetheless, an era of semi-isolation was ended. No longer would St. Paul, "impatient as a young widow waiting for her nuptials," have to depend for its "outside" news on Burbank and Company's stage line in winter and steamboats in summer. James Madison Goodhue, who had written "we need and *must have* here, the telegraphic wires from the south," would have been pleased. The telegraph was to make more immediate much of the content of Minnesota's newspapers, even as the news that it brought was to signify the state's involvement in the Civil War.

CHAPTER 6

Epilogue

ONE YEAR AND A DECADE: 1849 to 1860. So little time and all of it crowded by the pressures of physical development. Get there first with your Washington hand press, grind out the lures of the land to attract more settlers, maneuver for government patronage so you can pay the paper supplier and the type foundry, get a new power press and bring out a daily, fight the competition to make your paper the voice of the party and your party the power in the emerging state, and promote railroad construction and a telegraph link to speed settlement and the gathering of news. The frontier press was an activist press, and if its editors had paused in the headlong rush to ask what is progress or why, it is doubtful that anyone would have been listening.

Activism was reflected in the greatest virtue of the Minnesota press in this pioneer period: the vigorous expression of strong-minded opinion. There were excesses, of course, but they were the excesses of a frontier society, and they were repeated in the pages of most newspapers on the edges of settlement, whether in Minnesota or Tennessee or Missouri.[1] A man had to believe mightily in himself to undertake the rigors of westward migration, whatever his objective — farming or land speculation or publishing a newspaper. An Earle Goodrich might be for sale, but most of the editors believed in the positions they so firmly supported. The best of them used their papers to extol the land with the enthusiasm, if rarely the grace, of a Goodhue, a Whiting, or a Donnelly, or to insist upon the worth of the individual with the fervor of a Newson, an Ames, or a Swisshelm. A year and a decade is a brief span, and the Minnesota career of none of these editors occupied more than a fraction of the interval. Yet they made their contribution by providing the press that a self-governing society needs in order to function.

As might be expected, the content and editorial emphasis of Minnesota newspapers changed after 1860. The Civil War, of course, imposed unique strains. A study of four Minnesota papers between 1861 and 1865 revealed that as much as "Eighty per cent of the content of the news matter reminded the reader in some manner that a war was in progress." Three of the newspapers — the *St. Paul Daily Press,* the *Winona Daily Republican,* and the *Faribault Central Republican* — received wire news through telegraph offices in or near their respective cities and supplemented it with letters from home-town soldiers at the front. The fourth paper, the *Chatfield Democrat,* lacking access to telegraphic dispatches, clipped stories from other papers both in Minnesota and in the East. None of the four papers had correspondents with the Union Army. The St. Paul, Winona, and Faribault papers were Republican and favored abolition; the *Chatfield Democrat* opposed it and was threatened with violence as a consequence. The shortage of manpower was a severe handicap for all of these papers, and three of them increased their advertising and circulation rates.[2]

After the Civil War, national, state, and foreign news and magazine material resumed their prewar dominance in Minnesota weeklies. These topics continued to account for a high proportion of the content of the papers until about 1890, partly because of the introduction and wide use of ready-print and boiler-plate material. After 1890 the proportion of such material steadily declined as the editors gave increasing attention to local news, including personal and society items, and reports of sports, civic, and political events — fields where the community weekly was less vulnerable to the challenge of the ever-growing circulation of magazines and metropolitan dailies.[3]

Changing times and increasing professionalism among Minnesota's newspapers may also be observed in the history of the first thirty years of what is now the Minnesota Newspaper Association. Firmly reborn in 1867 primarily as a social organization, it developed slowly and unevenly into a business and professional group, urging upon its members ethical standards and more efficient business procedures. Foreshadowing the association's eventual vigor was the fact that a national organization of editors and publishers was proposed by Harlan P. Hall of the *St. Paul Globe* in 1870 and realized in 1885–86 through the efforts of Benjamin B. Herbert of the *Red Wing Daily Republican,* who was then president of the Minnesota association. Herbert became the first president of the National Editorial Association, one of six Minnesotans who have served in that office. The others were: Paul V. Collins of the *Minneapolis Agriculturist* in 1903, Herbert C. Hotaling of the *Mapleton Enterprise* in 1917, Will Wilke of the *Grey Eagle Gazette* in 1920, Herman Roe of the *Northfield News* in 1927, and Alan C. McIntosh of the *Rock County Star-Herald* (Luverne) in 1953.[4]

In the development of its association and in many other aspects, the press of Minnesota matured along the lines followed by the nation's press as a whole. Professor Edwin Emery has summarized the dominant trends during the second half of the nineteenth century as: more impartial handling of news, increasing independence of editorial opinion from partisan pressures, "active and planned crusading in the community interest," popularization of content, increased technical proficiency through mechanization, and decreasing personal influence of the editor with the development of corporate structures. In the twentieth century he has noted two major trends — consolidation of ownership and growth of the interpretive function.[5]

Numerically Minnesota papers reflected the expansion of the nation's press, although they multiplied faster than the nation's press as a whole until consolidation set in during the 1920s. Between 1870 and 1900 Minnesota papers — both daily and weekly — increased more than sixfold. While the number of dailies in the whole country was quadrupling, Minnesota's jumped from 6 to 44. In the same period, while the nation's weeklies tripled, Minnesota's advanced from 72 to 493. In 1920, the peak year for dailies in the state, the number reached 45. The depression decade of the 1930s saw the greatest decrease: from 43 in 1930 to 36 ten years later. By 1950 the number had stabilized at 31; it was 30 in 1960. Weeklies in Minnesota, however, were most numerous in 1910 when they totaled 641. Each decade since that time has seen a decline: 622 in 1920, 500 in 1930, 464 in 1940, 419 in 1950, and 377 in 1960. For the weeklies the greatest rate of attrition coincided with the agricultural slump of the 1920s rather than with the deepening depression of the 1930s.[6]

In St. Paul and Minneapolis, the area's printing centers in the pioneer period, the succeeding century has seen the rise of the state's largest metropolitan dailies. The evolution of corporate ownership of newspapers as well as their gradual emergence from partisan domination are observable in the development of the present dailies in both cities. In St. Paul the *Pioneer and Democrat* lost prestige as a Democratic paper in a predominantly Republican era after Earle Goodrich sold it in 1865. In addition it faced formidable competition from a strong Republican newcomer, the *St. Paul Daily Press,* which published its first number on January 1, 1861. In 1875 the two papers merged, and the evolution of today's *St. Paul Pioneer Press,* which traces its lineage back to Goodhue's *Minnesota Pioneer,* took place under the editorial direction of Joseph A. Wheelock and the business management of Frederick Driscoll.[7]

Wheelock, who was to dominate the journalism of St. Paul and the Northwest for almost half a century, arrived in the Minnesota capital from Boston in 1850 as a sickly and impoverished youth of nineteen. In 1854, after holding various other jobs, he became the editor of banker Charles Parker's *St. Paul Financial & Real Estate Advertiser.* Wheelock later purchased the *Advertiser,* which he continued to edit until he sold it to the *Pioneer and Democrat* in 1858. He then joined the *Pioneer and Democrat* staff as an associate editor under Goodrich. The following year he accepted an appointment as commissioner of statistics for the state.[8]

Wheelock's opportunity came in 1861 when the *St. Paul Daily Press* was established with William R. Marshall as editor in chief and Newton Bradley as business manager. The prime mover in the enterprise, however, was Wheelock, who assumed full editorial control in 1862 when Marshall joined the Union Army. The *Press* was founded because leaders of the Republican party in Minnesota wanted a single strong organ in the capital. After the fusion of the *Times* and *Minnesotian* in 1859 had proved abortive, they knew they were not going to get it with Newson and Foster. Thus the *Daily Press* was born. The *Times* ceased publication, and the *Press* purchased its equipment.[9]

The paper was a success from the outset largely because Republican leaders wanted it to be. The *Daily Press* got the state printing contract in its first year, and had ample capital to pay more than its competitors for telegraphic dispatches — charges which were soon to mount to the then impressive sum of $125 a week. But the new paper was not without challengers. It was little more than a year old when a Republican faction backed Cyrus W. Aldrich for the United States Senate against regular Republican Alexander Ramsey. To oppose Ramsey, Driscoll founded the *St. Paul Daily Union* in 1862. The *Union* captured the state printing, but Ramsey got the Senate seat and Republicans decided that the schism should be healed. Thus on February 28, 1863, Driscoll discontinued the *Union,* bought a half interest in the *Press* for $4,000, and later became its business manager, although he and Wheelock were barely on speaking terms for many months.[10]

Throughout the Civil War, the *Press* was unswerving in its support of Lincoln and, like the Republican party, the paper continued to gain adherents. The times were less favorable for its Democratic opposition, the *Pioneer and Democrat.* In 1865 Earle Goodrich sold the paper to John X. Davidson and Harlan P. Hall, and in the next nine years the *Pioneer* changed hands five times, passing in 1874 to David Blakely, who was a Republican. Then on April 11, 1875, the *Pioneer* was merged with the *Press.* A story on page one quoted from the private agreement on which consolidation was based: "it is agreed that in general the paper shall be independent of party; that is to say, that with whatever party it may or shall generally sympathize, it shall be *pledged* to the support of none, but reserve to itself at all times the privilege of supporting such platforms and such candidates as to the editors and proprietors seem best to accord with their conscience and views of the public weal."[11]

Of the editorial policy of the *Pioneer Press* from 1875 to 1900, Quintus C. Wilson, Wheelock's biographer, says: "Liberal but

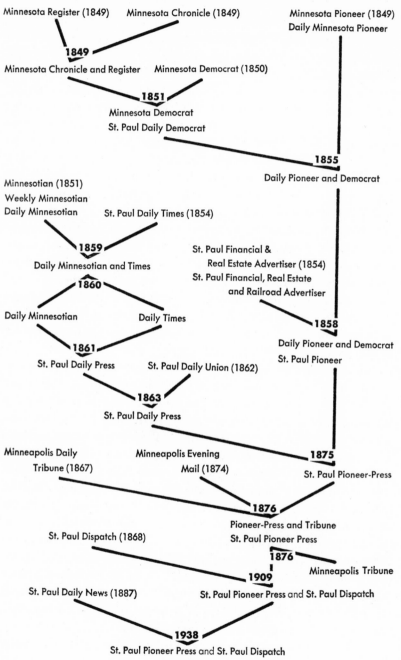

Minnesota Register (1849)   Minnesota Chronicle (1849)   Minnesota Pioneer (1849)
                                                              Daily Minnesota Pioneer

1849
Minnesota Chronicle and Register   Minnesota Democrat (1850)

1851
Minnesota Democrat
St. Paul Daily Democrat

1855
Daily Pioneer and Democrat

Minnesotian (1851)
Weekly Minnesotian
Daily Minnesotian   St. Paul Daily Times (1854)

1859
Daily Minnesotian and Times   St. Paul Financial &
                                   Real Estate Advertiser (1854)
1860   St. Paul Financial, Real Estate
                                       and Railroad Advertiser
Daily Minnesotian   Daily Times

1858
1861
St. Paul Daily Press   St. Paul Daily Union (1862)   Daily Pioneer and Democrat
                                                           St. Paul Pioneer

1863
St. Paul Daily Press

Minneapolis Daily   Minneapolis Evening   **1875**
Tribune (1867)   Mail (1874)   St. Paul Pioneer-Press

1876
Pioneer-Press and Tribune
St. Paul Pioneer Press

St. Paul Dispatch (1868)   St. Paul Pioneer Press
                                1876
                                              Minneapolis Tribune
                                1909
St. Paul Daily News (1887)   St. Paul Pioneer Press and St. Paul Dispatch

1938
St. Paul Pioneer Press and St. Paul Dispatch

THE GENEALOGY OF THE ST. PAUL PIONEER PRESS

opposed to the extreme Populists, the *Pioneer Press* edited by Joseph Wheelock sought to lead its readers along a central path to health and wealth." In national affairs the paper advocated the adoption of a nonpartisan civil service and the reduction of public expenditures, and it opposed cheap money. In the state it urged the regulation of trusts, advocated forest preservation and the diversification of farming, supported education, and recognized the right of labor to organize (but condemned Eugene V. Debs in the 1894 Pullman strike).[12]

Throughout his long career, which terminated with death in 1906, Wheelock was primarily interested in the editorial page of his newspaper. He insisted on publishing and commenting on the news as fast as it broke, to the chagrin of his press operators who were occasionally kept waiting while the boss prepared his dicta concerning the latest dispatch from Washington. He also changed the face of the city where he made his home for over fifty years. Before and after his election to the St. Paul park board in 1893, Wheelock was an ardent proponent of parks, playgrounds, and boulevards. The St. Paul park system is largely the result of his foresight and energy.[13]

Although the *St. Paul Pioneer Press* became the city's leading morning paper under Wheelock, it was not without competitors. One of them — Harlan P. Hall — gave Wheelock considerable trouble. Hall, who has been characterized as "a political and journalistic maverick," arrived in St. Paul from Ohio in 1862. As we have seen he was one of the purchasers of the *Pioneer and Democrat* in 1865. Five years later he founded another Democratic paper, the *St. Paul Dispatch*. In 1876 he sold it to a stock company, which made its policies Republican. "The changed allegiance of the *Dispatch* left St. Paul Democrats, who were an overwhelming majority of the city's voting population, without a journalistic voice." Hall remedied this in 1878 by founding the *St. Paul Globe* as the journalistic spokesman for the Democrats. The ever-restless Hall sold the *Globe* in 1881 to a joint stock company, of which Henry H. Sibley was a prominent member. About four years later a new set of owners incorporated with a board of directors that included Sibley and Norman W. Kittson. Changes of ownership were even more frequent in the mid-

1890s when both the economy and the Democratic party in Minnesota knew lean years. The *Globe's* last owner, from 1896 to 1905 when it folded in part for lack of advertising support, was James J. Hill of railroad fame.[14]

Consolidation of St. Paul's dailies was brought about gradually during the thirty years following the death of Wheelock. George Thompson, who in 1885 had acquired the *St. Paul Dispatch,* the city's dominant evening paper, purchased the *Pioneer Press* in 1909. Thompson and later his widow controlled both papers until 1923, when Charles K. Blandin became the owner. On October 4, 1927, Blandin sold the papers to New York's B. H. Ridder publishing family. The Ridders also gained control of a third paper, the *St. Paul Daily News,* in 1933, and five years later discontinued it. Today Northwest Publications, of which B. H. Ridder, Sr., is president, continues to publish the *Pioneer Press* and *Dispatch* with B. H. Ridder, Jr., as editor and publisher of both papers.[15]

The Ridder family figures importantly also in recent chapters of the history of journalism at the head of Lake Superior. Here, too, is a tangled skein of ownerships, starting with individual, partisan enterprises which merged into increasingly consolidated corporate holdings. There is a familiar name, also, at the inception, that of the acid-tongued Dr. Thomas Foster.

After Civil War service and unsuccessful efforts at journalism and medical practice in Minneapolis, St. Paul, and Sleepy Eye, Foster moved to Duluth. There in 1869 he launched the city's first paper, the *Duluth Minnesotian,* which was a weekly. On September 11, 1875, the *Minnesotian* merged with the *Duluth Herald,* which had been published sporadically for four years, to become the *Duluth Minnesotian-Herald.* The *Herald* was Duluth's first daily, having begun to publish six days a week in July, 1871. Thus today's *Duluth Herald* and *Duluth News-Tribune,* now owned by the Ridder family's Northwest Publications, can trace their ancestry not only to the city's first daily but also to the *Minnesotian,* Duluth's first newspaper.

Other papers in the genealogy are the *Duluth Tribune,* begun as a weekly in 1870 by Robert C. Mitchell and converted to a daily publication — the *Evening Tribune* — on May 15, 1872;

and the *Lake Superior Weekly News,* begun in 1878 by William
S. Woodbridge and converted by him into the *Duluth Daily
News* on July 1, 1886. The *News* and the *Tribune* were merged
by Myron A. Hays on October 5, 1892. They passed through
three ownerships before being acquired by M. Francis Hanson
and Paul Block and merged with the *Herald* on December 1,
1929. The Ridders took over from Hanson and Block on July 23,
1936.[16]

In Minneapolis, the course of the *Tribune* is the mainstream
to which many a tributary — most notably the *Minneapolis Star*
and the *Minneapolis Journal* — found its way over the last century. The first major confluence in that mainstream, as noted in
Chapter 4, occurred in 1867 when a pre-Civil War paper, the
State Atlas, merged with the postwar *Minneapolis Chronicle* to
produce the *Tribune.* One writer observed that "The *Tribune*
went through six ownership changes in the first 24 years of its
history." For a brief time in the 1870s, for example, the *Tribune*
was controlled by the *St. Paul Pioneer Press.* In May, 1876, the
Pioneer Press purchased both the *Tribune* and the *Minneapolis
Evening Mail,* and for a year the *Tribune* was issued as an
evening subsidiary of the St. Paul paper. The morning slot was
filled by the *Pioneer Press,* which ran for six months as the
Pioneer-Press and Tribune and carried the dateline "Saint Paul
and Minneapolis." Thus, as one writer put it, "citizens of Minneapolis suffered the indignity of a 'Twin Cities newspaper' controlled by Wheelock and Driscoll."[17]

It was a businessman who brought stability to the *Tribune*
and advanced it to pre-eminence among Midwest newspapers.
William J. Murphy, a native of Hudson, Wisconsin, had practiced law, invested in electric utilities, and published the Grand
Forks, North Dakota, *Plain Dealer* for nine years before he and
Senator Gilbert A. Pierce of North Dakota purchased the *Tribune* in 1891 for $450,000. Two years later Murphy became the
sole owner and publisher. In a recent study of the paper's development, Bradley L. Morison wrote that "A Tribune associate
who knew Murphy well describes him as distinguished in appearance, aloof in most of his employe relationships, shrewd in
business dealings and relentless in his determination to keep the

Tribune abreast of modern publishing techniques." During the first decade of his control, the *Tribune* installed Minneapolis' first Mergenthaler typesetting machines, experimented with color, and published its first cartoon and its first halftone engraving—suitably enough a photograph of that citadel of local government, the city hall and courthouse.[18]

The business side was Murphy's primary concern, and Morison noted that as long as news and editorial policies "reflected a plainly discernible Republican bias," the publisher was "likely to consider them highly satisfactory." Sometimes the bias was more than discernible even in the news columns, as the paper supported Republican candidates, urged sound money policies, and opposed government intervention in the economic sphere. In international affairs it pursued a course that ranged from disinterest to qualified approval of the events that led up to the intervention in Cuba and the Spanish-American War in 1898. During World War I, the *Tribune* emerged from preoccupation with its own region, both in news and editorials, to responsible coverage of world events without neglecting its own area. By that time, one student noted, the paper "could find promise in a league of nations that didn't compromise the United States' sovereignty."[19]

When William J. Murphy died in 1918, the *Tribune's* circulation was twice that of its morning rival in St. Paul. Later developments have made the paper less his monument than is William J. Murphy Hall, home of the University of Minnesota's School of Journalism and Mass Communication. Murphy's will left $350,000 to the university to establish and maintain a school of journalism—a bequest for such a purpose second only to Joseph Pulitzer's endowment of Columbia University. Murphy Hall was dedicated in 1940.[20]

After a brief interregnum ending in 1921, William J.'s younger brother, Frederick J. Murphy, became the publisher of the *Tribune,* a post he was to fill until his death in 1940. Fred Murphy was devoted to the Republican party, but he was even more devoted to the cause of agriculture, and when the Smoot-Hawley tariff favored the East's industry over the Midwest's agriculture, the *Tribune* attacked the party repeatedly for failing to keep its

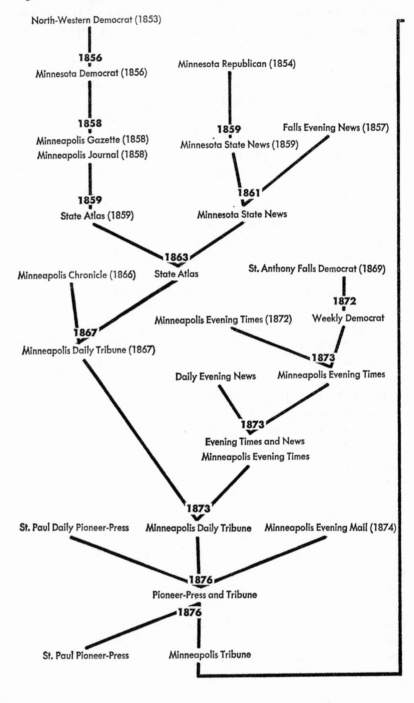

North-Western Democrat (1853)

1856
Minnesota Democrat (1856)

Minnesota Republican (1854)

1858
Minneapolis Gazette (1858)
Minneapolis Journal (1858)

1859
Minnesota State News (1859)

Falls Evening News (1857)

1859
State Atlas (1859)

1861
Minnesota State News

1863
Minneapolis Chronicle (1866)   State Atlas

St. Anthony Falls Democrat (1869)

1872
Weekly Democrat

Minneapolis Evening Times (1872)

1867
Minneapolis Daily Tribune (1867)

1873
Daily Evening News   Minneapolis Evening Times

1873
Evening Times and News
Minneapolis Evening Times

1873
St. Paul Daily Pioneer-Press   Minneapolis Daily Tribune   Minneapolis Evening Mail (1874)

1876
Pioneer-Press and Tribune

1876
St. Paul Pioneer-Press   Minneapolis Tribune

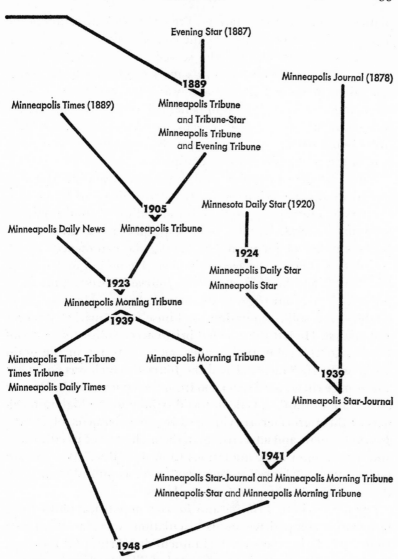

Evening Star (1887)

Minneapolis Journal (1878)

1889
Minneapolis Tribune
and Tribune-Star
Minneapolis Tribune
and Evening Tribune

Minneapolis Times (1889)

Minnesota Daily Star (1920)

1905
Minneapolis Daily News   Minneapolis Tribune

1924
Minneapolis Daily Star
Minneapolis Star

1923
Minneapolis Morning Tribune

1939
Minneapolis Times-Tribune   Minneapolis Morning Tribune
Times Tribune
Minneapolis Daily Times

1939
Minneapolis Star-Journal

1941
Minneapolis Star-Journal and Minneapolis Morning Tribune
Minneapolis Star and Minneapolis Morning Tribune

1948
Minneapolis Star and Minneapolis Morning Tribune

THE GENEALOGY OF THE MINNEAPOLIS STAR AND TRIBUNE

platform promises to the farmer. Fred Murphy's direction of the
Tribune was almost as long as the concurrent career of the leg-
endary Thomas J. Dillon, who served as editor in chief from
1920 until 1945. "The Tribune's most spectacularly successful
campaign, in those Dillon years" was one in which the paper
co-operated with a political opponent, Floyd B. Olson, Hennepin County district attorney, to send four Minneapolis aldermen
to the penitentiary for accepting payoffs in the issuing of licenses
and in the purchasing of city equipment.[21]

The *Tribune's* principal rival during the years the Murphys
owned it was the *Minneapolis Journal,* which had followed a
similarly conservative, pro-Republican, editorial course since its
founding in 1878. Its most notable publisher was Herschel V.
Jones, a native of Jefferson, New York, who had owned the village weekly there at the age of eighteen. He moved to Minneapolis in 1885 and became one of the *Journal's* three reporters (it
published only four pages in those days). In time Herschel Jones
established a solid reputation for himself as a market reporter
and analyst. He left the *Journal* briefly to establish *Commercial
West,* a local weekly trade paper, and to engage in the grain
business. In 1908 he purchased the *Journal,* which was no longer
a four-page sheet, for $1,200,000 from the estate of E. B. Haskell
of Boston. Edward C. Gale has paid tribute to the high-minded-
ness of this publisher as evidenced by "the character of its [*the
Journal's*] news and advertising, in the high level of its editorials,
and in its almost daily quotations from the Bible." When death
ended Herschel Jones's twenty-year career as publisher in 1928,
the post passed to his son, Carl W. Jones.[22]

Opposed to both *Tribune* and *Journal* in political philosophy,
but hardly competitive in its circulation, was the *Minnesota
Daily Star.* This paper was the brainchild of Arthur C. Townley,
head of the Nonpartisan League, and of Thomas Van Lear, onetime Socialist mayor of Minneapolis. The *Star* was launched on
August 19, 1920, as mouthpiece, educator, and champion of the
workingman and the farmer. Its stock was held by more than
20,000 members of the Nonpartisan League and the Socialist
party. Four years later the *Star* went into receivership and was
sold on June 1, 1924. One student has theorized that the paper

sponsored by the Nonpartisan League failed largely because it did not attract the advertising of local businessmen, because of unwise business decisions, and because its news bias became more extreme with each election campaign. Beginning on July 1, 1924, it continued publication as the *Minneapolis Daily Star,* an orthodox daily with John Thompson as publisher.[23]

In 1935 the *Star* was a weak third, trailing both the *Tribune* and *Journal* in circulation and advertising linage. In that year it was purchased by the Cowles family, publishers of Iowa's *Des Moines Register* and *Des Moines Tribune.* The new owners' aggressive policies almost immediately threatened the *Journal,* and in August, 1939, the two papers merged as the *Star-Journal.* The *Tribune,* which in turn felt threatened, renamed its evening edition the *Minneapolis Times-Tribune* in the hope of attracting former readers of the *Journal.* But just when a greater competitive effort was needed, Fred Murphy died in 1940. In May, 1941, *Tribune* stockholders agreed to a merger. Thus John Cowles became the publisher of all three Minneapolis newspapers. On July 15, 1946, he changed the name of the *Star-Journal* to the *Minneapolis Star,* and in 1948 he discontinued the *Times.* He continued to issue the surviving *Tribune* and *Star* as morning and evening papers respectively, a status they hold to this day.[24]

The Cowles achievement in forging the two thriving papers that dominate Minnesota journalism today was the result of shrewd editorial and business management, concentration on local news, more attractive type and make-up, brighter writing, more aggressive promotion, and improved distribution. But other factors also operated in the elimination of competition — the stodginess of the opposition, especially on the part of the *Tribune;* the greater efficiency of twenty-four-hour operation of a single plant; and the preference of advertisers for wide coverage of the market in single strong morning and evening papers rather than overlapping coverage in two or more.[25]

Ironically, it is not the name of such Minnesota publishers as Cowles, Murphy, Ridder, or Wheelock that is writ large in the legal annals of the nation's press in the first half of the twentieth century. Rather, it was the editor of a scurvy little sheet called the *Saturday Press* who focused attention on Minnesota because his name became attached to a historic Supreme Court decision. The case was Near *v*. Minnesota, and the decision made history because it was the first to apply the guarantee of liberty in the Fourteenth Amendment to a newspaper enjoined from publication under a state law. The Minnesota "gag law," as it came to be known, was enacted by the state legislature in 1925, perhaps in an effort to curb the scandal sheets which enjoyed a certain vogue in the 1920s. It passed the Senate without dissent, the House by a vote of eighty-two to twenty-two, and was signed by Governor Theodore Christianson without stirring a ripple among the newspapers reporting the session. The law's preamble described it as "An act declaring a nuisance, the business . . . of regularly or customarily producing, publishing, or circulating an obscene, lewd, and lascivious newspaper, magazine, or other periodical, and providing for injunction and other proceedings." [26]

The *Saturday Press* had been launched in Minneapolis on September 24, 1927, by Jay M. Near and Howard A. Guilford. Both men had previously edited the *Twin City Reporter*, a weekly whose staples were "sex, attacks on public officials and prominent private citizens, and vicious baiting of minority groups." The *Saturday Press* eschewed sex to concentrate on baiting public officials and Jews.

Three days after the publication of the first issue, Guilford was shot as he drove away from his Robbinsdale home. He identified two men who were arrested as his assailants but he refused to press charges. At the same time from his hospital bed he attacked Floyd B. Olson, who was then serving as Hennepin County attorney, for failing to prosecute criminals. Olson's answer was to ask the Hennepin County district court to enjoin the *Saturday Press* from publishing on the grounds that it violated the provisions of the 1925 gag law. Near and Guilford demurred, contending that the law was unconstitutional. When they were overruled in the district court and restrained from publication, they twice appealed to the state supreme court, which twice held that the law was a legitimate exercise of the state's police power.

With the support of Colonel Robert R. McCormick, publisher of the *Chicago Tribune* and chairman of the American Newspaper Publishers Association's committee on freedom of the press, Near appealed to the United States Supreme Court.[27] On June 1, 1931, the high court in a five to four decision declared the gag law unconstitutional. Chief Justice Charles E. Hughes and Justices Louis O. Brandeis, Oliver Wendell Holmes, Owen J. Roberts, and Harlan F. Stone held the law to be a previous restraint — in effect, censorship. Hughes declared in the majority opinion that the remedy for the ills the law was designed to correct was action for libel. Justice Pierce Butler, a native Minnesotan, wrote the minority opinion in which Justices Willis Van Devanter, George Sutherland, and James C. McReynolds concurred. They argued that the court's decision "declares Minnesota and every other state powerless to restrain by legislative action the business of publishing and circulating . . . malicious and defamatory periodicals."

In the wake of the Supreme Court's decision, Near resumed publication of the *Saturday Press,* but its tone was markedly restrained. Guilford, after a short flyer with a new weekly called the *Pink Sheet,* returned to the *Saturday Press,* from which he was severed by an assassin's bullet on September 6, 1934. Near died without violence in 1936, and the *Saturday Press* expired not long afterward.

Eighty-two years after the publication of the first newspaper in Minnesota, another weekly, disreputable rather than dedicated, had become the agency for expanding the constitutional guarantee of press freedom. The irony of the episode was sharpened by the fact that Floyd B. Olson, the man who initiated the prosecution, deserves his place in history as Minnesota's most liberal governor, while McCormick, the publisher who carried the fight, is remembered as the Midwest's, if not the nation's, most conservative newspaper owner. It is not incongruous that other circumstances surrounding the episode recalled the violence of the frontier more than three-quarters of a century earlier when James Madison Goodhue set out to make the nation aware of Minnesota.

Minnesota Newspapers 1849–1860

Newspapers are listed alphabetically under the year in which they were first established. The abbreviation MHS refers to the collections of the Minnesota Historical Society.

1849

MINNESOTA CHRONICLE, St. Paul (weekly) — First issue May 31, 1849. Last issue August 9, 1849. Merged August, 1849, with Minnesota Register to become Minnesota Chronicle and Register.

MINNESOTA CHRONICLE AND REGISTER, St. Paul (weekly) — First issue August 25, 1849. Last issue February 10, 1851. Absorbed by Minnesota Democrat, No. 1, in 1851.

MINNESOTA PIONEER, St. Paul (weekly) — First issue April 28, 1849. Last issue November 1, 1855. Merged November 1, 1855, with Minnesota Democrat to become St. Paul Weekly Pioneer and Democrat. See 1855 below.

MINNESOTA REGISTER, St. Paul (weekly) — First issue printed in Cincinnati, Ohio, on April 7 or 27, 1849; second issue printed in Minnesota on July 14, 1849. Last issue August 18, 1849. Merged August, 1849, with Minnesota Chronicle to become Minnesota Chronicle and Register.

1850

DAKOTA TAWAXITKU KIN, OR THE DAKOTA FRIEND, St. Paul (monthly) — First issue November, 1850. Last issue August, 1852. Suspended November, December, 1851.

MINNESOTA DEMOCRAT, No. 1, St. Paul (weekly) — First issue December 10, 1850. Last issue October 31, 1855. Absorbed Minnesota Chronicle and Register, 1851. Merged November 1, 1855, with Minnesota Pioneer to become St. Paul Weekly Pioneer and Democrat. See 1855 below.

1851

The MINNESOTIAN, St. Paul (weekly) — First issue September 17, 1851. Last issue January 25, 1861. Name changed to Weekly Minnesotian May 8, 1852; to St. Paul Weekly Minnesotian May 1, 1858. Merged with Minnesota Weekly Times to form Weekly Minnesotian and Times from December 17, 1859, to about June 13, 1860. Resumed separate publication from about June 29, 1860, to January 25, 1861, when it again merged with Times into St. Paul Weekly Press.

The ST. ANTHONY EXPRESS, St. Anthony (weekly)—First issue May 31, 1851. Last issue late in May, 1861. Name changed to Saint Anthony Weekly Express, April 21, 1860.

WATAB REVEILLE, St. Paul (weekly)—Three issues known: January 13, 29, February 10, 1851.

1853

NORTH-WESTERN DEMOCRAT, St. Anthony and Minneapolis (weekly)—First issue July 13, 1853. Last issue July, 1856. Moved to Minneapolis August 12, 1854. Became Minnesota Democrat, No. 2, July 19, 1856. See 1856 below.

1854

BOMB SHELL, Fort Ripley—Prospectus July 26, 1854; first issue August 16, 1854. Only known copies.

DAILY MINNESOTA PIONEER, St. Paul (daily) — First issue May 1, 1854. Last issue October 31, 1855. Merged November 1, 1855, with St. Paul Daily Democrat to become St. Paul Pioneer and Democrat. See 1855 below.

DAILY MINNESOTIAN, St. Paul (daily)—First issue May 11, 1854. Last issue January 25, 1861. Name changed to St. Paul Daily Minnesotian May 11, 1858. Merged with St. Paul Daily Times to form daily Minnesotian and Times from December 14, 1859, to June 17, 1860. Resumed separate publication from June 21, 1860, to January 25, 1861, when it merged again with Times to form St. Paul Press.

The MINNESOTA REPUBLICAN, St. Anthony (weekly)—First issue October 5, 1854. Last issue December 24, 1858. Volume and numbering continued in Minnesota State News. See 1859 below.

MINNESOTA WEEKLY TIMES, St. Paul (weekly)—First issue May 23, 1854. Last issue January 3, 1861. Merged with Weekly

Minnesotian to form Weekly Minnesotian and Times from December 17, 1859, to about June 13, 1860. Resumed separate publication from about June 27, 1860, to January 3, 1861, when it merged again with Minnesotian to form St. Paul Weekly Press.

ST. CROIX UNION, Stillwater (weekly)—First issue October 23, 1854. Last issue November 13, 1857.

ST. PAUL DAILY DEMOCRAT, St. Paul (daily)—First issue May 1, 1854. Last issue October 31, 1855. Merged November 1, 1855, with Daily Minnesota Pioneer to become Daily Pioneer and Democrat. See 1855 below.

ST. PAUL DAILY TIMES, St. Paul (daily) — First issue May 15, 1854. Last issue December 30, 1860. Merged with St. Paul Daily Minnesotian to form daily Minnesotian and Times from December 14, 1859, to June 17, 1860. Resumed separate publication as Daily Times from June 21, 1860, to December 30, 1860, when it merged again with Minnesotian to form St. Paul Press.

ST. PAUL FINANCIAL & REAL ESTATE ADVERTISER, St. Paul (weekly)—First issue November 3, 1854. Last issue June 19, 1858. Name changed January 26, 1856, to St. Paul Financial, Real Estate and Railroad Advertiser. Absorbed by St. Paul Pioneer and Democrat, 1858.

The WINONA ARGUS, Winona (weekly)—First issue October 11, 1854. Last issue about September 3, 1857.

1855

The DAILY PIONEER AND DEMOCRAT, St. Paul (daily)—First issue November 1, 1855. Merged April 11, 1875, with St. Paul Daily Press and continued as St. Paul Daily Pioneer-Press. Still published in 1967 as St. Paul Pioneer Press.

DIE MINNESOTA DEUTSCHE ZEITUNG, St. Paul (German-language weekly)—First issue November 19, 1855. Suspended November, 1856; revived January, 1857. Became Minnesota Staats-Zeitung July 24, 1858. See 1858 below.

MINNESOTA WEEKLY FREE PRESS, St. Paul (weekly)—First issue about August 30, 1855. Last issue about May 16, 1856. Weekly edition of Saint Paul Daily Free Press. No MHS file.

RED-WING SENTINEL, No. 1, Red Wing (weekly)—First issue July 20, 1855. Last issue May, 1856. No MHS file. Volume and numbering continued in Red Wing Sentinel, No. 2. See 1857 below.

RUBE'S ADVOCATE, Stillwater (irregular)—Established January 1, 1855. Last issue in MHS file February 24, 1855.

The SAINT PAUL DAILY FREE PRESS, St. Paul (daily) — First issue about August 30, 1855. Last issue about May 16, 1856. Last issue in MHS file April 5, 1856.

ST. PAUL WEEKLY PIONEER AND DEMOCRAT, St. Paul (weekly)—First issue November 8, 1855. Last issue November 10, 1865, when it became St. Paul Weekly Pioneer.

SAINT PETER'S COURIER, St. Peter (weekly)—First issue January 4, 1855. Name changed to Saint Peter Weekly Courier, November 6, 1855, to April 22, 1856. Last issue in MHS file January 1, 1858. Discontinued about July, 1858.

SAUK RAPIDS FRONTIERMAN, Sauk Rapids (weekly)—First issue April 26, 1855. Last issue January 5, 1860. Publication suspended November 19, 1857, to about February 4, 1858; July 1, 1858, to September 22, 1859.

SHAKOPEE INDEPENDENT, Shakopee (weekly)—First issue November 3, 1855. Last issue September 17, 1856. Became Valley Herald about September 24, 1856. See 1856 below.

SOUTHERN MINNESOTA HERALD, Brownsville (weekly)—First issue June 23, 1855. Last issue June 4, 1859. Moved to Fairy Rock, Houston County, in 1859.

The WINONA REPUBLICAN, Winona (weekly)—First issue November 20, 1855. Name changed to Winona Weekly Republican August 13, 1862. Last issue February 18, 1901, when it merged with Winona Herald.

The WINONA WEEKLY EXPRESS, Winona (weekly)—First issue August 14, 1855. Last issue in MHS file October 16, 1855.

1856

CANNON FALLS GAZETTE, Cannon Falls (weekly)—First issue about August 1, 1856. Last issue about May 15, 1857.

CARIMONA TELEGRAPH, Carimona (weekly)—First issue October, 1856. Last issue about May 20, 1857. No MHS file.

CHATFIELD DEMOCRAT, Chatfield (weekly)—First issue about October 1, 1856. Suspended before August, 1857. Resumed September 11, 1857. Merged with Chatfield News to become Chatfield News-Democrat May 22, 1902. Still published in 1967 as Chatfield News.

CHATFIELD REPUBLICAN, Chatfield (weekly)—First issue October 25, 1856. Last issue in MHS file October 15, 1861.

DAKOTA WEEKLY JOURNAL, Hastings (weekly)—First issue

May 24, 1856. Last issue in MHS file September 27, 1857. Probably ran until November 19, 1857.

EMIGRANT AID JOURNAL, Nininger (weekly)—First issue published at Philadelphia December 1, 1856. Second issue published at Nininger June 20, 1857. Last issue in MHS file May 5, 1858.

FILLMORE COUNTY PIONEER, Carimona (weekly)—First issue about January 15, 1856. Discontinued about October, 1856.

The HENDERSON DEMOCRAT, Henderson (weekly)—First issue April 3, 1856. Last issue in MHS file May 4, 1861. Name changed to Henderson Weekly Democrat August 10, 1859.

MINNESOTA DEMOCRAT, No. 2, Minneapolis (weekly)—First issue July 19, 1856. Last issue in MHS file October 17, 1857. Continuation of North-Western Democrat. See 1850, 1853 above.

MINNESOTA GAZETTE, Red Wing (weekly)—First issue about June 25, 1856. Last issue about July 25, 1857. No MHS file.

MONTICELLO JOURNAL, Monticello (weekly)—First issue about mid-December, 1856. Last issue May, 1857. No MHS file.

NORTHERN HERALD, Watab and Little Falls (weekly)—First issue published at Watab about November 15, 1856. Moved to Little Falls before January 14, 1857. Last issue in MHS file October 28, 1857.

ORONOCO COURIER, Oronoco (weekly) — First issue about December 15, 1856. Last issue about December 20, 1857.

OWATONNA WATCHMAN AND REGISTER, Owatonna (weekly)—First issue about July 22, 1856. Name changed to Owatonna Register about December 15, 1856. Discontinued winter of 1857–58. Owatonna Register, No. 2, published in 1867–68.

PRESTON JOURNAL, Preston (weekly?)—First issue July 15 or 21, 1856. Only known number. No MHS file.

REPUBLICAN ADVOCATE, Shakopee (weekly)—First issue about September 27, 1856. Suspended November, 1857. Resumed and thought to have discontinued about February 20, 1860. No MHS file.

RICE COUNTY HERALD, Faribault (weekly)—First issue October 22, 1856. Last issue February 26, 1857. Became Faribault Herald. See 1857 below.

STILLWATER MESSENGER, No. 1, Stillwater (weekly) —First issue September 15, 1856. Last issue in MHS file March 11, 1868. Stillwater Messenger, No. 2, began publication in 1870.

VALLEY HERALD, Shakopee (weekly)—First issue about September 24, 1856. Name changed to Weekly Valley Herald August 26,

1857. Suspended soon after October 28, 1857 (last issue in MHS file), reappeared in September, 1858, and discontinued soon after that. See also Shakopee Independent above, 1855.

WABASHAW JOURNAL, No. 1, Read's Landing and Wabasha (weekly)—First issue published at Read's Landing about July 12, 1856. Moved to Wabasha spring, 1857. Last issue about December 20, 1858. See 1859 below.

1857

BANCROFT PIONEER, Bancroft (weekly)—First issue October 17, 1857. Last issue about September 23, 1858. No MHS file.

BELLE PLAINE ENQUIRER, Belle Plaine (weekly)—First issue December 3, 1857. Last issue October 5, 1861. Name changed to Belle Plaine Weekly Enquirer, April 6, 1861, to October 5, 1861.

CANNON FALLS BULLETIN, Cannon Falls (weekly)—First issue early August, 1857. Last issue about April, 1858. No MHS file.

FALLS EVENING NEWS, St. Anthony (daily, triweekly)—First issue September 28, 1857. Last issue May 18, 1861. Daily to December 7, 1857; triweekly thereafter.

FARIBAULT HERALD, Faribault (weekly)—First issue March 12, 1857. Last issue June 16, 1858. Continued as Faribault Central Republican, June 23, 1858. See 1858 below. See also Rice County Herald above, 1856.

FOLKETS RÖST, St. Paul (Norwegian-language semimonthly) — First issue about October, 1857. Second issue July 10, 1858 (vol. 1, no. 1). Last issue in MHS file November 20, 1858.

The GLENCOE REGISTER, No. 1, Glencoe (weekly)—First issue August 8, 1857. Last issue in MHS file under this name April 2, 1868. From July 21, 1862, to January 10, 1863, name changed to Glencoe Register and Soldier's Budget. Suspended September, 1862, to January, 1863. Became Glencoe Weekly Register from about July, 1866, to April 2, 1868. Became McLeod County Register from April 9, 1868, to July 2, 1868. A second Glencoe Register ran from February 25, 1869, to February 1, 1907.

HASTINGS INDEPENDENT, Hastings (weekly)—First issue July 27, 1857. Last issue in MHS file November 8, 1866. Merged with Hastings Conserver November 13, 1866, and still published in 1967 as Hastings Gazette.

HOKAH CHIEF, Hokah (weekly)—First issue about July 15, 1857. Probably suspended early 1859. Revived April 26, 1859, to May 23,

1865. Volume and numbering continued in August, 1882. Became Houston County Chief, January, 1894; Hokah Chief, 1927–1953.

LAKE CITY TRIBUNE, Lake City (weekly)—First issue January 3, 1857. Last issue about March 1, 1861. Suspended January 10, 1859, to February 10, 1859.

MANKATO INDEPENDENT, Mankato (weekly, semiweekly) — First issue about June 13, 1857. Semiweekly August 9, 1860, to December 30, 1862. Last issue July 11, 1863. Became Mankato Weekly Union, July 17, 1863; consolidated with Mankato Record to become Mankato Free Press in 1879. Still published in 1967 as daily.

MANTORVILLE EXPRESS, Mantorville (weekly)—First issue July 16, 1857. Ran as Mantorville and Kasson Express, September 3, 1880, to October 22, 1886. Still published in 1967.

MINNESOTA ADVERTISER, St. Cloud (weekly)—First issue about January 15, 1857. Last issue in MHS file August 27, 1857. Followed by St. Cloud Visiter. See below.

MINNESOTA FREE PRESS, St. Peter (weekly)—First issue May 27, 1857. Publication suspended November 24, 1858, to April 13, 1859. Name changed and publication resumed April 20, 1859, as Saint Peter Free Press, No. 1. Last issue in MHS file December 7, 1859. Suspended about December 21, 1859. St. Peter Free Press, No. 2, published 1894–1925.

MINNESOTA NATIONAL DEMOKRAT, St. Paul (German-language weekly)—First issue about June 6, 1857. Last issue in MHS file October 8, 1859.

MINNESOTA POSTEN, Red Wing (Swedish-language weekly)— First issue November 7, 1857. Last issue October 13, 1858, when it merged with Hemlandet of Galesburg, Illinois.

MINNESOTA THALBOTEN, Chaska (German-language weekly)— First issue about June 1, 1857. Last issue about March or June, 1858. No MHS file.

MONTICELLO TIMES, No. 1, Monticello (weekly)—First issue May 21, 1857. Last issue April 6, 1859. Another paper of same name appeared in 1906.

OLMSTED JOURNAL, Rochester (weekly)—First issue about March 26, 1857. Last issue about September 1, 1857.

RED WING REPUBLICAN, Red Wing (weekly)—First issue September 4, 1857. Last issue November 22, 1884. Name changed to Goodhue County Republican from August 19, 1859, to July 29, 1880. Became a daily October 12, 1885.

RED WING SENTINEL, No. 2, Red Wing (weekly)—First issue of

about August 1, 1857, continued numbering of Red-Wing Sentinel, No. 1. See 1855 above. Last issue April 24, 1861.

ROCHESTER DEMOCRAT, Rochester (weekly)—First issue August 6, 1857. Last issue in MHS file October 21, 1858. Removed to Winona and continued as Democrat. See 1858 below.

ST. CLOUD VISITER, St. Cloud (weekly)—First issue December 10, 1857. Last issue July 29, 1858. Suspended March 24, 1858, to May 13, 1858, except for one issue on April 1, 1858. Became St. Cloud Democrat. See 1858 below.

SOUTHERN MINNESOTA STAR, Albert Lea (weekly)—First issue July 9, 1857. Last issue May 25, 1858.

TRAVERSE DES SIOUX REPORTER, Traverse des Sioux (weekly)—First issue about September 17, 1857. Last issue about November 15, 1857. No MHS file.

The WABASHAW COUNTY HERALD, Read's Landing and Wabasha (weekly, semiweekly) — Began as Waumadee Herald August 15, 1857. See below. Moved to Wabasha December 8, 1860. Ran as Wabashaw County Herald and Weekly Journal from December 15, 1860, to December 29, 1860. Name changed to Wabashaw County Herald, January 5, 1861. Ran as semiweekly from January 30, 1861, to October 8, 1862. Still published in 1967.

WASIOJA GAZETTE, Wasioja (weekly)—First issue July 17, 1857. Last issue in MHS file September 9, 1859.

WAUMADEE HERALD, Read's Landing (weekly)—First and perhaps only issue May 9, 1857. Publication resumed August 15, 1857; about this time name changed to Wabashaw County Herald. See above.

WESTERN TRANSCRIPT, Carimona (weekly)—First issue about May 25, 1857. Last issue about June 25, 1857. No MHS file.

1858

CLEVELAND LEADER, Cleveland (weekly)—First issue about July, 1858. Ran until fall, 1860. No MHS file.

CLEVELAND WEEKLY HERALD, Cleveland (weekly)—First issue about May 15, 1858. Last issue April or May, 1860. No MHS file.

DEMOCRAT, No. 1, Winona (weekly) — First issue November 20, 1858. Last issue about February 1, 1861. Last issue in MHS file November 17, 1860. Continuation of Rochester Democrat. See 1857 above. Another paper of same name published from September, 1864, to sometime in 1866.

FARIBAULT CENTRAL REPUBLICAN, Faribault (weekly?)—

First issue June 23, 1858. Last issue May 18, 1870. See Rice County Herald, 1856, above.

FREEBORN COUNTY EAGLE, Albert Lea (weekly)—First issue September 18, 1858. Last issue May 19, 1860.

HASTINGS DAILY LEDGER, Hastings (daily)—First issue May 10, 1858. Last issue about March 12, 1859. Continued as weekly to October 8, 1859. No MHS file.

MEDFORD VALLEY ARGUS, No. 1?, Medford (weekly)—First issue August, 1858. Lasted a few months. No MHS file. A second Medford Valley Argus may have run from March, 1859, to about June 20, 1859, or later.

MINNEAPOLIS GAZETTE, Minneapolis (weekly)—First issue February 2, 1858. Last issue in MHS file October 15, 1858. Absorbed by Minneapolis Journal, No. 1. See below.

MINNEAPOLIS JOURNAL, No. 1, Minneapolis (weekly)—First issue about September 30, 1858. Last issue in MHS file December 30, 1858. Absorbed by State Atlas. See 1859 below. Minneapolis Journal, No. 2, established in 1878.

MINNESOTA MIRROR—see Mower County Mirror.

MINNESOTA PATRIOT, Wabasha (weekly)—First issue December 25, 1858. Last issue in MHS file October 1, 1859.

MINNESOTA STAATS-ZEITUNG, St. Paul (German-language weekly, triweekly)—First issue July 24, 1858. Last issue September 4, 1877. Merged with Volksblatt to form Die Volkzeitung in September, 1877.

MINNESOTA STATESMAN, St. Peter (weekly)—First issue June 11, 1858. Last issue about April 1, 1865. Last issue in MHS file November 15, 1861.

MOWER COUNTY MIRROR, Austin (weekly)—First issue September 30, 1858. Name changed September 22, 1859, to Minnesota Mirror. Last issue in MHS file October 13, 1859. Moved soon after and became Rochester City Post. See 1859 below.

NEU-ULM PIONIER, New Ulm (German-language weekly)—First issue January 1, 1858. Last issue August 16, 1862.

NORTHFIELD JOURNAL, Northfield (weekly)—First issue about June 1, 1858. Last issue about March 1, 1861.

NORTH SHORE ADVOCATE, Buchanan (semimonthly)—First issue about January 1, 1858. Last issue about May, 1859. Ran weekly from June, 1858, to May, 1859. No MHS file.

The ROCHESTER FREE PRESS, Rochester (weekly)—First issue February 3, 1858. Last issue August 20, 1859.

ST. CLOUD DEMOCRAT, St. Cloud (weekly)—First issue August 5, 1858. Last issue September 6, 1866. Followed by St. Cloud Journal (1866–1876) and by St. Cloud Journal-Press (1876–1918). Still published in 1967 as St. Cloud Daily Times. See also St. Cloud Visiter above, 1857.

SHAKOPEE REPORTER, Shakopee (weekly)—First issue about March 25, 1858. Last issue about June 12, 1858.

STEELE COUNTY NEWS LETTER, No. 1, Owatonna (weekly)— First issue about December 4, 1858. Last issue about January 1, 1859. No MHS file. See 1860 below.

STILLWATER DEMOCRAT, No. 1, Stillwater (weekly)—First issue December 11, 1858. Last issue about February 2, 1861. Second paper of same name begun January 1, 1887.

WINONA TIMES, Winona (weekly)—First issue January 30, 1858. Last issue in MHS file July 17, 1858.

1859

CARVER COUNTY DEMOCRAT, Carver (weekly)—First issue May 10, 1859. Last issue about September 25, 1859. Last issue in MHS file August 3, 1859.

DAKOTA SENTINEL, Nininger (weekly)—First issue April 30, 1859. Last issue probably about June, 1859.

HASTINGS DEMOCRAT, No. 1, Hastings (weekly)—First issue December 3, 1859. Last issue April 27, 1861. A second paper of same name begun 1886.

HASTINGS WEEKLY LEDGER, Hastings (weekly)—First issue March 12, 1859. Last issue October 8, 1859.

LA CRESCENT BANNER, La Crescent (weekly)—First issue about March 12, 1859. Absorbed by La Crosse Democrat (Wis.) about July 23, 1859. No MHS file.

MANKATO RECORD, Mankato (weekly, semiweekly)—First issue July 5, 1859. Last issue October 25, 1879. Ran semiweekly June 3, 1860, to December 27, 1862. Consolidated with Mankato Weekly Union to become Mankato Free Press, 1879. Still published in 1967 as daily.

MEDFORD VALLEY ARGUS, No. 2?—See 1858 above.

MINNESOTA BEACON, Minneapolis and Wasioja (semimonthly)— First issue about December 1, 1859. Moved to Wasioja by August, 1860. Last issue September 15, 1860. Followed by Rural Minnesotian. See 1860 below.

MINNESOTA STATE NEWS, St. Anthony and Minneapolis (weekly)—First issue January 7, 1859. Last issue about November 4, 1863. Continued volume and numbering of Minnesota Republican. See 1854 above. Published in Minneapolis at least from May 9, 1863, to July 4, 1863. Absorbed by State Atlas (see 1859 below) about November, 1863.

MINNESOTIAN AND TIMES, St. Paul (daily)—First issue December 14, 1859. Name changed to Daily Minnesotian and Times about January 1–5, 1860. Last issue June 17, 1860, when merger dissolved and papers returned to separate publication until absorbed by St. Paul Press in 1861. See 1854 above.

OWATONNA JOURNAL, No. 1, Owatonna (weekly)—First issue about April 1, 1859. Last issue about March 1, 1860. No MHS file. Second paper of same name established in 1863.

PLAINDEALER, Minneapolis (weekly)—First issue May 14, 1859. Last issue in MHS file October 27, 1860.

ROCHESTER CITY NEWS, Rochester (weekly)—First issue November 2, 1859. Last issue about October 31, 1860.

ROCHESTER CITY POST, Rochester (weekly)—First issue November 5, 1859. Last issue January 27, 1899. Absorbed Rochester Republican, June, 1867. Successor of Mower County Mirror. See 1858 above. Title varies: Rochester City Post, November 5, 1859, to about November 20, 1865; Rochester Post from about November 20, 1865, to January 27, 1899. Merged with Record and Union to form Post and Record, 1899. Published daily from September 4, 1893, to January 28, 1899. Still published in 1967 as Rochester Post-Bulletin.

ST. ANTHONY ADVERTISER, St. Anthony (semiweekly)—First issue about February 1, 1859. Last issue soon after June 1, 1859. No MHS file.

ST. PETER ADVERTISER, St. Peter (weekly)—First issue about April, 1859. Still in existence April, 1867. No MHS file.

SAINT PETER FREE PRESS—See Minnesota Free Press above, 1857.

SCOTT COUNTY DEMOCRAT, Shakopee (weekly)—First issue February 12, 1859. Last issue August 24, 1861.

STATE ATLAS, Minneapolis (weekly)—First issue May 28, 1859. Last issue May 8, 1867. Merged May 25, 1867, with Minneapolis Tribune. Atlas issued daily between November 27, 1860, and February 20, 1861. See 1860 below.

WABASHAW WEEKLY JOURNAL, No. 2, Wabasha (weekly)—First issue October 29, 1859. Last issue December 8, 1860. Moved to Lake City and ran as Weekly Journal from about January 3, 1861, to about August 31, 1861.

WEEKLY MINNESOTIAN AND TIMES, St. Paul—First issue December 17, 1859. Last issue about June 13, 1860, when merger dissolved and papers returned to separate publication until absorbed by St. Paul Weekly Press in 1861. See 1854 above.

WINONA DAILY REPUBLICAN, Winona (daily)—First issue December 19, 1859. Last issue February 16, 1901. Merged February, 1901, with Winona Daily Herald and still published in 1967 as Winona Republican-Herald.

WINONA REVIEW, Winona (daily)—First issue November 19, 1859. Last issue December 18, 1859. Continued December 19, 1859, as Winona Daily Republican. See above.

WRIGHT COUNTY REPUBLICAN, Monticello (weekly)—First issue June 30, 1859. Last issue November 23, 1861.

1860

ANOKA REPUBLICAN, Anoka (weekly)—First issue August 25, 1860. Last issue about September 12, 1863. Suspended from May 31, 1863, to about July 8, 1863.

The DAILY JOURNAL, Wabasha (daily)—First issue April 30, 1860. Only known issue.

DAILY MORNING ATLAS, Minneapolis (daily)—First issue about November 27, 1860. Last issue February 20, 1861.

DODGE COUNTY DEMOCRAT, Mantorville (weekly?)—First issue about April 19, 1860. Last issue about February, 1861. Last issue in MHS file October 25, 1860.

FREEBORN COUNTY HERALD, Itasca (also known as Freeborn Springs), (weekly)—First issue about August 21, 1860. Last issue November, 1860. No MHS file.

FREEBORN COUNTY STANDARD, Albert Lea (weekly)—First issue May 26, 1860. Last issue April 30, 1931. Suspended July 4, 1864, to April 6, 1865. Semiweekly May 14, 1916, to March 31, 1921.

LA CRESCENT PLAIN DEALER, La Crescent (weekly)—First issue November 26, 1860. Last issue about November 11, 1862.

LE SUEUR COUNTY HERALD, Cleveland (weekly)—First issue about December 1, 1860. Last issue about July 15, 1862. No MHS file.

LITTLE GIANT, St. Peter (weekly)—No. 1 published by S. W. Smith from about August 4, 1860, to about October 15, 1860. No. 2

published by Thomas M. Perry from about September 8, 1860, to about November 10, 1860. No MHS files.

MINNESOTA COURIER, Austin (weekly)—First issue about December 15, 1860. Last issue January 6, 1864.

NEW ERA, Sauk Rapids (weekly)—First issue January 12, 1860. Last issue about June 15, 1861.

NORTHWESTERN FREE WILL BAPTIST, Wasioja (monthly)— First issue March, 1860. Last issue November, 1862.

REPRESENTATIVE, Owatonna (weekly)—First issue about December 12, 1860. Last issue in MHS file March 13, 1861.

RURAL MINNESOTIAN, Wasioja (weekly)—First issue about November 15, 1860. Last issue about August 29, 1861.

SAINT PETER TRIBUNE (weekly)—First issue February 15, 1860. Last issue January 21, 1920. Merged with St. Peter Herald, which was still published in 1967.

STAR OF THE NORTH, St. Paul (daily)—First issue July 28, 1860. Last issue November, 1860.

STEELE COUNTY NEWS LETTER, No. 2, Owatonna (weekly)— First issue about March 6, 1860. Discontinued about December 1, 1861. No MHS file. News Letter, No. 3, published January 6, 1863, to about May 1, 1863. See also 1858 above.

TAYLOR'S FALLS REPORTER (weekly)—First issue February 23, 1860. Last issue July 11, 1873. Followed by Taylors Falls Journal.

WASECA CITIZEN, Wilton (weekly)—First issue December 26, 1860. Last issue in MHS file March 27, 1861.

WASECA HOME VIEWS, Owatonna, Wilton, Faribault (weekly)— First issue March 13, 1860. Last issue about November 1, 1863. Last issue in MHS file September 26, 1861. Printed at Owatonna until March, 1861; printed at Wilton until autumn, 1861; printed at Faribault until suspension.

Notes

CHAPTER 1 — *Pioneers and Printers*

[1] The Minnesota Historical Society has a copy of volume 1, number 1, of the *Register*, which is dated April 27, 1849. Its collections also contain a photostat of a second copy of the same issue, bearing the same volume and number, which is dated April 7, 1849. The original of the latter is in the Western Reserve Historical Society, Cleveland, Ohio. The second issue of the *Register* was published in St. Paul about three months later on July 14, 1849, using a press taken to the territory by John P. Owens, who was associated with Randall. Andrew Randall, a native of Ohio, had traveled to Minnesota in 1847, but he did not return to the territory after a trip east in the winter of 1848. Instead he sold the *Register*, while still in Cincinnati, to Nathaniel McLean, who reached Minnesota the following August. Randall was murdered on a San Francisco street on July 24, 1856. On Randall and the origins of the *Register*, see Mary W. Berthel, *Horns of Thunder: The Life and Times of James M. Goodhue*, 36 (St. Paul, 1948); C. C. Andrews, ed., *History of St. Paul*, 342 (Syracuse, N.Y., 1890); J. Fletcher Williams, "The Press of Minnesota," in Minnesota Editorial Association, *Proceedings, 1870*, p. 33, 39 (St. Paul, 1871). Unless otherwise noted, all newspapers cited in this book are in the collections of the Minnesota Historical Society.

[2] The *Pioneer* continues today in the *St. Paul Pioneer Press*. In addition to the *Pioneer*, the seven weeklies which began publication from 1849 through 1853 were: *1849: Minnesota Register* (Whig), *Minnesota Chronicle* (Whig), which became the *Chronicle and Register* in August, 1849; *1850: Minnesota Democrat* (Democrat), which absorbed the *Chronicle and Register* (Whig) in February, 1851; *1851: Watab Reveille, St. Anthony Express* (Whig), *Minnesotian* (Whig); and *1853: North-Western Democrat* of St. Anthony (Democrat). See Appendix, below. The *Reveille*, which appears to have been more prank than newspaper, said on January 13, 1851, in the first of its three known issues that it was prepared to adopt whatever political label was necessary to get the contract for territorial printing. See note 21, below.

[3] On Goodhue and the organization of Minnesota Territory, here and below, see Berthel, *Horns of Thunder*, 3–24; William W. Folwell, *A History of Minnesota*, 1:246 (St. Paul, 1956). See also Douglas C. McMurtrie, "The Printing Press Moves Westward," in *Minnesota History*, 15:1–3 (March, 1934).

[4] The first two quotations are from a reminiscent article in the *Pioneer*

of April 15, 1852, reprinted in Berthel, *Horns of Thunder*, 246–260. For the locations of the various buildings occupied by the *Pioneer* in 1849–50, see Berthel, *Horns of Thunder*, 25–27.

⁵ See Berthel, *Horns of Thunder*, 248. For additional information on the first three papers, see Daniel S. B. Johnston, "Minnesota Journalism in the Territorial Period," in *Minnesota Historical Collections*, vol. 10, part 1, p. 253–256 (St. Paul, 1905).

⁶ St. Anthony and Minneapolis combined in 1872. For the beginnings of the *Express*, the *North-Western Democrat*, the *Minnesota Democrat*, and the *Minnesotian*, see Johnston, in *Collections*, vol. 10, part 1, p. 256, 260–266.

⁷ *Pioneer*, July 4, 1850.

⁸ On the Rum River, see *Express*, February 11, 1855.

⁹ Old Bets repaid the settlers' charity by helping white prisoners in the Sioux Uprising of 1862. See J. Fletcher Williams, *A History of the City of Saint Paul*, 252–254 (*Minnesota Historical Collections*, vol. 4 — St. Paul, 1876). On the first court sessions in the sentence below, see *Pioneer*, August 16, 1849, January 30, 1850.

¹⁰ The controversy between St. Paul and St. Anthony over the possibility of steamboat navigation up to the Falls of St. Anthony began in 1850. For a detailed account, see Lucile M. Kane, "Rivalry for a River: The Twin Cities and the Mississippi," in *Minnesota History*, 37:309–323 (December, 1961). The *Pioneer* so consistently belittled St. Anthony's bid for river commerce that at a celebration marking a successful second trip to Cheever's Landing (near the present site of the University of Minnesota) of the "Dr. Franklin No. 2" in 1852, a toast was drunk to "Col. Goodhue: The man who put the 'boulders' in the Mississippi above St. Paul." See *Express*, July 2, 1852.

¹¹ The St. Anthony piece, for example, was reprinted in the *Pioneer's* next issue on August 16, 1849.

¹² *Express*, June 7, 21, August, 2, 1851. The booster spirit was also evident in the newsboys' greetings published by the *Express* for New Year's in 1853 and in those of the *Daily Minnesotian* of 1856. On this little-known aspect of newspapering, see June D. Holmquist, "Minnesota Newsboys' Greetings for the New Year," in *Minnesota History*, 33:164–168 (Winter, 1952).

¹³ The poem also appeared in the *Express* of July 5, 1851. On Mrs. Sigourney, who was the author of sixty-five books of prose and poetry, the first of which was published in 1851, see James D. Hart, *The Popular Book*, 133 (New York, 1950).

¹⁴ *Pioneer*, March 13, 1850.

¹⁵ The first lodges of Odd Fellows in the territory were organized about this time. See *Chronicle*, July 12, 1849; Williams, *History of Saint Paul*, 234.

¹⁶ *Pioneer*, August 21, 1851.

¹⁷ An exception was the *Dakota Friend*, a monthly missionary paper printed in English and Dakota. The fourth paper to be established in the territory, it was printed in the *Chronicle* shop from 1850 to 1852. Its editor was the Reverend Gideon H. Pond. The Minnesota Historical Society library has a complete file. See Appendix, below, and Johnston, in *Collec-*

tions, vol. 10, part 1, p. 256. It may be of interest to note also that one of the earliest printing presses to reach Minnesota was taken in 1849 to a Chippewa mission at Cass Lake, where it was devoted to the service of religion. See McMurtrie, in *Minnesota History,* 15:20.

18 On Randall, see note 1, above. On McLean and Hughes, see Andrews, ed., *History of St. Paul,* 350, 351; on Babcock and Henniss, see Johnston, in *Collections,* vol. 10, part 1, p. 254, 291; Andrews, ed., *History of St. Paul,* 347, 351. Le Duc's brief editing career from September 30 to November 11, 1850, has been almost entirely obscured by his activities as a railroad builder, Civil War officer, and commissioner of agriculture under President Rutherford B. Hayes from 1877 to 1881. See *Chronicle and Register,* September 30, 1850; *Pioneer,* November 21, 1850; Thomas M. Newson, *Pen Pictures of St. Paul, Minnesota and Biographical Sketches of Old Settlers,* 222 (St. Paul, 1886). On Owens' long career in Minnesota newspapering, see Johnston, in *Collections,* vol. 10, part 1, p. 255, 263, 274–276, 329; Newson, *Pen Pictures,* 116; Andrews, ed., *History of St. Paul,* 353.

19 On Robertson, see Warren Upham and Rose B. Dunlap, comps., *Minnesota Biographies, 1655–1912,* 648 (*Minnesota Historical Collections,* vol. 14 — St. Paul, 1912); Johnston, in *Collections,* vol. 10, part 1, p. 256, 258. On Terry and Moore, see Andrews, ed., *History of St. Paul,* 352; Newson, *Pen Pictures,* 168; Johnston, vol. 10, part 1, p. 263, 266, 520. On Prescott, see George R. Metcalf, ed., *The Golden Jubilee: A Chronicle of the Semi-Centennial Observance of the Founding of the [Masonic] Grand Lodge of . . . Minnesota,* 50 (St. Paul, 1903); Upham and Dunlap, *Minnesota Biographies,* 615; Newson, *Pen Pictures,* 394. Newson described Prescott as "a journalist of a great deal of ability."

20 Tyler's association with the paper was short-lived — May 31 to August 2, 1851. On the latter date the paper bore the names of "Woodbury & Hollister" as publishers and proprietors. Two months later on October 1, it listed "H. & J. P. Woodbury, Editors and Proprietors." Atwater, too, put money into the venture, seemingly from its beginning. See Atwater, *History of the City of Minneapolis,* 355, 359 (New York, 1893). Atwater assumed full editorial control of the paper on August 4, 1855. Two years later he sold a third interest to Charles H. Slocum, and in 1857 or 1859 another third to Daniel S. B. Johnston. When the paper suspended in 1861, Johnston was the sole proprietor. See Marion D. Shutter, ed., *History of Minneapolis,* 1:436 (Chicago and Minneapolis, 1923); Johnston, in *Collections,* vol. 10, part 1, p. 260.

21 On Goodhue's death, see page 39, below. On Owens, see note 18, above. The most fleeting and obscure editor of all was "J. W. Chaskarak" of the *Watab Reveille,* a paper said to have been edited by J. W. Vincent and printed and circulated by Henniss from the office of the *Chronicle and Register.* See *Pioneer,* February 6, 1851; Johnston, in *Collections,* vol. 10, part 1, p. 259. A denial that Owens had anything to do with the *Reveille* appears in the *Daily Minnesotian,* September 27, 1854.

22 The first engraver of whom a record has been found was J. H. Felch, who founded his business in St. Paul in August, 1858. See Marjorie Kreidberg, *Fragments of Early Printing,* 24 (St. Paul, 1958). Before 1858 the

rare appearances of cuts were largely limited to ads which ran for a year at a time. Such engravings were probably sent by eastern advertisers or were "stock cuts" purchased by a printer when he bought his type.

23 *Pioneer*, May 29, June 5, November 20, 1851.

24 For detailed information on advertising in St. Paul and St. Anthony newspapers from 1849 to 1851, see Theodore C. Blegen, "Minnesota Pioneer Life as Revealed in Newspaper Advertisements," in *Minnesota History*, 7: 99–121 (June, 1926). Examples of territorial ads are reproduced in the article.

25 On the Washington hand press, see Robert Hoe, *A Short History of the Printing Press*, 9–11 (New York, 1902); J. Luther Ringwalt, *American Encyclopaedia of Printing*, 490 (Philadelphia, 1871); Kreidberg, *Fragments of Early Printing*, 7. The linotype machine was unknown at this time. It was not patented in the United States until 1885. On the *Pioneer's* subscription list, see the issue of April 13, 1854.

26 See McMurtrie, in *Minnesota History*, 15:1–25. On Goodhue's presses and paper, see Berthel, *Horns of Thunder*, 26n, 46; *Pioneer*, August 30, November 8, 1849.

27 Charles G. Ames, "Reminiscences of an Old-Time Editor," in Minnesota Editors and Publishers Association, *Proceedings*, 1887, p. 26 (St. Paul, 1888); Kreidberg, *Fragments of Early Printing*, 11–14; Lucile M. Kane, *The Waterfall That Built a City: The Falls of St. Anthony in Minneapolis*, 60 (St. Paul, 1966).

The first printing press "manufactured" in Minnesota was apparently a wooden one built by soldiers at Fort Ripley. Using wooden type whittled by hand with a pocketknife, the soldiers issued in 1854 a paper called the *Bomb Shell*. See *Minnesota Democrat*, August 23, 1854. Two copies of the *Bomb Shell* are in the collections of the Minnesota Historical Society — a prospectus, dated July 26, and the first number, issued August 16, 1854.

28 The three papers at the time were the *Pioneer*, the *Minnesotian*, and the *Minnesota Democrat*. The latter had absorbed the *Chronicle and Register* on February 10, 1851. On the importance of job printing in sustaining the early frontier papers, see Kreidberg, *Fragments of Early Printing*, 20.

29 Goodhue to Henry H. Sibley, February 10, 1851, in the Sibley Papers owned by the Minnesota Historical Society; *Pioneer*, June 10, 1852. Fifty-five printers are listed in the *St. Paul City Directory* of 1858–59.

30 *Pioneer*, November 20, 1851.

31 *Pioneer*, August 23, 1849.

32 The quotations appear respectively in the *Pioneer* of February 27 and July 18, 1850. For additional information on the content of the papers, see Richard B. Eide, "Minnesota Pioneer Life as Reflected in the Press," in *Minnesota History*, 12:391–403 (December, 1931) which draws its examples from the territorial press; Willoughby M. Babcock, "Smoke Signals to Telephone," in Lawrence M. Brings, ed., *Minnesota Heritage: A Panoramic Narrative of the Historical Development of the North Star State*, 307 (Minneapolis, 1960).

33 On the incorporation, see Williams, *History of Saint Paul*, 186–188, 241, 349; Minnesota, *Laws*, 1849, p. 99.

34 A notable exception was the publication of Judge David Cooper's

charge to the grand jury of the third district court at Mendota, which ran for four columns in the *Chronicle and Register* of September 1, 1851.

[35] For additional information on the first district court, see Aaron Goodrich, "Early Courts of Minnesota," in *Minnesota Historical Collections,* 1:56 (St. Paul, 1902). The docket, covering the six-day term in 1849, is preserved in the office of the clerk of district court, Washington County Courthouse, Stillwater.

CHAPTER 2 — *Pioneers and Partisans*

[1] For detailed information on the Sibley-Rice rivalry and politics in Minnesota Territory, see Erling Jorstad, "Personal Politics in the Origin of Minnesota's Democratic Party," in *Minnesota History,* 36:259–271 (September, 1959); John C. Haugland, "Alexander Ramsey and the Birth of Party Politics in Minnesota," in *Minnesota History,* 39:37–48 (Summer, 1964).

[2] Berthel, *Horns of Thunder,* 16, 24. The first contest for delegate preceded the organization of Minnesota Territory. See Folwell, *Minnesota,* 1:236–241.

[3] See Folwell, *Minnesota,* 1:247, 253; United States, *Statutes at Large,* 9:416, 787. Gideon H. Pond to Sibley, August [September ?] 6, 1849; James Goodhue to Sibley, September 30, 1849; Isaac Goodhue to Sibley, August 27, 1849; Henry Lambert to Sibley, January 26, 1850 — all in the Sibley Papers. Isaac's name was listed with his brother's on the *Pioneer* masthead from October 11, 1849, to October 31, 1850. After James died in 1852, Isaac assisted his brother's widow with the paper, but his name did not again appear on the masthead. Indeed, James M. Goodhue's name remained there for a full year after his death. Not until September 1, 1853, did the *Pioneer* carry the name of Joseph R. Brown as publisher, although he had become its editor in February, 1853. See *Pioneer,* February 2, 1854.

[4] On the convention, see Jorstad, in *Minnesota History,* 36:264. On Sibley's re-election in 1849, see Folwell, *Minnesota,* 1:252. Sibley received all of the 682 votes cast. The quotation is from Goodhue to Sibley, November 26, 1849, Sibley Papers.

[5] Goodhue to Sibley, November 26, December 11, 1849, January 22, 1850, Sibley Papers; *Pioneer,* November 8, 1849. McLean and Owens presented bills for printing totaling $2,542, which amount was later reduced to $2,050. See Smith to Elisha Whittlesey, June 27, 29, 1850, in Minnesota Territory, Secretary's Letter Book, p. 8, in the Minnesota State Archives, St. Paul. For Goodhue's total bill, see note 13, below.

[6] Goodhue to Sibley, November 26, December 11, 1849, Sibley Papers.

[7] Goodhue to Sibley, February 19, 1850; James S. Norris to Sibley, February 25, 1850 — Sibley Papers.

[8] Brown to Sibley, December 21, 1849; John H. Stevens to Sibley, January 6, 1850 [1851] — Sibley Papers.

[9] Minnesota Territory, *Statutes, 1849–1858,* 533, 543, 734, 759, 760; Cyrus Aldrich *v.* The Press Printing Company (1864), in 9 *Minnesota* 131 (Gil. 123). It is interesting to note that only one suit for slander came before the

territorial supreme court. In it that body upheld a finding that an accusation of stealing was slanderous and ruled that "a verdict of $212.50 was not excessive." See Pascal St. Martin v. Stephen Desnoyer, in 1 *Minnesota* 156 (Gil. 131).

10 Potts to Sibley, January 15, 1850; Brown to Sibley, February 4, 1850; Steele to Sibley, March 12, 1850; Goodhue to Sibley, February 5, 19, March 10, 18, June 15, 1850 — all in Sibley Papers.

11 *Pioneer,* August 8, 15, 1850; "Address of Henry H. Sibley to the People of Minnesota Territory," July 29, 1850, Sibley Papers; Folwell, *Minnesota,* 1:370; Jorstad, in *Minnesota History,* 36:266–270; *Chronicle and Register,* August 2, 1850.

12 Although Olmsted presumably owned the paper, it was the name of Lorenzo A. Babcock (the territorial attorney general who owed his appointment to Ramsey) that replaced those of McLean and Owens in the masthead on August 12, 1850. See *Pioneer,* December 5, 1850; Owens' statement in the *Minnesotian,* April 2, 1853. See also Folwell, *Minnesota,* 1:370–372; Jorstad, in *Minnesota History,* 36:270; Haugland, in *Minnesota History,* 39:45.

13 Goodhue to Sibley, July 30, 1850; Brown in a postscript to a letter from Fred B. Sibley to Sibley, August 11, 1850 — Sibley Papers. For the vote, see *Pioneer,* October 16, 1850. As late as June 29, 1850, Goodhue had been paid only $1,300, and his total bill of $5,642.06 had been reduced to $3,964.16 by the federal comptroller of the treasury on the grounds that his rates were more than twice those of Washington printers. See Smith to Whittlesey, June 27, 29, 1850, in Minnesota Territory, Secretary's Letter Book, p. 10, 14.

14 Folwell, *Minnesota,* 1:371; Fred Sibley to Sibley, September 15, 1850; Goodhue to Sibley, September 14, 1850; Brown to Sibley, September 4, 1850 — Sibley Papers.

15 Potts to Sibley, January 21, 1851; Brown to Sibley, December 2, 1850 — Sibley Papers.

16 Brown to Sibley, December 2, 1850, Sibley Papers.

17 See Folwell, *Minnesota,* 1:260; Berthel, *Horns of Thunder,* 60, 71; *Pioneer,* February 13, 1851; Alexander Ramsey Diary, January 14, 1851, Allen Pierse to Ramsey, April 23, 1851, Ramsey Papers; Potts to Sibley, January 14, 1851, Goodhue to Sibley (quote), February 6, 1851, Sibley Papers; H. L. Tilden to John H. Stevens, March 9, 1851, D. B. Loomis to Stevens, March 10, 1851, Stevens Papers — all in the collections of the Minnesota Historical Society.

18 See Robert C. Voight, "Aaron Goodrich: Stormy Petrel of the Territorial Bench," in *Minnesota History,* 39:141–152 (Winter, 1964).

19 This piece appeared in the *Pioneer* of January 16, 1851, which according to Berthel, *Horns of Thunder,* 66, hit the streets on January 14, two days early. Berthel quotes Goodhue's diatribe on pages 63–66.

20 In that day the word "groceries" was used to refer to barrooms as well as to intoxicating liquors.

21 Berthel, *Horns of Thunder,* 66–70; *Chronicle and Register,* January 20, 21, 1851; *Pioneer,* January 23, February 6, 13, 1851; Potts to Sibley, January 21, 1851, Brown to Sibley, January 24, 1851 — Sibley Papers.

22 Potts to Sibley, January 21, 1851, Sibley Papers.

23 Goodrich was replaced as territorial chief justice in October, 1851, by

Jerome Fuller rather than by Cooper. The latter served as associate justice until 1853.

24 Goodhue to Sibley, February 10, 1851, Sibley Papers. The Ramsey letter quoted below is also in the Sibley Papers.

25 Minnesota Territory, Secretary's Ledger, p. 17, in Minnesota State Archives; Berthel, *Horns of Thunder*, 71, 202, 259.

26 *Pioneer*, September 2, 1852; *Minnesota Democrat*, September 1, 1852; *Express*, September 3, 1852.

27 See note 3, above; Folwell, *Minnesota*, 1:231–237, 403; *Pioneer*, March 16, October 4, 1854. Brown also founded and owned the *Henderson Democrat*, which began publication on April 3, 1856. See Johnson, in *Collections*, vol. 10, part 1, p. 292.

28 See p. 15, above; Newson, *Pen Pictures*, 217; Upham and Dunlap, comps., *Minnesota Biographies*, 648; Charles E. Flandrau, *Encyclopedia of Biography of Minnesota*, 431 (Chicago, 1900); William E. Kelley, "Reminiscences of Persons and Events in the Early Days of the Minnesota Historical Society," in *Minnesota Historical Collections*, 8:420 (St. Paul, 1898); "Obituaries," in *Collections*, 8:530; Johnston, in *Collections*, vol. 10, part 1, p. 258. A typewritten copy of Robertson's arguments before the Ohio convention on May 22, 1850, is in the Robertson Papers of the Minnesota Historical Society. Robertson edited the *Democrat* until June 29, 1853, when David Olmsted took over the paper.

29 The celebration on June 26 is described in *Minnesota Democrat*, June 30, 1852; *Pioneer*, July 1, 1852; *Minnesotian*, July 3, 1852. For a discussion of the complicated problems of the treaties of 1851 touched on here and below, see Lucile M. Kane, "The Sioux Treaties and the Traders," in *Minnesota History*, 32:65–80 (June, 1951).

30 *Minnesotian*, December 18, 1852–February 19, 1853; *Express*, December 24, 31, 1852, January 28, 1853; *Pioneer*, February 3, 17, 1853.

31 *Minnesota Democrat*, December 22, 1852–May 4, 1853; *Minnesotian*, February 5, 1853. See also note 34, below.

32 Dodge to Sibley, March 31, April 1, 1853, Sibley Papers. In a series of satirical "correspondence," the *Pioneer* described Robertson's "triumphal progress" to the nation's capital, noting that he arrived in Washington with the president-elect in his party. "The inaugural address for the President has been written by Robertson. . . . It is not yet decided whether the President or the Col. will deliver it," Brown remarked in the *Pioneer* of March 3, 1853.

33 Folwell, *Minnesota*, 1:373, 379; Robertson to Ramsey, and Ramsey to Robertson, January 25, 1854 — Ramsey Papers.

34 For a detailed account of the investigation, see Folwell, *Minnesota*, 1:462–470.

CHAPTER 3 — *The Dailies Take Over*

1 Eastman to Sibley, February 3, 1854, Sibley Papers. Six days later Eastman again wrote Sibley on Goodrich's behalf, revealing that Mrs. Goodrich "is one of the best of women and a sister to one of my brother's wives."

2 The *Daily Free Press* began publication on October 5, 1855; the last issue in the Minnesota Historical Society's file is dated April 5, 1856. The *Pioneer* and the *Democrat* combined in 1855, and the *Minnesotian* and the *Times* merged for a short time in 1859. See pages 114–115, below.

3 The *Falls Evening News* ceased publication on April 13, 1861, although it continued to issue legal advertisements in the form of a single sheet until May 18, 1861. On Clark and on Croffut, who went on to a distinguished newspaper career in New York and Washington, D.C., see Johnston, in *Collections,* vol. 10, part 1, p. 336–339; and Johnston, "Minnesota Journalism from 1858 to 1865," in *Collections,* 12:193 (St. Paul, 1908). The *Winona Republican* and other weeklies begun in this period are more fully discussed in Chapter 4, below. On the *Winona Daily Review,* see *Winona Daily News,* November 19, 1955, p. 3A. The first issue of the *Review* appeared on November 19, 1859.

4 *Daily Times,* December 6, 7, 8, 12, 1855. On the spreading of newspapers, see Edwin H. Ford, "Southern Minnesota Pioneer Journalism: A Study of Four Newspapers of the 1850's," in *Minnesota History,* 27:1–10 (March, 1946). All newspapers quoted and cited in this chapter are daily editions unless otherwise specified.

5 On Olmsted, see Williams, *History of Saint Paul,* 349; Folwell, *Minnesota,* 1:276. Emerson edited the weekly and daily *Democrat* from September, 1854, to August, 1855; Brown from August to October 31, 1855, when the paper merged with the *Pioneer.*

6 Newson, *Pen Pictures,* 116.

7 See Foster to Ramsey, June 1, July 19, 1854; Newson to Ramsey, October 15, 1856, January 24, March 6, November 2, 1857 — all in Ramsey Papers. Notes for which Newson asked Ramsey's endorsement were in the amounts of $200, $1,000, $500, and $273.27. On Foster and Newson, see Johnston, in *Collections,* vol. 10, part 1, p. 264, 265 (quote), 268, 270; Andrews, ed., *History of St. Paul,* 355. Foster was to remain associated with the *Minnesotian* until 1861. After the Civil War he returned to the state to edit, at various times, the *Minneapolis Chronicle* and the *St. Paul Dispatch* and to found the *Duluth Minnesotian* on April 24, 1869. See p. 129, below.

For the beginnings of the Republican party, see Eugene V. Smalley, *A History of the Republican Party,* 20, 148–154, 324 (St. Paul, 1896); "The Genesis of the Republican Party," in *Minnesota History,* 2:24–30 (February, 1917). The *Times* was not the first Republican paper in the territory. That distinction belongs to the *Minnesota Republican,* a weekly which appeared in St. Anthony on October 5, 1854. See Chapter 4, below.

8 On steam presses of the period, see Hoe, *Short History of the Printing Press,* 10–20. The *Pioneer* of December 16, 1854, announced that it was "PRINTED BY STEAM," and by 1858 the *Pioneer and Democrat* boasted that it had four steam presses. See Kreidberg, *Fragments of Early Printing,* broadside opposite p. 5.

9 *Democrat,* June 14, 1854.

10 Sibley to Goodrich, July 21, 1854, in Sibley Letter Books, Sibley Papers.

11 Parker's column first appeared in the *Times* of December 2, 1854. Parker also established a weekly newspaper, the *St. Paul Financial & Real Estate Advertiser,* in 1854. Its editor was Joseph A. Wheelock, who was

later to gain prominence as a long-time editor of the *St. Paul Pioneer Press.*
The *Advertiser* was independent in politics and much of its circulation was
in the East. In 1856 its name was lengthened to *St. Paul Financial, Real
Estate and Railroad Advertiser,* and in 1858 it was acquired by the *Pioneer
and Democrat.* See Johnston, in *Collections,* vol. 10, part 1, p. 272.

[12] See *Daily Minnesotian,* April 5, 21, 1858 (quotes); *Weekly Minnesotian,*
April 3, 20, 1858. The first unions were not very stable. According to the
Chronicle and Register of September 22, 1849, journeymen printers of St.
Paul had "organized a Typographical Association, and established a bill
of prices." Apparently the first effort did not take, and the group reorganized
in 1856. During the Civil War, the charters of both locals were dropped by
the national group. The St. Paul chapter was again reorganized in 1870
and achieved stability in 1882. See George B. Engberg, "The Rise of Organized Labor in Minnesota," in *Minnesota History,* 21:375-378, 385 (December, 1940).

[13] *Times,* March 16, 1855.

[14] On Goodrich, see Johnston, in *Collections,* vol. 10, part 1, p. 268.
Letters cited here and below are in the Sibley Papers.

[15] Notice of the dissolution of the partnership appears in the *Pioneer,*
October 4, 1854. See also *Times,* October 5, 1854.

[16] On this election, see Folwell, *Minnesota,* 1:375-377.

[17] The letter made it clear that the man to whom Goodrich referred was
Frederick Somers, who was introduced to readers of the *Pioneer* on November 1, 1855.

[18] *Pioneer,* August 2, 6, 20, 1855. The *Times* and *Minnesotian,* both of
which supported Marshall, were equally vehement in their denunciations
of Rice. See, for example, *Times,* August 2, September 6, 8, October 9, 1855;
Minnesotian, August 7, 14, 25, September 7, 11, 19, 1855.

[19] *Times,* February 2, 1857; *Pioneer,* February 3, 1857; Eastman to Sibley,
October 19, 1855, Sibley Papers. Goodrich signed a chattel mortgage for
$6,500 on the *Pioneer's* equipment in favor of Sibley on September 28, 1855.
The satisfaction of the mortgage, dated July 22, 1859, is in the Sibley Papers.
Goodrich continued to edit the *Pioneer* until 1865. For an assessment of his
career, see Richard B. Eide, *The Influence of Editorship and Other Forces on
the Growth of the St. Paul Pioneer-Press, 1849–1909,* 18–28 ([Minneapolis],
1939).

[20] Smalley, *History of the Republican Party,* 153.

[21] On the later development of this movement and newspaper reaction
to it, see Frank Klement, "The Abolition Movement in Minnesota," in
Minnesota History, 32:15-33 (March, 1951).

[22] On Douglas' visit, see *Pioneer and Democrat,* August 14–16, 18, 19, 25,
1857. On the Lecompton constitution, see the issues of March 26, April 6,
1858.

[23] *Pioneer and Democrat,* February 23, 24, 1857; *Minnesotian,* February 24, 1857; *Times,* February 14, 20, 1857. For a more detailed account
of the capital removal attempt, see Folwell, *Minnesota,* 1:382-387.

[24] For fuller discussions of the complex events of the constitutional convention touched on here and below, see Folwell, *Minnesota,* 1:394-421;

William Anderson, "Minnesota Frames a Constitution," in *Minnesota History*, 36:1–12 (March, 1958). In addition to Foster, printers and editors who were members of the constitutional convention included L. A. Babcock, Joseph R. Brown, H. W. Holley, William F. Russell, N. B. Robbins, Jr., and John Q. A. Ward.

25 *Minnesotian*, August 1, 1857; *Pioneer and Democrat*, August 9, 1857.

26 *Pioneer and Democrat*, July 14, 26, August 25, 1857; *Minnesotian*, August 7, 1857.

27 On Congressional difficulties over Minnesota's admission, see Folwell, *Minnesota*, 2:9–18; *Pioneer and Democrat*, April 1–6, 8, 10, 13, 14, 16, 27 (quote), 1858; *Minnesotian*, April 28, 1858.

28 For other newspaper comment on the event, see Bertha L. Heilbron, "Minnesota Statehood Editorials," in *Minnesota History*, 14:173–191 (June, 1933).

CHAPTER 4 – *The Weeklies Disperse*

1 Between 1849 and 1858 land offices were located at various periods in Stillwater, Sauk Rapids, Brownsville, Minneapolis, Winona, Red Wing, Chatfield, Forest City, Henderson, Faribault, St. Peter, St. Cloud, Cambridge, and Buchanan. At least twelve of these towns also had newspapers at the time. See J. W. Bond, *Minnesota and Its Resources*, 388–393 (Chicago, 1856); Minnesota Commissioner of Statistics, *Annual Report, 1860*, 163–167 (Hartford, Conn., 1860).

Although material on the beginnings of specific weekly papers can be found in many histories of Minnesota counties, relatively few general studies have been made of weeklies in the territorial period. The most useful of these, not cited elsewhere in this chapter, are: Richard B. Eide, "Minnesota Journalism, 1849–55" (University of Iowa, master's thesis, 1930); Eide, in *Minnesota History*, 12:391–403; Herman Roe, "The Frontier Press in Minnesota," in *Minnesota History*, 14:393–410 (December, 1933). Irene B. Taeuber, "Changes in the Content and Presentation of Reading Material in Minnesota Weekly Newspapers, 1860–1929" (University of Minnesota, Ph.D. thesis, 1931) touches on the territorial period, as does the digest of her thesis, "Weekly Newspapers in Pioneer Minnesota," in *Minnesota History*, 14:411–415 (December, 1933). See also "The Frontier Press: Two Communications," in *Minnesota History*, 15:86–89 (March, 1934), which corrects Johnston's material on the *Wabasha County Herald-Standard* and the *Mankato Independent* as presented in *Collections*, vol. 10, part 1.

2 Strictly speaking, the first foreign-language newspaper in Minnesota was Gideon Pond's missionary journal, the *Dakota Friend*. See Chapter 1, note 17, above.

3 On Orthwein, see Andrews, ed., *History of St. Paul*, 369. *Die Minnesota Deutsche Zeitung*, which began publication on November 19, 1855 (according to the *Daily Minnesotian* of November 20, 1855) became the *Minnesota Staatszeitung* in 1858. On these papers and the men associated with them, see Johnston, in *Collections*, vol. 10, part 1, p. 286–289; Lynwood G. Downs, "The Writings of Albert Wolff," in *Minnesota History*, 27:327–329 (Decem-

ber, 1946); Hildegard B. Johnson, "The Election of 1860 and the Germans in Minnesota," in *Minnesota History*, 28:22 (March, 1947).

Although no issues have been found and nothing is known of it, a fifth German paper, *Pfälzische Volkszeitung*, may have been started in the territory in 1856. See Karl J. R. Arndt and May E. Olson, *German-American Newspapers and Periodicals, 1732–1955,* 230 (Heidelberg, Ger., 1961).

4 Norelius was later the editor and one of the three proprietors of the Swedish language weekly, *Skaffaren*, founded in Red Wing in 1877 and removed to St. Paul in 1879. A file of this paper may be found in the Denkman Library, Augustana College, Rock Island, Illinois. Norelius was also the founder of a private school at Red Wing which was later moved to St. Peter and became Gustavus Adolphus College. See George E. Warner and Charles M. Foote, eds., *History of Ramsey County and the City of St. Paul,* 361 (Minneapolis, 1881); Upham and Dunlap, comps., *Minnesota Biographies,* 552.

5 There is some confusion over the first issue of *Folkets Röst*. The *Daily Pioneer and Democrat* of September 29, 1857, announced that 5,000 copies of the Norwegian paper were to be printed, and *Emigranten* (Madison, Wis.), November 18, 1857, refers to such a paper, so perhaps at least one issue was published about October, 1857. Volume 1, number 1, in the files of the Minnesota Historical Society, however, is dated July 10, 1858. On Nelson, see Minnesota Editorial Association, *Proceedings*, 1870, p. 44. A complete file of the *Neu-Ulm Pionier* may be found in the collections of the Brown County Historical Society, New Ulm.

6 Ames, in Minnesota Editors and Publishers Association, *Proceedings,* 1887, p. 25. Ames returned to New England in 1859, changed his religious affiliation, and later became well known as a Unitarian minister. See Allen Johnson, ed., *Dictionary of American Biography,* 1:240 (New York, 1928).

7 Ames, in Minnesota Editors and Publishers, *Proceedings,* 1887, p. 26.

8 *Falls Evening News*, November 5, 1859; *Minnesota State News*, January 7, 1859; *State Atlas*, March 4, 1863.

9 For the tangled lineage of the *Minneapolis Tribune*, see Chapter 6, below; Johnston, in *Collections*, vol. 10, part 1, p. 266, 271, 337, 347, and 12:192–194, 198–200; Edwin Emery, "The Mass Media Mature," in Brings, ed., *Minnesota Heritage*, 318–320; *North-Western Democrat*, July 12, 1856. The *Chronicle* began as a weekly on June 9, 1866, and became a daily the following September 20.

10 See Johnston, in *Collections*, 12:184. The quotations below are from the *Mantorville Express*, June 12, 1858. Similar accounts of the meeting were published in the *Red Wing Republican*, June 11, 1858, and the *Chatfield Democrat*, June 12, 1858.

11 Johnston, in *Collections*, 12:184. A second editorial convention, which also proved to be an abortive effort at permanent organization, was held at Mankato on June 4, 1862. Not until February, 1867, did a third convention succeed in launching the permanent organization which changed its name to the Minnesota Newspaper Association in 1959. See Minnesota Editor's and Publisher's Association, *Proceedings*, 1867 (St. Paul, 1867).

12 These sums of money did not materialize. Rohr, who was a musician, did not move to Minnesota until 1859, and then he settled in St. Paul. See

Dudley S. Brainard, "Nininger, A Boom Town of the Fifties," in *Minnesota History*, 13:131, 132 (June, 1932); Donnelly to George O. Robertson, October 4, 10, 1856; to MacDonald, December 11, 1856 — Donnelly Papers, vol. 72, in the Minnesota Historical Society.

13 See Brainard, in *Minnesota History*, 13:136. Only volume 1, number 1, of the *Dakota Sentinel*, dated April 30, 1859, is in the Minnesota Historical Society's collections. For information on Donnelly's later career and his rise to national prominence, see Martin Ridge, *Ignatius Donnelly: The Portrait of a Politician* (Chicago, 1962).

14 On the founding of these papers, see Margaret Snyder, *The Chosen Valley: The Story of a Pioneer Town*, 52 (New York, 1948). The *Democrat* began publication in October, 1856, and apparently suspended before August, 1857. Copies of the second *Democrat* in the Minnesota Historical Society's collection begin on September 11, 1857, with volume 1, number 1, of the new series. For additional information on the paper's content, see Ford, in *Minnesota History*, 27:1–20.

15 *Chatfield Democrat*, September 30, 1857.

16 On King, Foster, Dye and Company, see Franklyn Curtiss-Wedge, *A History of Winona County*, 246 (Chicago, 1913). On Whiting, see *Winona Daily News*, November 19, 1955, 9A; Mrs. W. J. Arnold, *The Poets and Poetry of Minnesota*, 291–297 (Chicago, 1864); Curtiss-Wedge, *History of Winona County*, 245.

17 Ford, in *Minnesota History*, 27:12.

18 Whiting's name disappeared from the paper after the issue of March 25, 1856. He was succeeded for a brief interim by Edwin C. Bearce. Whiting returned to the *Argus* as assistant editor until it suspended publication in 1857. During the Civil War, he commanded a ship captured by the Confederacy. He died a suicide in a New York sailors' home in 1882. See Johnston, in *Collections*, vol. 10, part 1, p. 274; *Winona Daily News*, November 19, 1955, 2A, 11A.

19 On the changes in ownership, see Curtiss-Wedge, *History of Winona County*, 246. On Sinclair, see H. P. Hall, "History of the Minnesota Editors and Publishers Association," 69, 73, in the Association's *Proceedings*, 1896, (St. Paul, 1896).

20 *St. Cloud Visiter*, May 13, 1858.

21 For background on Mrs. Swisshelm here and below, see Arthur J. Larsen, *Crusader and Feminist: Letters of Jane Grey Swisshelm 1858–1865*, 1–32 (St. Paul, 1934).

22 See Mrs. Swisshelm's autobiography, *Half a Century*, 37 (Chicago, 1880).

23 *Visiter*, December 24, 1857, January 14, February 18, June 17, July 22, 1858.

24 Larsen, *Crusader and Feminist*, 11.

25 *Visiter*, March 4, 1858.

26 Quotations here and below are from the *Visiter*, May 13, 1858.

27 *Daily Pioneer and Democrat*, April 2, 1858. On April 1, 1858, one issue of the *St. Cloud Visiter* appeared in the form of a single sheet printed on one side only, although regular publication was not resumed until May.

28 Mrs. Swisshelm's last issue of the *Democrat* appeared on June 4, 1863; Mitchell's first number was published on June 11, 1863.

CHAPTER 5 — *Conflict: From Railroads to Prize Ring*

[1] For a fuller discussion of these two articles, see George S. Hage, "The Railroad: Carrier of a Common Ideology," in *Minnesota History*, 38:45–52 (June, 1962).

[2] See William J. Petersen, "The Rock Island Railroad Excursion of 1854," in *Minnesota History*, 15:405–420 (December, 1934).

[3] Neill's talk was printed in the *Daily Minnesotian*, June 14, 1854. All quotations and citations in this chapter are from the daily editions of the various papers.

[4] On the first railroad train to operate in Minnesota, see "The 'William Crooks,'" in Sue E. Holbert and June D. Holmquist, *A History Tour of 50 Twin City Landmarks*, 7 (*Minnesota Historic Sites Pamphlet Series No. 2* — St. Paul, 1966).

[5] For a thorough discussion of this grant and the events which followed, see Folwell, *Minnesota*, 1:329–350. For the chartering of the Minnesota and North Western, see Minnesota, *Laws*, 1854, p. 121.

[6] On Emerson, see Newson, *Pen Pictures*, 429. For examples of letters from Congressmen, see issues of the *Democrat* and *Minnesotian* for September 26–28, 1854.

[7] *Times*, November 28, December 15, 1854; *Pioneer*, December 2, 1854; *Minnesotian*, December 4, 1854; *Democrat*, December 13, 1854. For the documents in the case, see 33 Congress, 2 session, *House Executive Documents*, no. 35 (serial 783). On Warren's dismissal, see Folwell, *Minnesota*, 1:342.

[8] *Times*, February 1, 9, 10, 17 (quote), 1855; *Minnesotian*, January 30, February 10, 17, 1855.

[9] *Minnesotian*, March 21, 1855.

[10] On the election, see Chapter 3, above.

[11] *Pioneer and Democrat*, January 28, 1857; United States, *Statutes at Large*, 11:195–197. On the proposed celebration, see *Minnesotian*, April 7, 8, 14, 1857; *Times*, April 10, 1857.

[12] For the subsequent history of the Minnesota and North Western, see Folwell, *Minnesota*, 1:349; *Pioneer and Democrat*, January 28, March 2, June 6–16, 1857, January 6, 1859; *Minnesotian*, July 20, August 3, 1858; *Times*, April 27, 1857, July 20, 1858. On the railroad act, see Minnesota, *Laws*, 1857 (extra session) 1–26; Folwell, *Minnesota*, 2:40–43 (St. Paul, 1961).

[13] *Minnesotian*, May 21, 1857; *Pioneer and Democrat*, May 21, 1857; *Times*, May 12, 1857.

[14] *Minnesotian*, February 15, 25, 1858. For a thorough discussion of the Five Million Dollar Loan, see Folwell, *Minnesota*, 2:44–58.

[15] The series of articles from the *Pioneer and Democrat* was also issued by the paper as a thirty-two-page pamphlet entitled *An Act Proposing a Loan of State Credit to the Land Grant Railroad Companies* (St. Paul, 1858). A copy of the law appears in the pamphlet as well as in *General Laws*, 1858, p. 9–13. For the expression "law of railroad progress," see *Pioneer and Democrat*, February 19, 1859.

[16] Neither extra is dated, but it is apparent that they appeared in April, 1858, just before the vote on the loan amendment. The *Minnesotian's* extra

listed the following papers as having taken no stand on the matter: *St. Cloud Visiter, Henderson Democrat, Southern Minnesota Herald* (Brownsville), *Glencoe Register, St. Peter Free Press,* and *Monticello Times.* The last two papers, however, had earlier been reported as against the loan by the *Minnesotian* of March 27, 30, 1858.

[17] For the vote, see Folwell, *Minnesota,* 2:48. The quotation appears in the *Minnesotian,* April 16, 1858.

[18] *Times,* March 3, 1859; *Pioneer and Democrat,* March 3, 1859.

[19] *Minnesotian,* March 9, 1859. Files of the *Minnesotian* for March, 1859, are broken; from March to December, 1859, they are missing entirely, so the long-range effects of the pressure cannot be determined.

[20] On the effects of the panic, see Sydney A. Patchin, "The Development of Banking in Minnesota," in *Minnesota History Bulletin,* 2:135–140 (August, 1917).

[21] See also *Times,* April 16–20, 27, May 4, 1857; *Minnesotian,* April 16–21, 1857; *Pioneer and Democrat,* March 25, April 17–21, 24, 28, 30, 1857.

[22] Volume 1, number 1, of the *Minnesotian and Times* is missing from the Minnesota Historical Society's files, so posterity is deprived of a salutatory that must have been a model of double talk. The two papers resumed separate publication on June 17, 1860.

[23] An earlier but less noteworthy innovation of the *Pioneer and Democrat* had been the publication of the first Sunday edition on April 5, 1857. It was less noteworthy because it varied little from the weekday papers, although Goodrich, in making the change, promised subscribers a "less secular" edition on Sunday. The Sunday paper replaced Monday's and was justified by Goodrich on the grounds that the twelve employees of the plant did not want to work on Sunday to put out the Monday edition. (". . . we especially ask the countenance of the moral and religious portion of [the] community in this attempt to rid our office of the shame and immorality of Sunday labor." *Pioneer and Democrat,* April 2, 1857.) The *Times* issued a Sunday edition in February, 1858, causing the *Minnesotian* of February 16, 1858, to comment: "Our piety has not yet reached the high point to which our contemporaries have attained."

[24] Mitchell V. Charnley, *Reporting,* 211 (New York, 1966).

[25] For a detailed account of the case, see Walter N. Trenerry, *Murder in Minnesota: A Collection of True Cases,* 25–41, 219 (St. Paul, 1962).

[26] The *Minnesotian and Times* of March 24, 1860, devoted only about a third as much space to the story and carried no interview with the prisoner.

[27] Edwin Emery, *The Press and America: An Interpretative History of Journalism,* 389 (Englewood Cliffs, N.J., 1962).

[28] *Pioneer and Democrat,* April 19, 22, 1860, quoting the *London Globe.*

[29] The *Pioneer and Democrat* of May 1, 1860, is missing from the Minnesota Historical Society's files.

[30] *Pioneer and Democrat,* May 18, 1860. At least one Minnesota newspaper refused to publish any account of the fight. The *Stillwater Messenger* of May 8, 1860, commented: "A large majority of our papers come to us with sickening details, in display type, of the prize fight between the champion bullies of England and America — Heenan and Sayers. We have no taste for that kind of literature. The affair is a burning disgrace to the two

governments, and we will not lumber our columns with a recital of the brutal collision."
[31] See Folwell, *Minnesota*, 2:66.

CHAPTER 6 — *Epilogue*

[1] See McMurtrie, in *Minnesota History*, 15:1–25; William H. Lyon, *The Pioneer Editor In Missouri 1808–1860* (Columbia, Mo., 1965).

[2] Vera W. Gillespie, "A Study of Four Minnesota Newspapers During the Civil War Period, 1861–1865," vi, 19, 135, 148, 151, 190 (quote), (University of Minnesota, master's thesis, 1946).

[3] Irene B. Taeuber, "Changes in the Content and Presentation of Reading Material in Minnesota Weekly Newspapers, 1860–1929," in *Journalism Quarterly*, 9:281–289 (September, 1932). The funnies were also born in the 1890s. See David M. White and Robert H. Abel, *The Funnies: An American Idiom*, 42 ([New York], 1963).

[4] Thomas F. Barnhart, "A History of the Minnesota Editorial Association," 89–99, 181–202 (University of Minnesota, master's thesis, 1937); Emery, in *Minnesota Heritage*, 323; Emery, *History of the American Newspaper Publishers Association*, 18 (Minneapolis, 1950).

[5] Emery, *The Press and America*, 317, 531, 622.

[6] For the 1870 figures, see *United States Census, 1870, Population*, 1:491. All others are from N. W. Ayer and Sons, *Directory of Newspapers and Periodicals*, 1920, p. 457; 1930, p. 479; 1940, p. 447; 1950, p. 476; 1960, p. 510.

[7] See Eide, *Influences . . . on the Growth of the St. Paul Pioneer-Press*, 29–32, 65; *Daily Press*, November 8, 1865. On Driscoll, see Johnston, in *Collections*, 12:240.

[8] Eide, *Influences*, 34; Quintus C. Wilson, "Joseph Albert Wheelock: A Study of His Life and the Impact of His Editorial Direction in St. Paul, Minnesota, and the Northwest," 52–62, 93 (University of Minnesota, Ph.D. thesis, 1953). For a summary of the editor's career, see also Eide's useful *North Star Editor: A Brief Sketch of Joseph A. Wheelock* (New York, 1944).

[9] Eide, *North Star Editor*, 15; Wilson, "Joseph Albert Wheelock," 128–130, 206. The *Daily Press* of January 1, 1861, contained the valedictory of Newson's *Times;* the *Minnesotian* held out only a little longer — until January 25, 1861.

[10] Wilson, "Joseph Albert Wheelock," 128, 132, 138n, 143, 144, 150, 151.

[11] Wilson, "Joseph Albert Wheelock," 152, 174, 185, 203, 205, 224; Eide, *Influences*, 65.

[12] Wilson, "Joseph Albert Wheelock," 269 (quote), 270, 283, 356. For other analyses of the paper's content, see Eide, *Influences*, 39–60; Eide, *North Star Editor*, 37.

[13] Wilson, "Joseph Albert Wheelock," 290, 402–410, 455, 459, 460, 462.

[14] Herbert Y. Weber, "The Story of the *St. Paul Globe*," in *Minnesota History*, 39:327–334 (Winter, 1965).

[15] Emery, in *Minnesota Heritage*, 318.

[16] Clarence N. Anderson, "Historical Aspects of the Development of the

Duluth Herald and News-Tribune," 1–13, Appendix, Table VI (University of Minnesota, master's thesis, 1956).

[17] Eide, *Influences,* 68; Emery, in *Minnesota Heritage,* 318; Johnston, in *Collections,* vol. 10, part 1, p. 342.

[18] Emery, in *Minnesota Heritage,* 318; Morison, *Sunlight on Your Doorstep: The Minneapolis Tribune's First Hundred Years,* 15–18 (Minneapolis, 1966).

[19] Morison, *Sunlight on Your Doorstep,* 15 (quote), 19; Marlin E. Aycock, "A Study of the News Coverage and Editorial Policies of the Minneapolis Tribune During the 1890's," 93–113 (University of Minnesota, master's thesis, 1956); Eileen W. Kuehn, "An Examination of the News and Editorial Function of the Minneapolis Tribune During World War I Years," 270 (quote), (University of Minnesota, master's thesis, 1966).

[20] Emery, in *Minnesota Heritage,* 318; James Gray, *The University of Minnesota 1851–1951,* 449–452 (Minneapolis, 1951); Morison, *Sunlight on Your Doorstep,* 23; Emery, *The Press and America,* 737.

[21] Morison, *Sunlight on Your Doorstep,* 31, 44–46.

[22] Edward C. Gale, "Herschel V. Jones," in *Minnesota History,* 10:27–32 (March, 1929); Emery, in *Minnesota Heritage,* 319.

[23] Harold L. Nelson, "A History of the Minnesota Daily Star," 44–56, 166–179 (University of Minnesota, master's thesis, 1950). See also Robert L. Morlan, *Political Prairie Fire: The Nonpartisan League, 1915–1922,* 280 (Minneapolis, 1955).

[24] Emery, in *Minnesota Heritage,* 320; Morison, *Sunlight on Your Doorstep,* 55–70.

[25] Paul Posel, "The End of Newspaper Competition in Minneapolis, 1935–1941," 122–136 (University of Minnesota, master's thesis, 1964). See also Morison, *Sunlight on Your Doorstep,* 71–78.

[26] The summary of the case, including quotations here and below, is drawn from John E. Hartmann, "The Minnesota Gag Law and the Fourteenth Amendment," in *Minnesota History,* 37:161–173 (December, 1960).

[27] In the meantime, the 1929 and 1931 Minnesota legislatures refused to repeal the law, the second time ignoring the request of Floyd B. Olson, who had become governor. See Hartmann, in *Minnesota History,* 37:169.

Index

About the Author

GEORGE S. HAGE is professor of journalism at the University of Minnesota, and a native of Madelia, Minnesota. Before starting his teaching career in 1946, he worked on the staff of the *Columbus* (Ohio) *Citizen* for several years.

In addition to his major field of journalism, he has been a continuing student of American social and intellectual history, and has taught courses in American Studies.

Mr. Hage and his family reside in Minneapolis. Interested in politics and civic affairs, he has served as president of the Minneapolis City Planning Commission. He also is an active member of various professional journalism organizations. This is his first book.